STRINGERS

D1530583

AN ONI PRESS PUBLICATION

STRIN

WRITTEN BY MARC GUGGENHEIM

COLORED BY RYAN HILL

ILLUSTRATED BY JUSTIN GREENWOOD

LETTERED BY CRANK!

FRIED PIE VARIANT COVER BY ROBBI RODRIGUEZ

EDITED BY JAMES LUCAS JONES AND ARI YARWOOD

DESIGNED BY HILARY THOMPSON

PUBLISHED BY ONI PRESS, INC.

JOE NOZEMACK, PUBLISHER

JAMES LUCAS JONES, EDITOR IN CHIEF

CHEYENNE ALLOTT, DIRECTOR OF SALES

AMBER O'NEILL, MARKETING COORDINATOR

RACHEL REED, PUBLICITY COORDINATOR

TROY LOOK, DIRECTOR OF DESIGN & PRODUCTION

HILARY THOMPSON, GRAPHIC DESIGNER

JARED JONES, DIGITAL ART TECHNICIAN

ARI YARWOOD, MANAGING EDITOR

CHARLIE CHU, SENIOR EDITOR

ROBIN HERRERA, EDITOR

BESS PALLARES, EDITORIAL ASSISTANT

BRAD ROOKS, DIRECTOR OF LOGISTICS

JUNG LEE, OFFICE ASSISTANT

ONIPRESS.COM
FACEBOOK.COM/ONIPRESS
TWITTER.COM/ONIPRESS
ONIPRESS.TUMBLR.COM
INSTAGRAM.COM/ONI PRESS

MARCGUGGENHEIM.TUMBLR.COM/@MGUGGENHEIM
JUSTINGREENWOODART.COM / @JKGREENWOOD_ART
@JOSEPHRYANHILL
@CCRANK

THIS VOLUME COLLECTS ISSUES #1-5 OF THE ONI PRESS SERIES *STRINGERS*.

FIRST EDITION: MARCH 2016

ISBN 978-1-62010-291-6
FRIED PIE ISBN 978-1-62010-310-4
EISBN 978-1-62010-292-3

PRINTED IN CHINA.

LIBRARY OF CONGRESS CONTROL NUMBER: 2015913628

1 2 3 4 5 6 7 8 9 10

For my parents, who are still wondering what use that law school tuition is going to be put to. This book won't help.

—MARC GUGGENHEIM

For my father, who taught me about the hustle, the value of friendship, and always told the best stories.

—JUSTIN GREENWOOD

And to Jill Beaton, one of *Stringers*' earliest parents. This book wouldn't exist without you.

INTRODUCTION

F*CK JAKE GYLLENHAAL.

I'm serious. F*ck him.

And while you're at it, f*ck Dan Gilroy, too.

I haven't met either gentleman, but f*ck 'em both.

I haven't seen their movie *Nightcrawler*, either. But really f*ck that movie. Like I said, I haven't seen it— scout's honor—but apparently it's not about a blue-skinned teleporting X-Man. Rumor has it, it's about a video freelancer—a stringer—working in Los Angeles.

See where I'm going with this?

Yeah, apparently Mssrs. Gilroy and Gyllenhaal were, as they say, "first to market."

F*ck 'em. We're doing something different here.

Nightcrawler was dark and moody and a penetrating character study set against the seedy underbelly of the City of Angels. This is not that. No, *Stringers* is a high octane, occasionally funny, hopefully exciting romp through, if not L.A.'s underbelly, one of its armpits.

Here follows its "secret origin": Ten years ago (has it been that long?!), I was driving to work at *CSI: Miami*,

listening to NPR (listening to NPR on one's way to work may or may not be a requirement of the driving regulations in southern California), and my attention was arrested by a piece on the freelance videogra-phers who hunt down the footage of the fires, chases, and shootings which to this day serve as the lifeblood of what constitutes "local news" in Los Angeles. (This is the piece. It's worth a listen/read: http://www.npr.org/templates/story/story.php?storyId=4717263.) I stayed in my car, listening to the story in my workplace's parking lot, growing more convinced with each passing syllable that there was a story to be told in and about this world. I wasn't sure whether it should be a TV show (my bread and butter at the time), a movie (wasn't writing 'em yet), or a comic book (I was just getting into the industry).

But I knew there was a story.

I quickly hit upon the characters of Nick and Paul. One irresponsible; the other diligent. One who got off on the adrenaline rush of their work; the other yearning for more respectable journalistic avenues. One an irrepressible horndog with a hard-on for the news producer they sell their wares to; the other happily married. This would be The Odd Couple in a radio-festooned SUV.

And then...

Nothing happened. The idea lay fallow as a file on my computer's hard-drive for years as I found myself distracted by my three-month-old daughter, travails at *CSI: Miami* (I'd quit three months later), and starting to write for Marvel Comics.

But somewhere in that interval I met the fine folks at Oni Press. Although it didn't end up being the first comic of mine to be published, Oni was the first comic company to buy a project from me: *Resurrection*— the story of what happens after an alien invasion. We lost our artist six issues in and planned a relaunch with a new artist.

Enter Justin Greenwood.

Justin worked tirelessly for years on *Resurrection*, penciling and inking I'velostcounthowmanypages and giving the book his all. And he did so with no ownership of this creator-owned property.

(Those shares were already spoken for by *Resurrection*'s original artist.)

And that didn't seem right.

So we decided to put *Resurrection* on hiatus so that I could create something new, a project Justin could have some equity in.

But what story should we tell?

The story had to be fast. It had to be funny. It had to fit with Justin's kinetic style, his specific artistic voice.

Stringers was, as the French say, *prêt-à-porter*. Ready to wear.

We announced the project at San Diego Comic-Con in 2010 and we were off to the races. Yes, I know 2010 was five years ago. The races took a while to coordinate, alright? Yes, I know Dan Gilroy was able to write, find financing for, direct, produce, post-produce, and distribute an entire movie in less time. Get off my back already, willya? Jeez.

Ten years is a long time to give birth to an idea. Here's hoping you think our baby's cute.

MARC GUGGENHEIM
AMERICAN AIRLINES FLIGHT 2381
30,000 FEET OVER SAN ANTONIO, TEXAS
MAY 2015

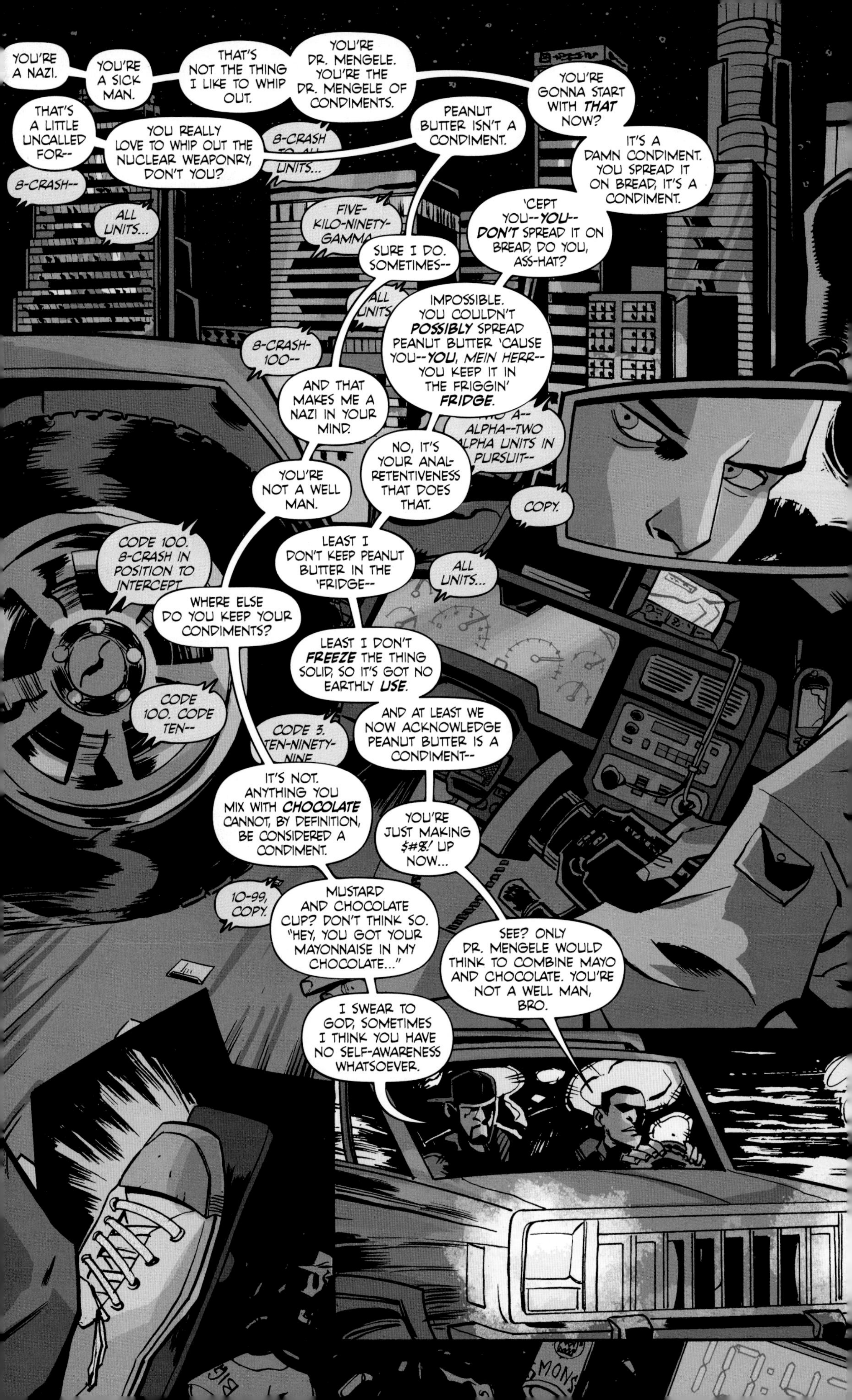
YOU'RE A NAZI.
YOU'RE A SICK MAN.
THAT'S NOT THE THING I LIKE TO WHIP OUT.
YOU'RE DR. MENGELE. YOU'RE THE DR. MENGELE OF CONDIMENTS.
YOU'RE GONNA START WITH *THAT* NOW?
THAT'S A LITTLE UNCALLED FOR--
8-CRASH--
YOU REALLY LOVE TO WHIP OUT THE NUCLEAR WEAPONRY, DON'T YOU?
8-CRASH
UNITS...
PEANUT BUTTER ISN'T A CONDIMENT.
IT'S A DAMN CONDIMENT. YOU SPREAD IT ON BREAD, IT'S A CONDIMENT.
ALL UNITS...
FIVE-KILO-NINETY-GAMMA
'CEPT YOU--*YOU*--*DON'T* SPREAD IT ON BREAD, DO YOU, ASS-HAT?
SURE I DO. SOMETIMES--
ALL UNITS
8-CRASH-100--
IMPOSSIBLE. YOU COULDN'T ***POSSIBLY*** SPREAD PEANUT BUTTER 'CAUSE YOU--*YOU*, *MEIN HERR*--YOU KEEP IT IN THE FRIGGIN' ***FRIDGE***.
AND THAT MAKES ME A NAZI IN YOUR MIND.
ALPHA--TWO ALPHA UNITS IN PURSUIT--
NO, IT'S YOUR ANAL-RETENTIVENESS THAT DOES THAT.
COPY.
YOU'RE NOT A WELL MAN.
CODE 100. 8-CRASH IN POSITION TO INTERCEPT
LEAST I DON'T KEEP PEANUT BUTTER IN THE 'FRIDGE--
ALL UNITS...
WHERE ELSE DO YOU KEEP YOUR CONDIMENTS?
LEAST I DON'T ***FREEZE*** THE THING SOLID, SO IT'S GOT NO EARTHLY ***USE***.
CODE 100. CODE TEN--
AND AT LEAST WE NOW ACKNOWLEDGE PEANUT BUTTER IS A CONDIMENT--
CODE 3. TEN-NINETY-NINE
IT'S NOT. ANYTHING YOU MIX WITH ***CHOCOLATE*** CANNOT, BY DEFINITION, BE CONSIDERED A CONDIMENT.
YOU'RE JUST MAKING $#%! UP NOW...
10-99, COPY.
MUSTARD AND CHOCOLATE CUP? DON'T THINK SO. "HEY, YOU GOT YOUR MAYONNAISE IN MY CHOCOLATE..."
SEE? ONLY DR. MENGELE WOULD THINK TO COMBINE MAYO AND CHOCOLATE. YOU'RE NOT A WELL MAN, BRO.
I SWEAR TO GOD, SOMETIMES I THINK YOU HAVE NO SELF-AWARENESS WHATSOEVER.

A NEAR COLLISION

YOU NEARLY GOT US KILLED JUST THEN, YOU KNOW.

THE CHICAGO CUBS HAVE "NEARLY" WON *SEVEN* WORLD SERIES IN THE LAST 104 YEARS.

TRY TO KEEP IT STEADY THIS TIME.

OKAY, I HAVE TO ADMIT, THIS IS ACTUALLY CHOICE.

OH, THIS IS MONEY. THIS IS LITERAL MONEY. I CAN ACTUALLY FEEL MY BANK ACCOUNT SWELLING.

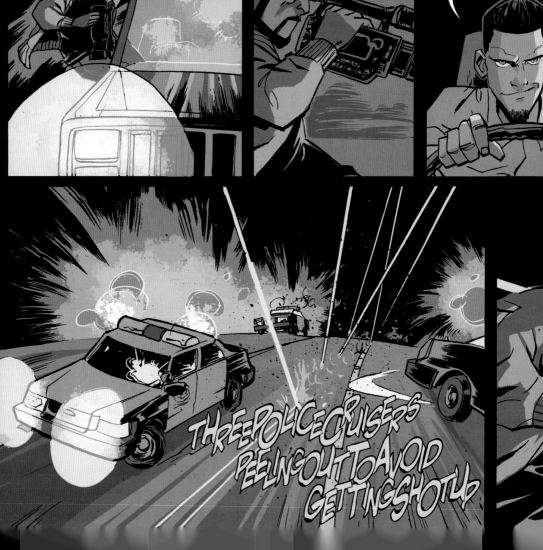

THREE POLICE CRUISERS PEELING OUT TO AVOID GETTING SHOT UP.

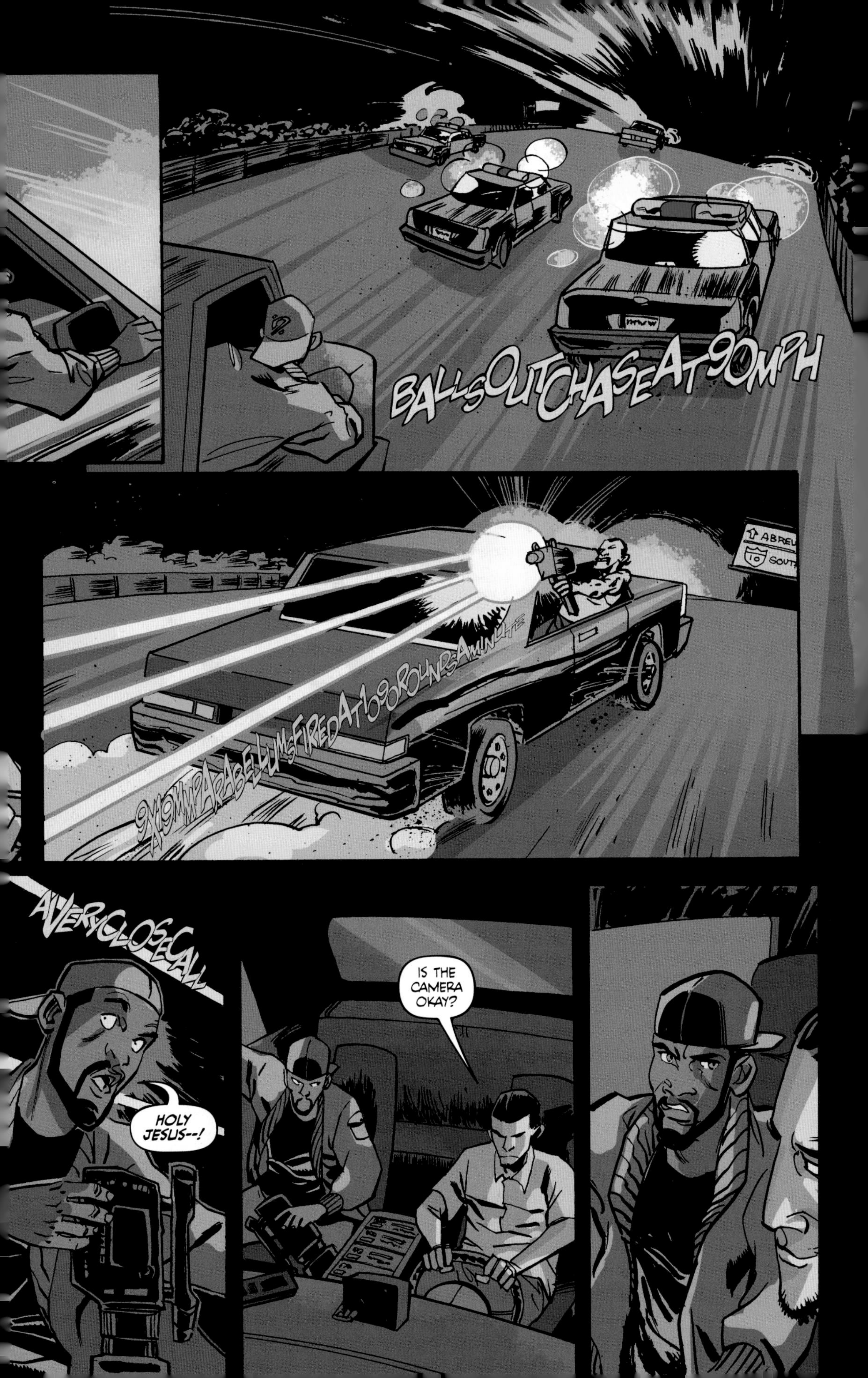
BALLS OUT CHASE AT 90 MPH
9X19MM PARABELLUMS FIRED AT 1090 ROUNDS A MINUTE
A VERY CLOSE CALL
HOLY JESUS--!
IS THE CAMERA OKAY?

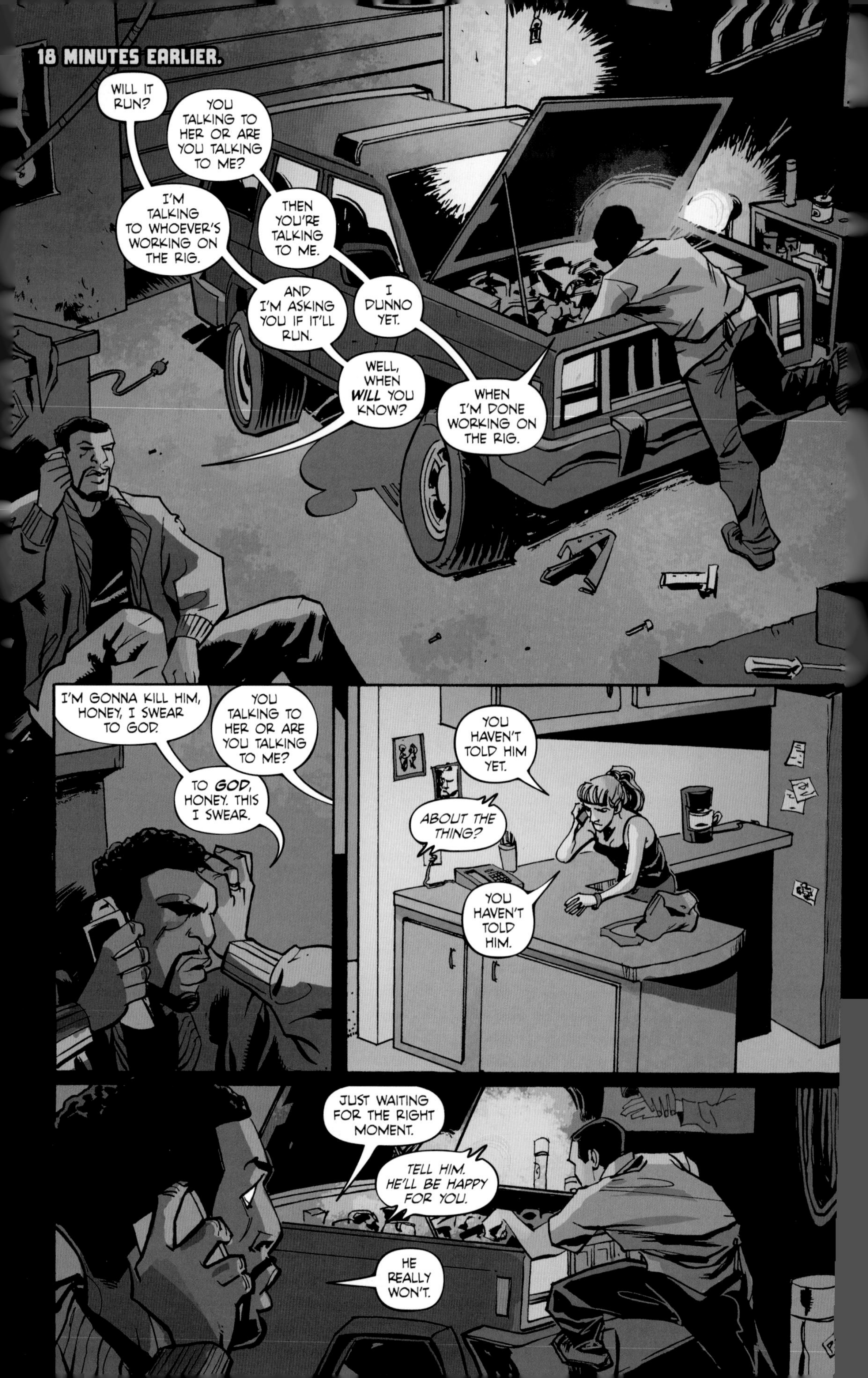
18 MINUTES EARLIER.
WILL IT RUN?
YOU TALKING TO HER OR ARE YOU TALKING TO ME?
I'M TALKING TO WHOEVER'S WORKING ON THE RIG.
THEN YOU'RE TALKING TO ME.
AND I'M ASKING YOU IF IT'LL RUN.
I DUNNO YET.
WELL, WHEN WILL YOU KNOW?
WHEN I'M DONE WORKING ON THE RIG.
I'M GONNA KILL HIM, HONEY, I SWEAR TO GOD.
YOU TALKING TO HER OR ARE YOU TALKING TO ME?
TO GOD, HONEY. THIS I SWEAR.
YOU HAVEN'T TOLD HIM YET.
ABOUT THE THING?
YOU HAVEN'T TOLD HIM.
JUST WAITING FOR THE RIGHT MOMENT.
TELL HIM. HE'LL BE HAPPY FOR YOU.
HE REALLY WON'T.

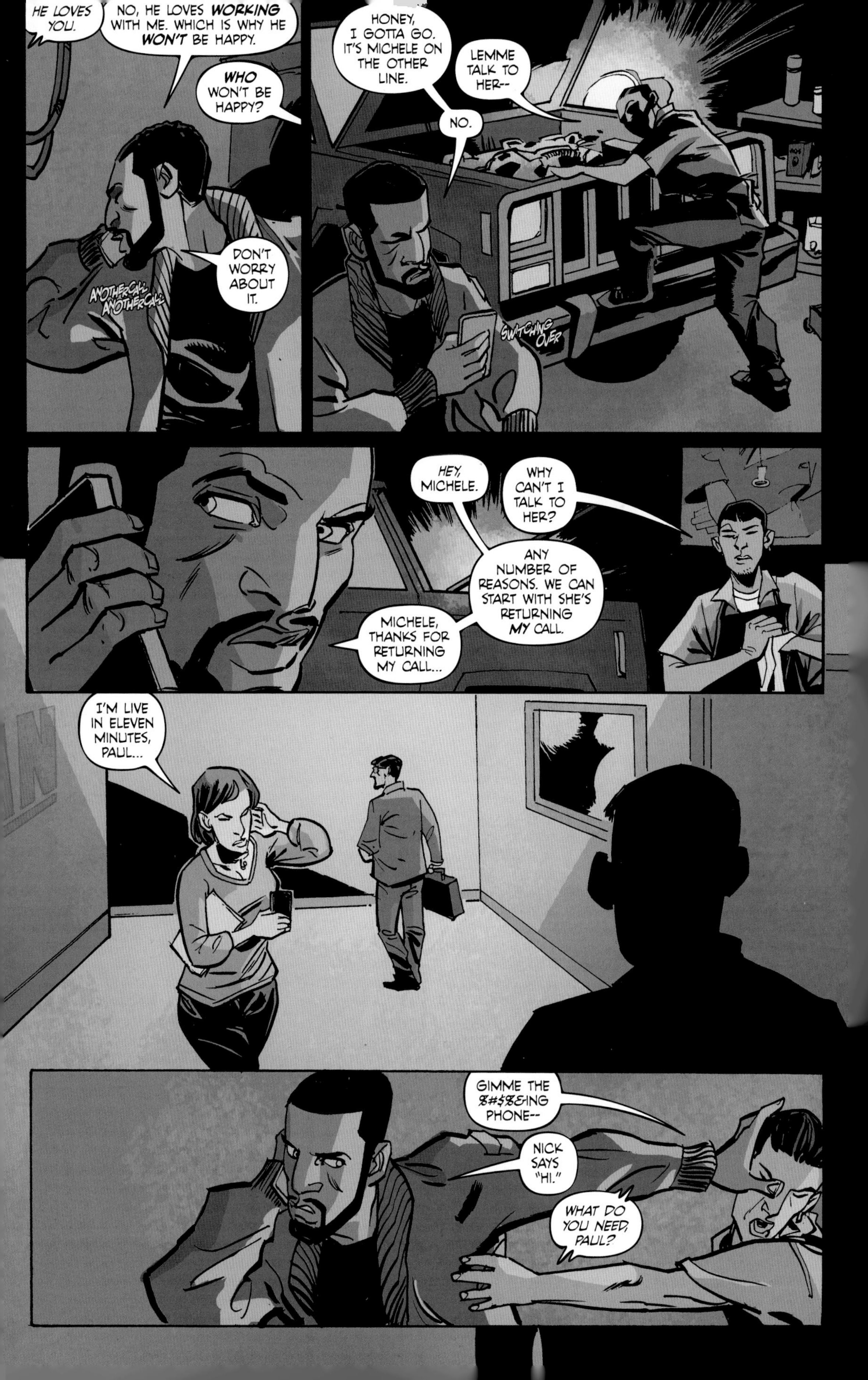

HE LOVES YOU.
NO, HE LOVES WORKING WITH ME. WHICH IS WHY HE WON'T BE HAPPY.
WHO WON'T BE HAPPY?
DON'T WORRY ABOUT IT.
ANOTHER CALL ANOTHER CALL
HONEY, I GOTTA GO. IT'S MICHELE ON THE OTHER LINE.
LEMME TALK TO HER--
NO.
SWITCHING OVER
HEY, MICHELE.
WHY CAN'T I TALK TO HER?
ANY NUMBER OF REASONS. WE CAN START WITH SHE'S RETURNING MY CALL.
MICHELE, THANKS FOR RETURNING MY CALL...
I'M LIVE IN ELEVEN MINUTES, PAUL...
GIMME THE %#$%&ING PHONE--
NICK SAYS "HI."
WHAT DO YOU NEED, PAUL?

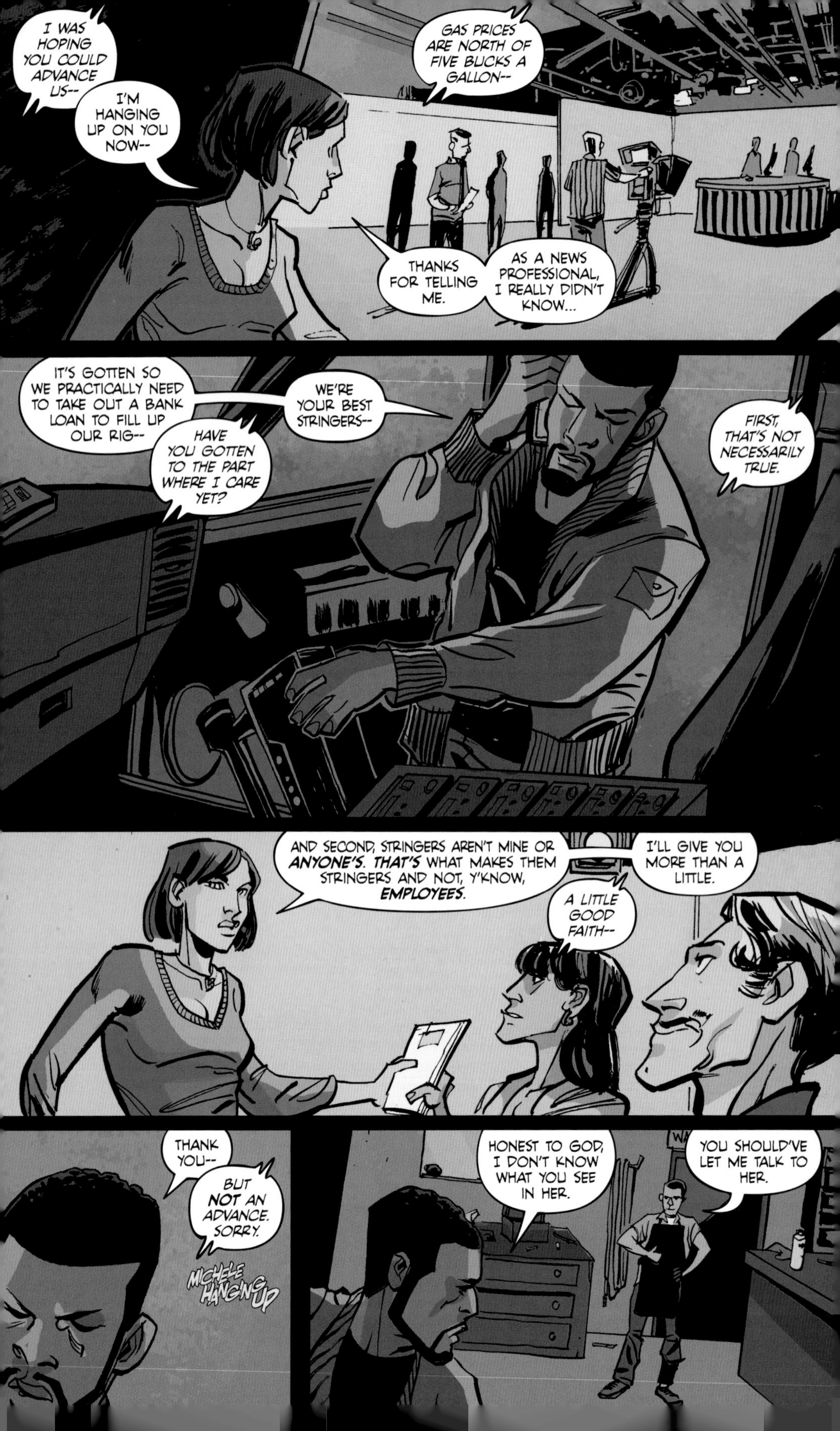
I WAS HOPING YOU COULD ADVANCE US--
I'M HANGING UP ON YOU NOW--
GAS PRICES ARE NORTH OF FIVE BUCKS A GALLON--
THANKS FOR TELLING ME.
AS A NEWS PROFESSIONAL, I REALLY DIDN'T KNOW...
IT'S GOTTEN SO WE PRACTICALLY NEED TO TAKE OUT A BANK LOAN TO FILL UP OUR RIG--
WE'RE YOUR BEST STRINGERS--
HAVE YOU GOTTEN TO THE PART WHERE I CARE YET?
FIRST, THAT'S NOT NECESSARILY TRUE.
AND SECOND, STRINGERS AREN'T MINE OR ANYONE'S. THAT'S WHAT MAKES THEM STRINGERS AND NOT, Y'KNOW, EMPLOYEES.
I'LL GIVE YOU MORE THAN A LITTLE.
A LITTLE GOOD FAITH--
THANK YOU--
BUT NOT AN ADVANCE. SORRY.
MICHELE HANGING UP
HONEST TO GOD, I DON'T KNOW WHAT YOU SEE IN HER.
YOU SHOULD'VE LET ME TALK TO HER.

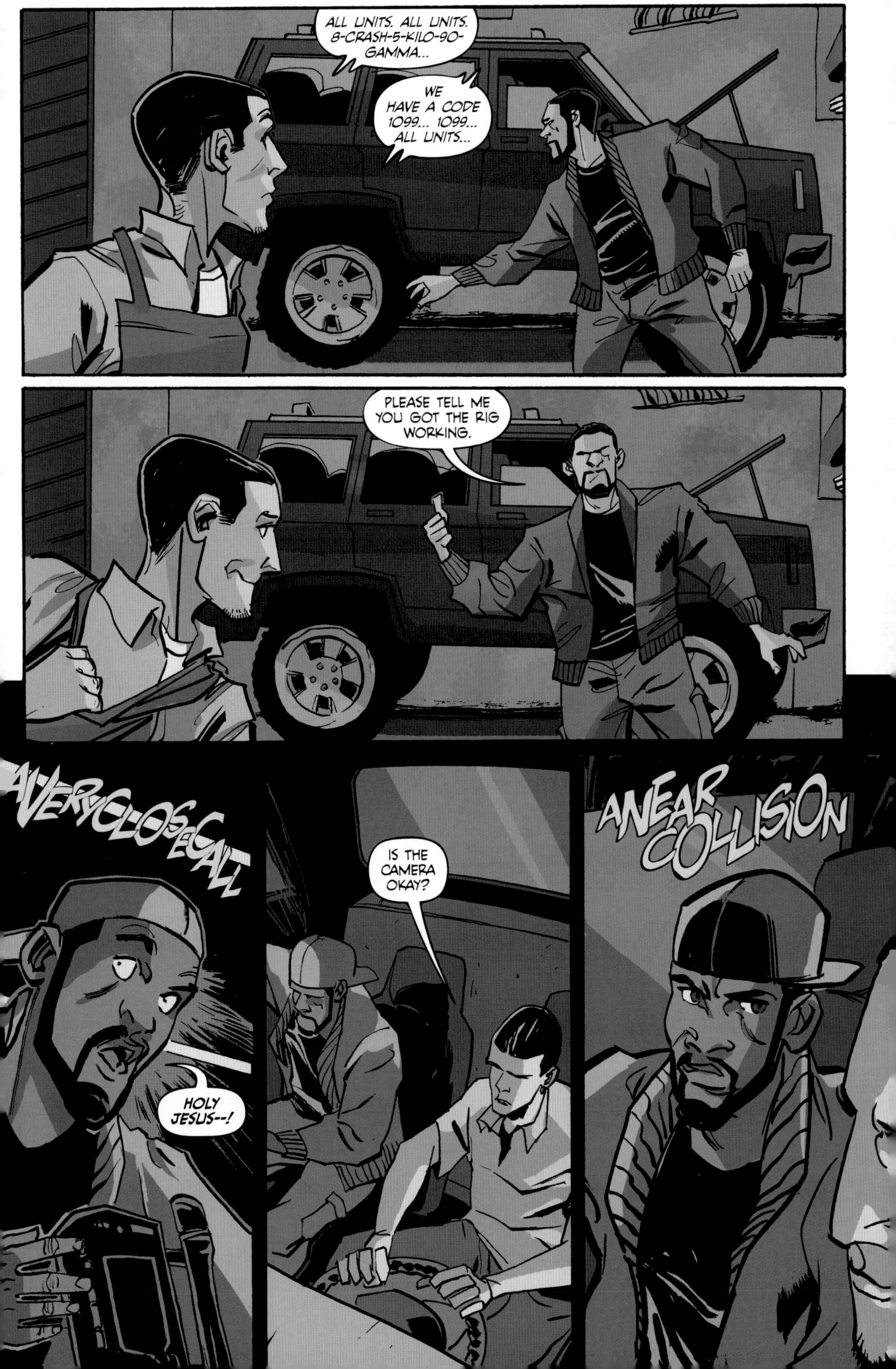
ALL UNITS. ALL UNITS. 8-CRASH-5-KILO-90-GAMMA...
WE HAVE A CODE 1099... 1099... ALL UNITS...
PLEASE TELL ME YOU GOT THE RIG WORKING.
A VERY CLOSE CALL
HOLY JESUS--!
IS THE CAMERA OKAY?
A NEAR COLLISION

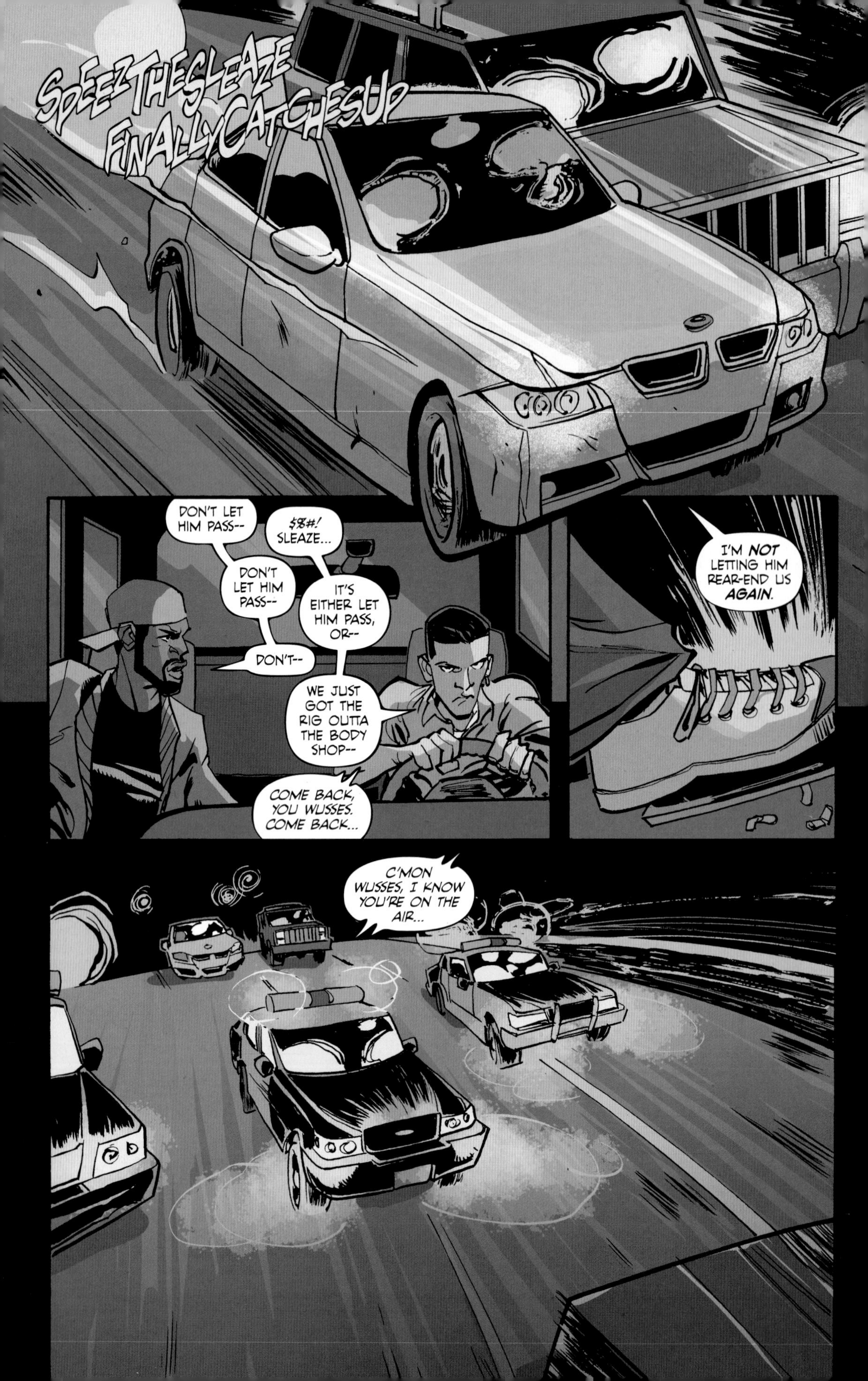
SPEEZ THE SLEAZE FINALLY CATCHES UP
DON'T LET HIM PASS--
$%#! SLEAZE...
DON'T LET HIM PASS--
IT'S EITHER LET HIM PASS, OR--
DON'T--
WE JUST GOT THE RIG OUTTA THE BODY SHOP--
COME BACK, YOU WUSSES. COME BACK...
I'M NOT LETTING HIM REAR-END US AGAIN.
C'MON WUSSES, I KNOW YOU'RE ON THE AIR...

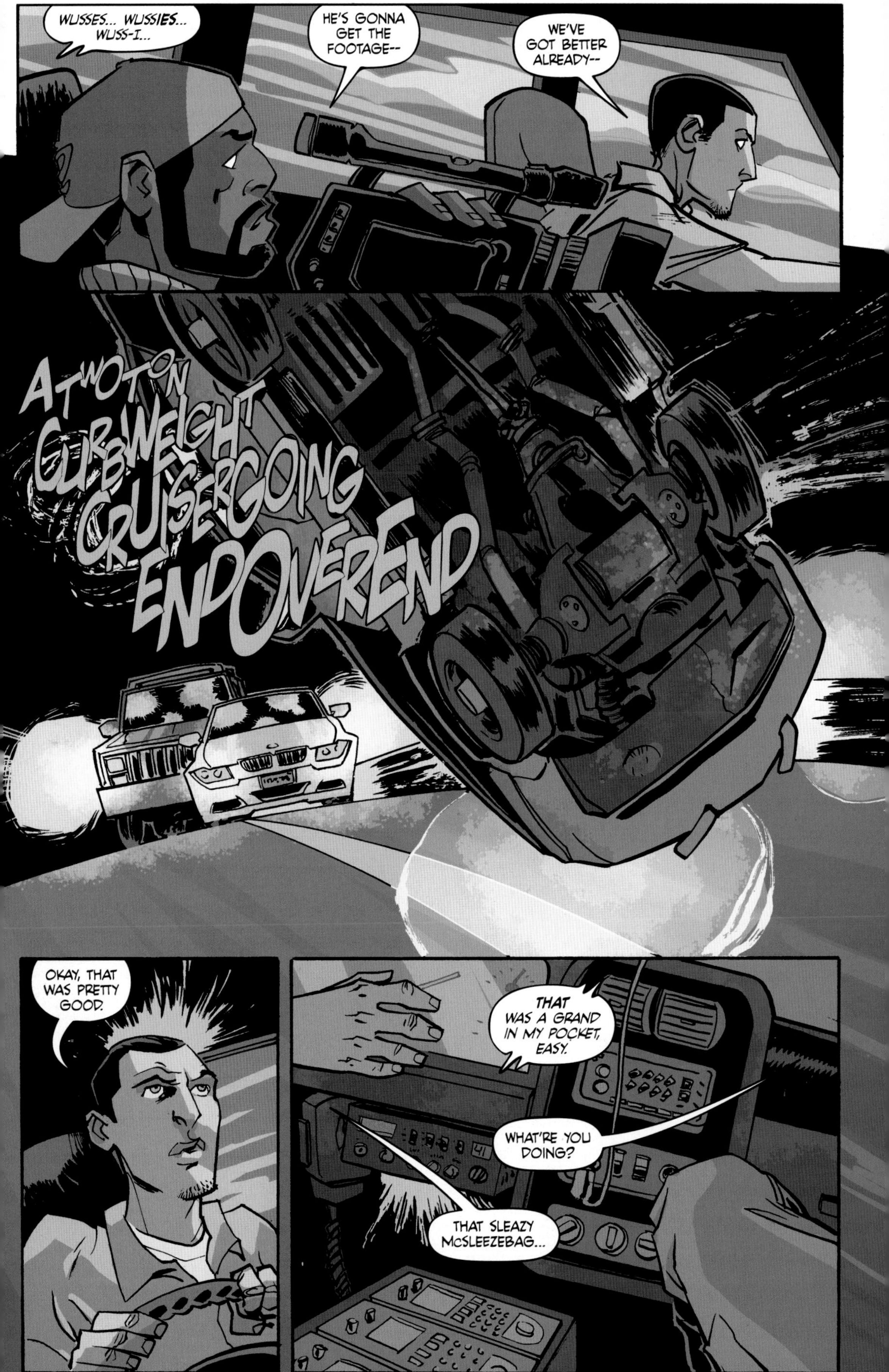
WUSSES... WUSSIES... WUSS-I...
HE'S GONNA GET THE FOOTAGE--
WE'VE GOT BETTER ALREADY--
A TWO TON CURBWEIGHT CRUISER GOING END OVER END
OKAY, THAT WAS PRETTY GOOD.
THAT WAS A GRAND IN MY POCKET, EASY.
WHAT'RE YOU DOING?
THAT SLEAZY McSLEEZEBAG...

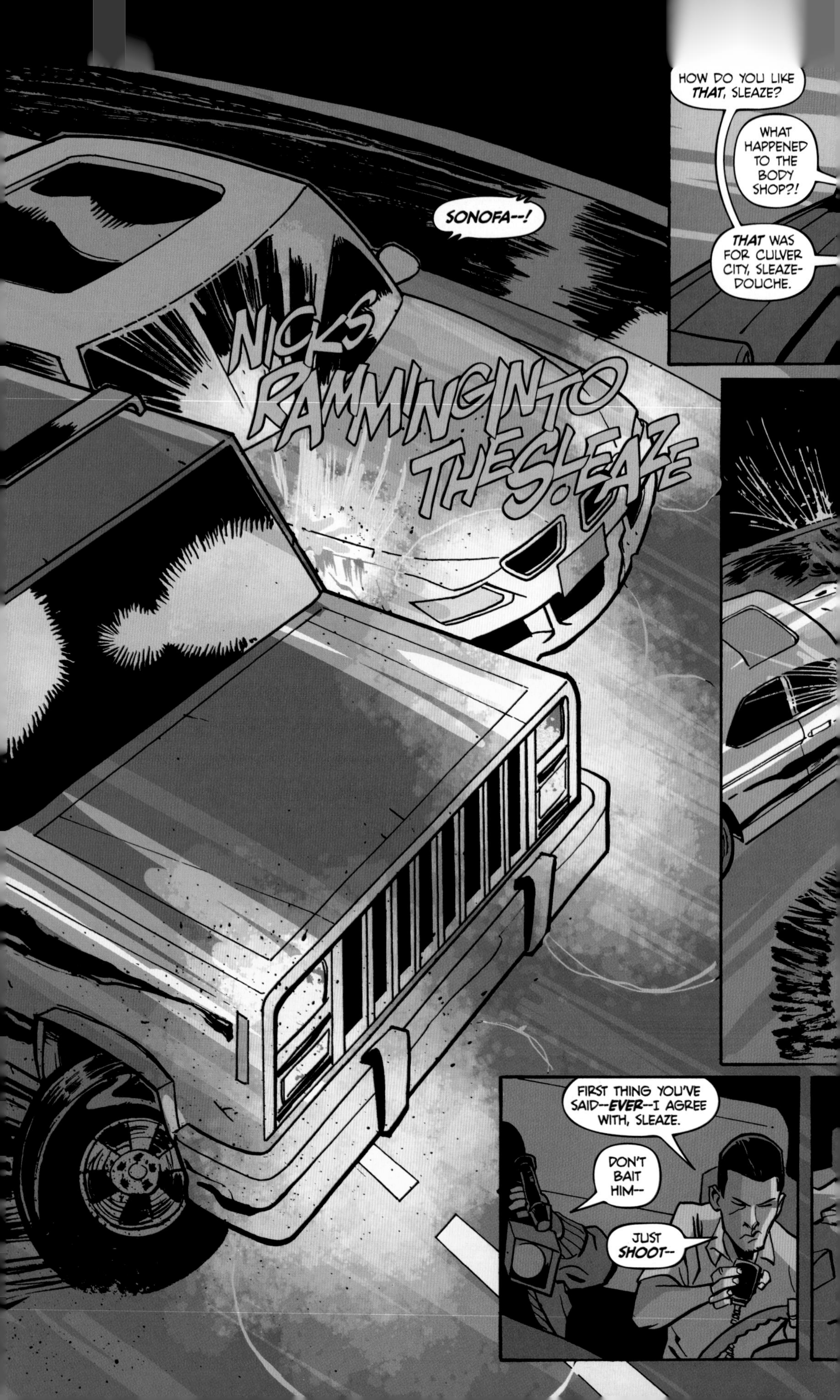
SONOFA--!
NICKS RAMMING INTO THE SLEAZE
HOW DO YOU LIKE THAT, SLEAZE?
WHAT HAPPENED TO THE BODY SHOP?!
THAT WAS FOR CULVER CITY, SLEAZE-DOUCHE.
FIRST THING YOU'VE SAID--EVER--I AGREE WITH, SLEAZE.
DON'T BAIT HIM--
JUST SHOOT--

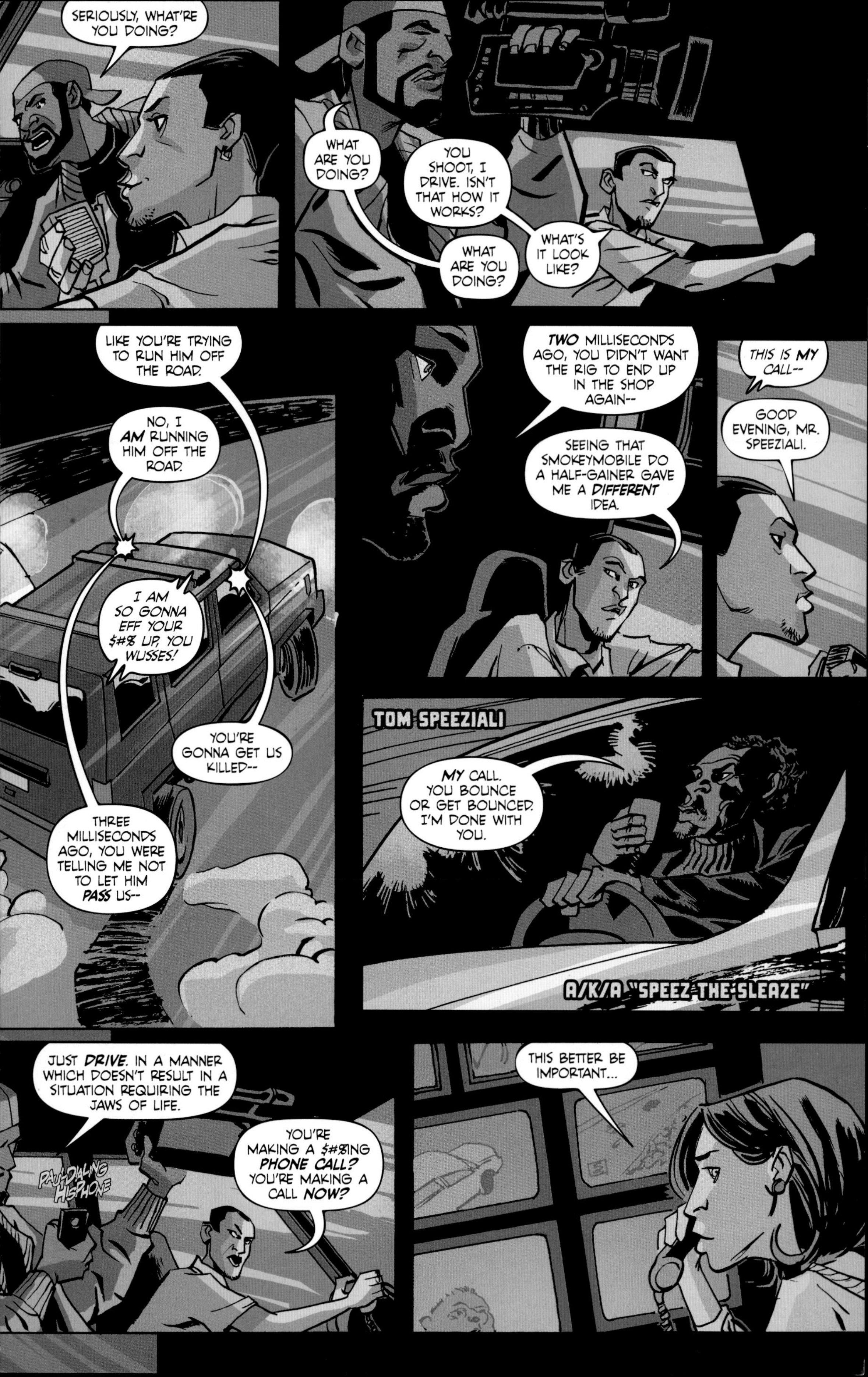
SERIOUSLY, WHAT'RE YOU DOING?
WHAT ARE YOU DOING?
YOU SHOOT, I DRIVE. ISN'T THAT HOW IT WORKS?
WHAT ARE YOU DOING?
WHAT'S IT LOOK LIKE?
LIKE YOU'RE TRYING TO RUN HIM OFF THE ROAD.
NO, I AM RUNNING HIM OFF THE ROAD.
I AM SO GONNA EFF YOUR $#% UP, YOU WUSSES!
YOU'RE GONNA GET US KILLED--
THREE MILLISECONDS AGO, YOU WERE TELLING ME NOT TO LET HIM PASS US--
TWO MILLISECONDS AGO, YOU DIDN'T WANT THE RIG TO END UP IN THE SHOP AGAIN--
SEEING THAT SMOKEYMOBILE DO A HALF-GAINER GAVE ME A DIFFERENT IDEA.
THIS IS MY CALL--
GOOD EVENING, MR. SPEEZIALI.
TOM SPEEZIALI
MY CALL. YOU BOUNCE OR GET BOUNCED. I'M DONE WITH YOU.
A/K/A "SPEEZ THE SLEAZE"
JUST DRIVE. IN A MANNER WHICH DOESN'T RESULT IN A SITUATION REQUIRING THE JAWS OF LIFE.
YOU'RE MAKING A $#%ING PHONE CALL? YOU'RE MAKING A CALL NOW?
THIS BETTER BE IMPORTANT...

THE 10 CHASE. I'VE GOT IT.

WE'VE BEEN RUNNING 'COPTER FOOTAGE--

SO'S CHANNELS 2, 4 AND 7. I'M ON SCENE.

IF THAT'S TRUE, THEN HOW DO YOU KNOW WHAT 2, 4 AND 7 ARE RUNNING?

THREE THOUSAND.

FIFTEEN HUNDRED. AND THAT'S ONLY IF YOU GET ME TAPE BY D-BLOCK.

TWENTY-FIVE HUNDRED. YOU GET EVERYTHING FOR THE DAYSIDE SHOWS.

MAKE SURE YOU SCRUB IT THROUGH AN AVID FIRST. I WANT SMOOTH FOOTAGE THIS TIME.

YOU GET ONE OF OUR OLD VG10s AND DON'T COMPLAIN.

AND I WANT GAS MONEY.

I'M GOING BACK TO PRODUCING A LOCAL NEWS SHOW NOW.

MICHELE ACTUALLY HUNG UP ON PAULA AGAIN

THE SLEAZE HAS LEFT THE BUILDING...

SHE'S GIVING US TWENTY-FIVE PLUS A SONY BETACAM.

I DON'T GET A "THANK YOU"?

WHERE'S *MY* THANK YOU?

FOR WHAT?

FOR GETTING US TWENTY-FIVE AND A SONY BETACAM.

WE DON'T GET IT 'LESS IT'S AN EXCLUSIVE. WHICH IT *WOULDN'T* BE IF I HADN'T TAKEN THE TRASH OUT JUST NOW.

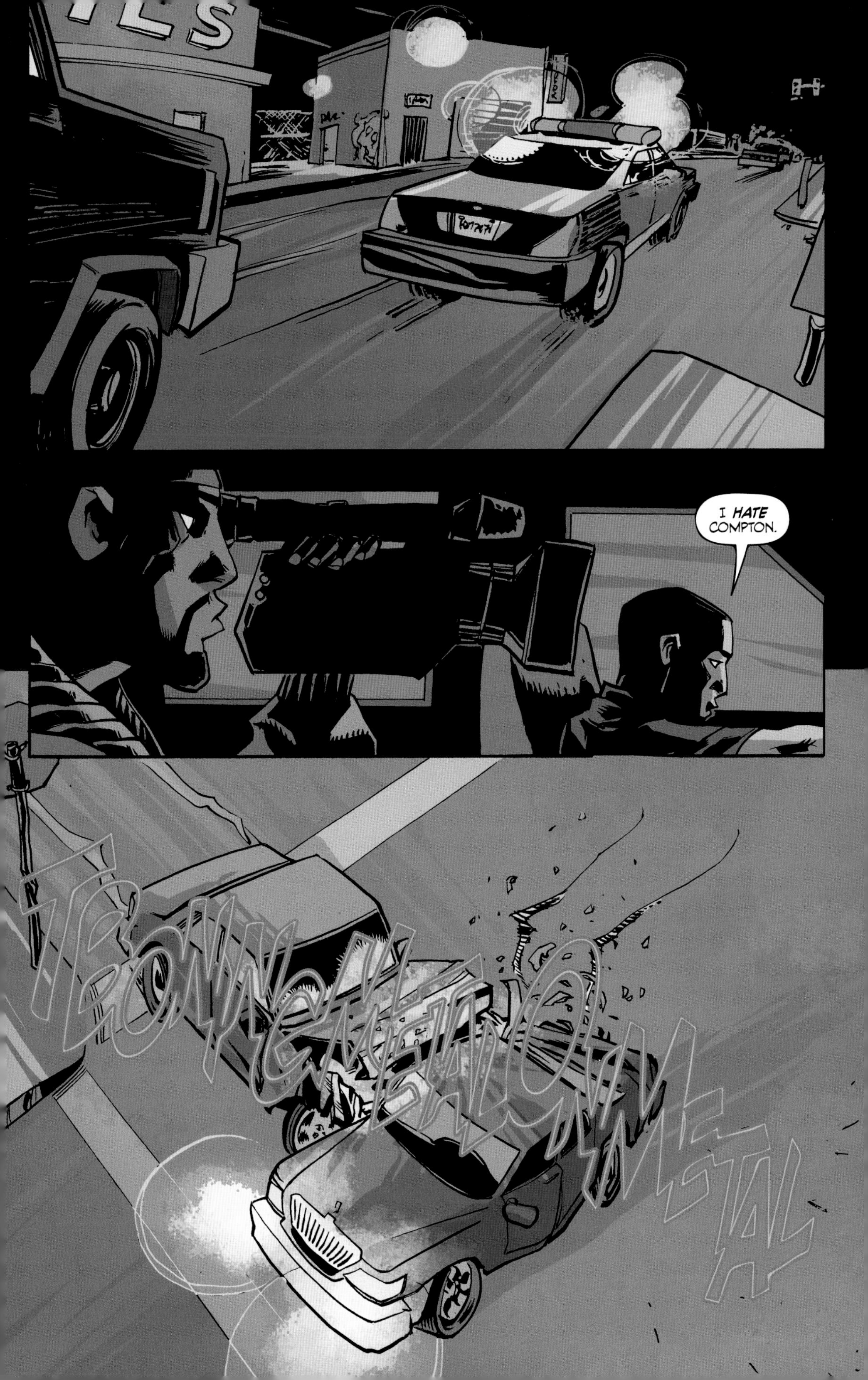
I *HATE* COMPTON.

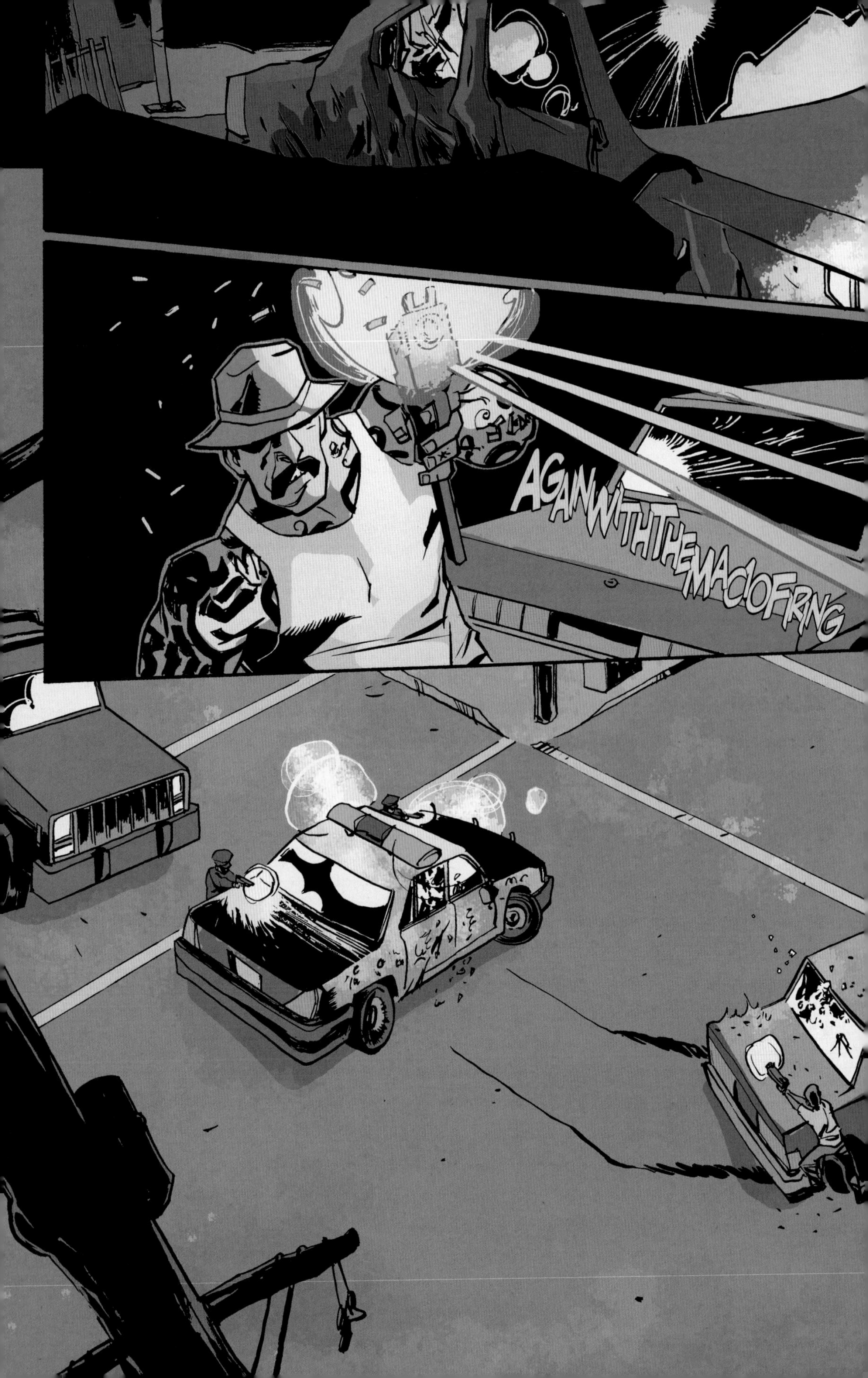
AGAINWITHTHEMAC10FIRING

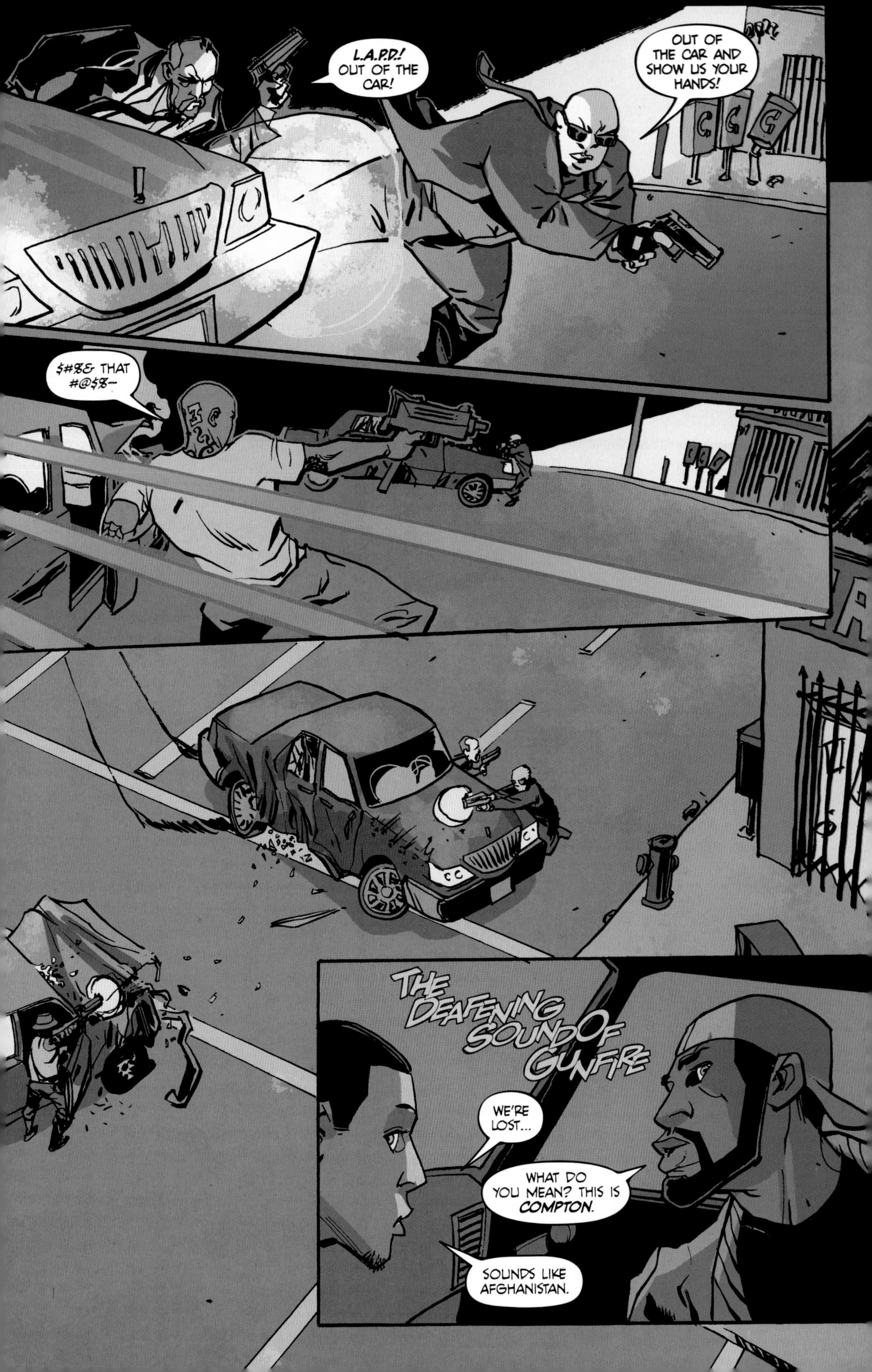
L.A.P.D.! OUT OF THE CAR!
OUT OF THE CAR AND SHOW US YOUR HANDS!
$#%& THAT #@$%–
THE DEAFENING SOUND OF GUNFIRE
WE'RE LOST...
WHAT DO YOU MEAN? THIS IS COMPTON.
SOUNDS LIKE AFGHANISTAN.

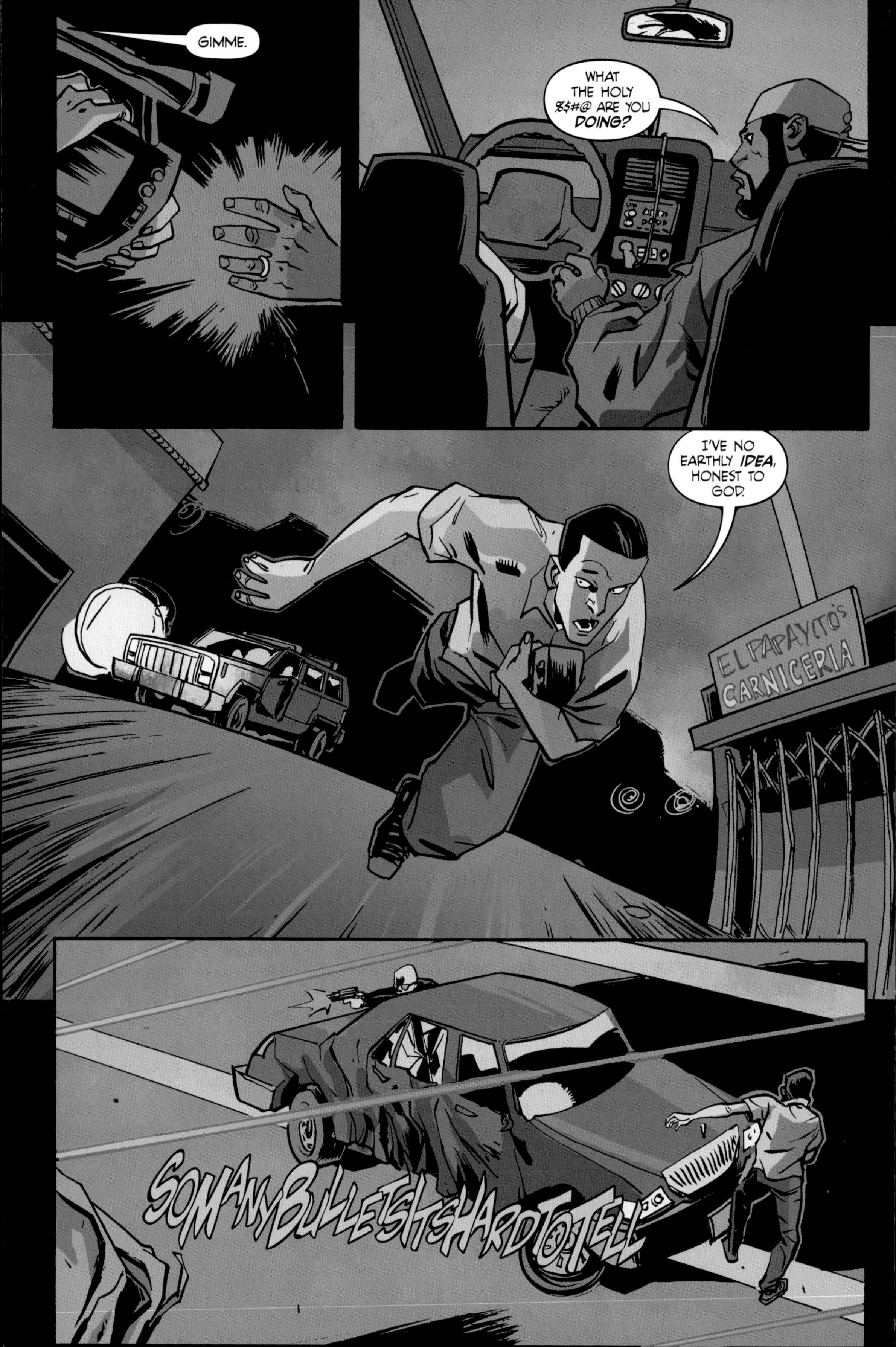
GIMME.
WHAT THE HOLY %$#@ ARE YOU DOING?
I'VE NO EARTHLY IDEA, HONEST TO GOD.
EL PAPAYITO'S CARNICERIA
SO MANY BULLETS IT'S HARD TO TELL

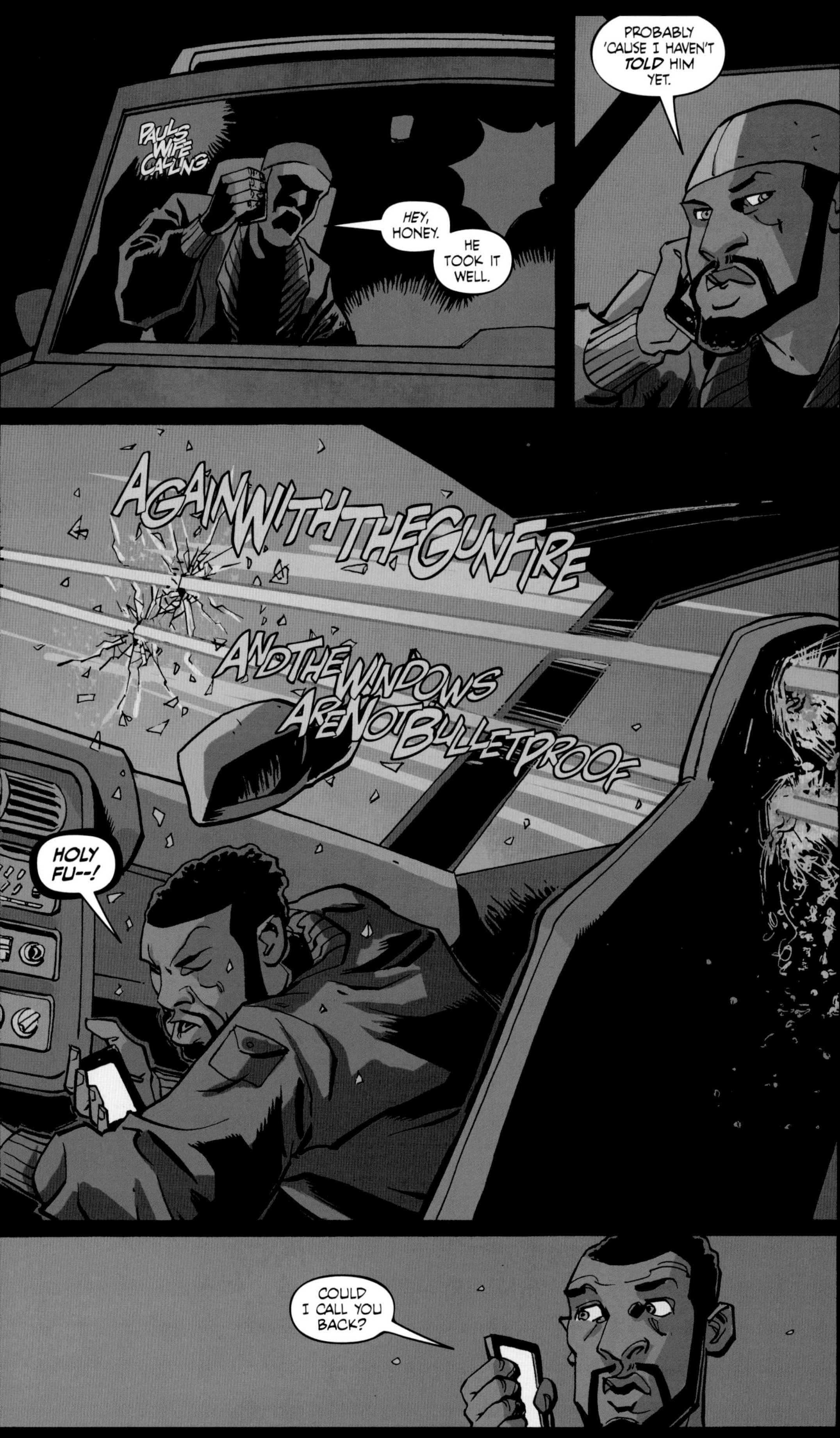
PAUL'S WIFE CALLING
HEY, HONEY.
HE TOOK IT WELL.
PROBABLY 'CAUSE I HAVEN'T TOLD HIM YET.
AGAIN WITH THE GUNFIRE
AND THE WINDOWS ARE NOT BULLETPROOF
HOLY FU--!
COULD I CALL YOU BACK?

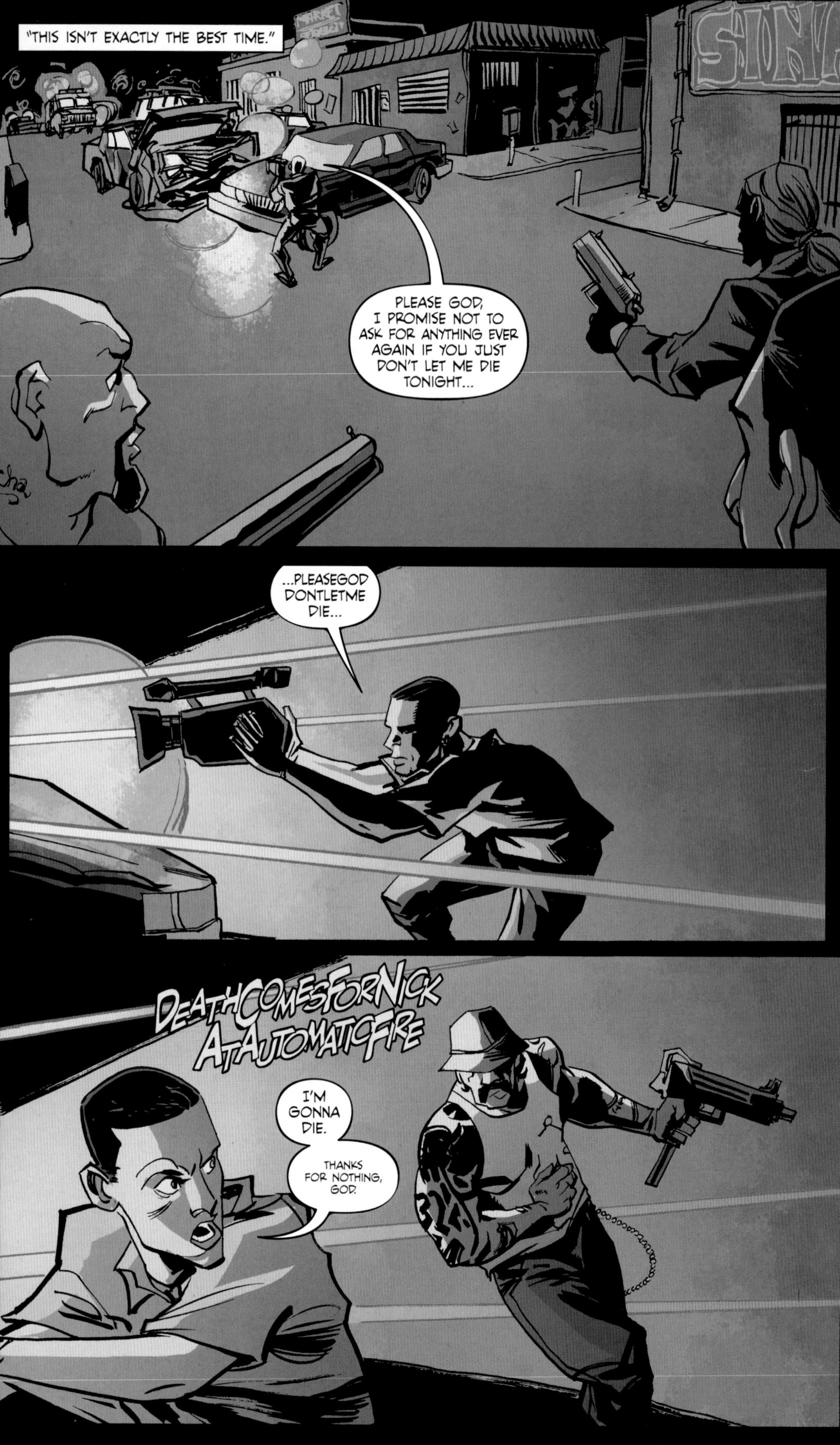
"THIS ISN'T EXACTLY THE BEST TIME."
PLEASE GOD, I PROMISE NOT TO ASK FOR ANYTHING EVER AGAIN IF YOU JUST DON'T LET ME DIE TONIGHT...
...PLEASEGOD DONTLETME DIE...
DEATHCOMESFORNICK ATAUTOMATICFIRE
I'M GONNA DIE.
THANKS FOR NOTHING, GOD.

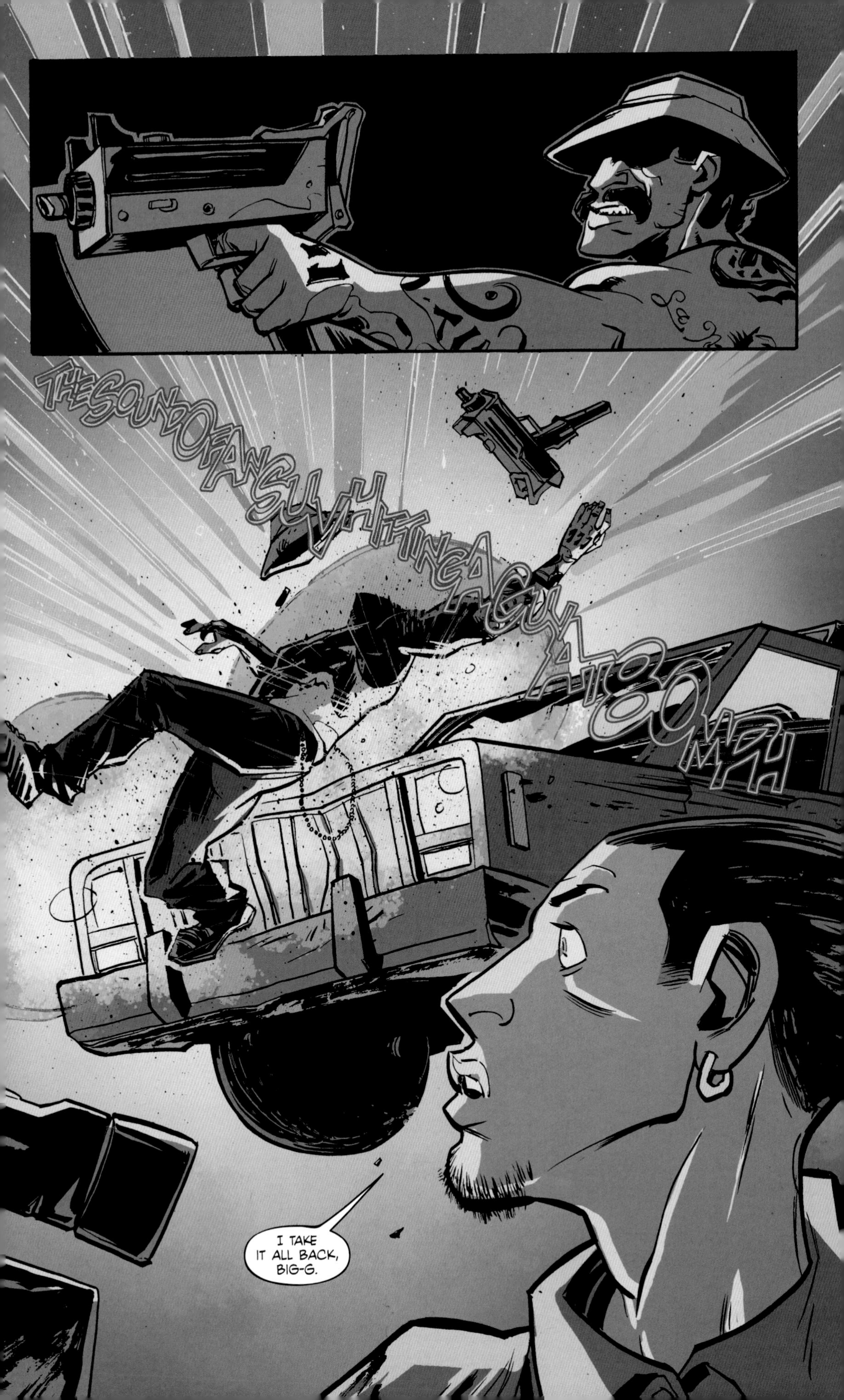
THE SOUND OF A GUY HITTING A GUY AT 80 MPH
I TAKE IT ALL BACK, BIG-G.

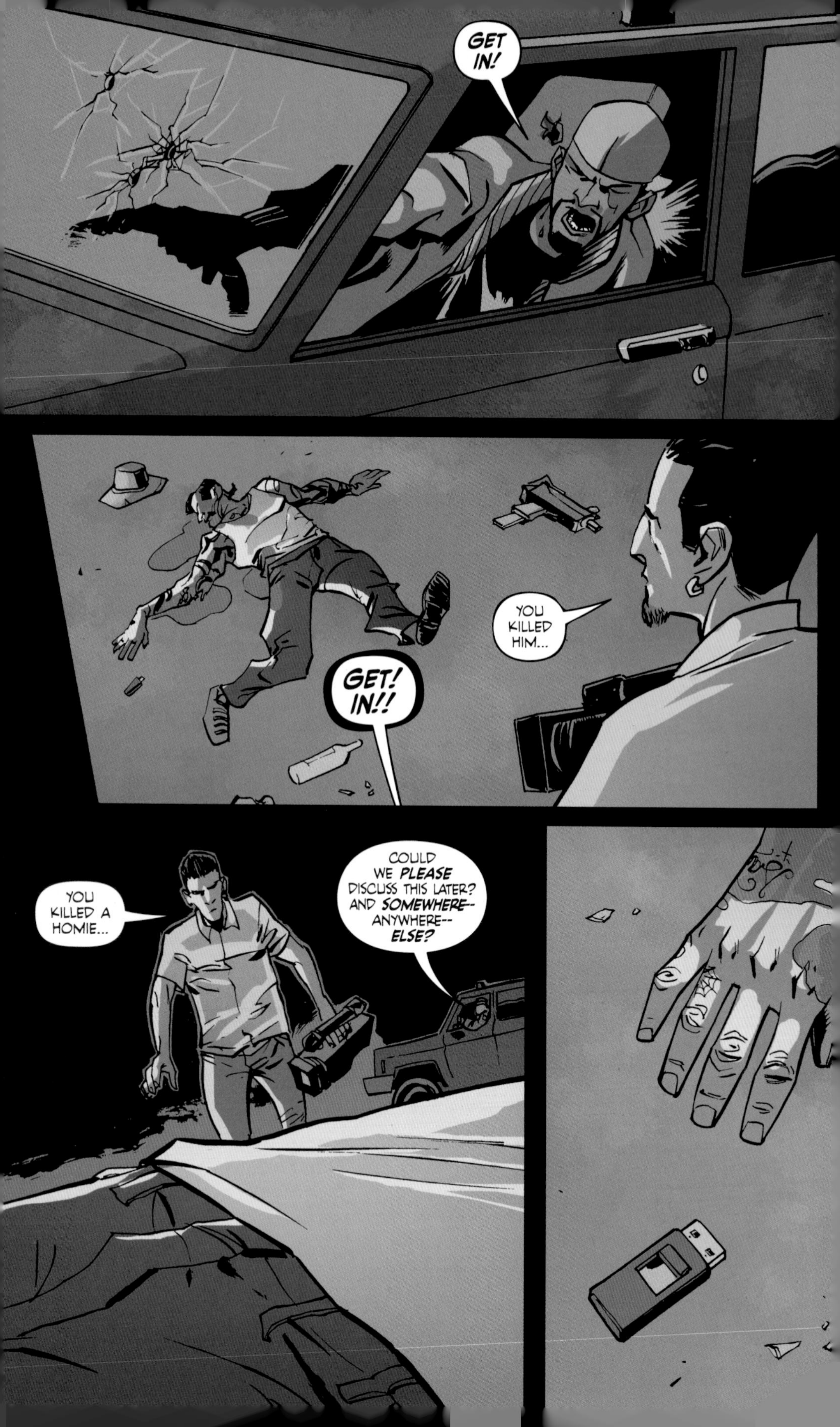
GET IN!
YOU KILLED HIM...
GET! IN!!
YOU KILLED A HOMIE...
COULD WE PLEASE DISCUSS THIS LATER? AND SOMEWHERE-- ANYWHERE-- ELSE?

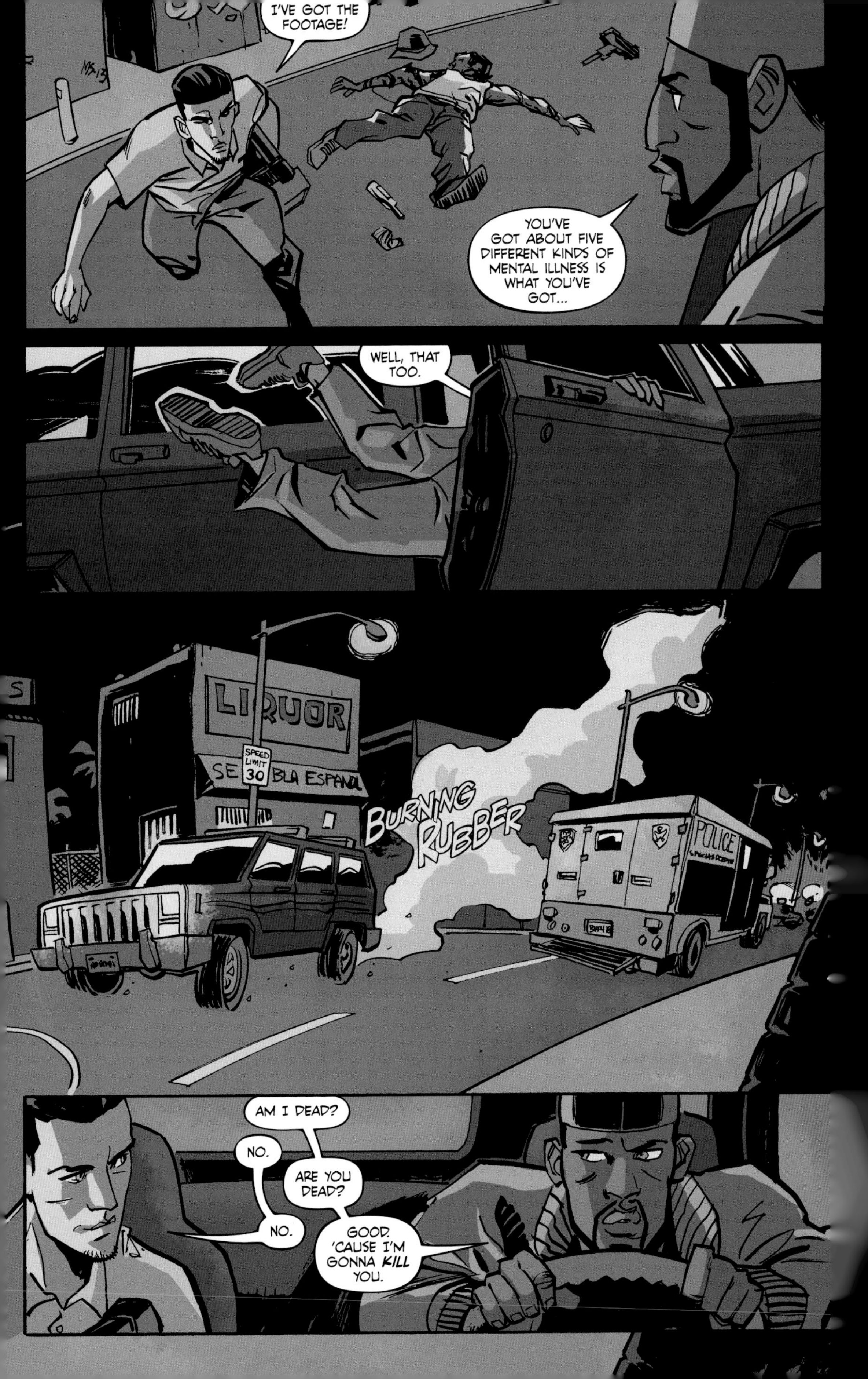
I'VE GOT THE FOOTAGE!
YOU'VE GOT ABOUT FIVE DIFFERENT KINDS OF MENTAL ILLNESS IS WHAT YOU'VE GOT...
WELL, THAT TOO.
LIQUOR
SE BLA ESPANOL
SPEED LIMIT 30
BURNING RUBBER
POLICE
AM I DEAD?
NO.
ARE YOU DEAD?
NO.
GOOD. 'CAUSE I'M GONNA **KILL** YOU.

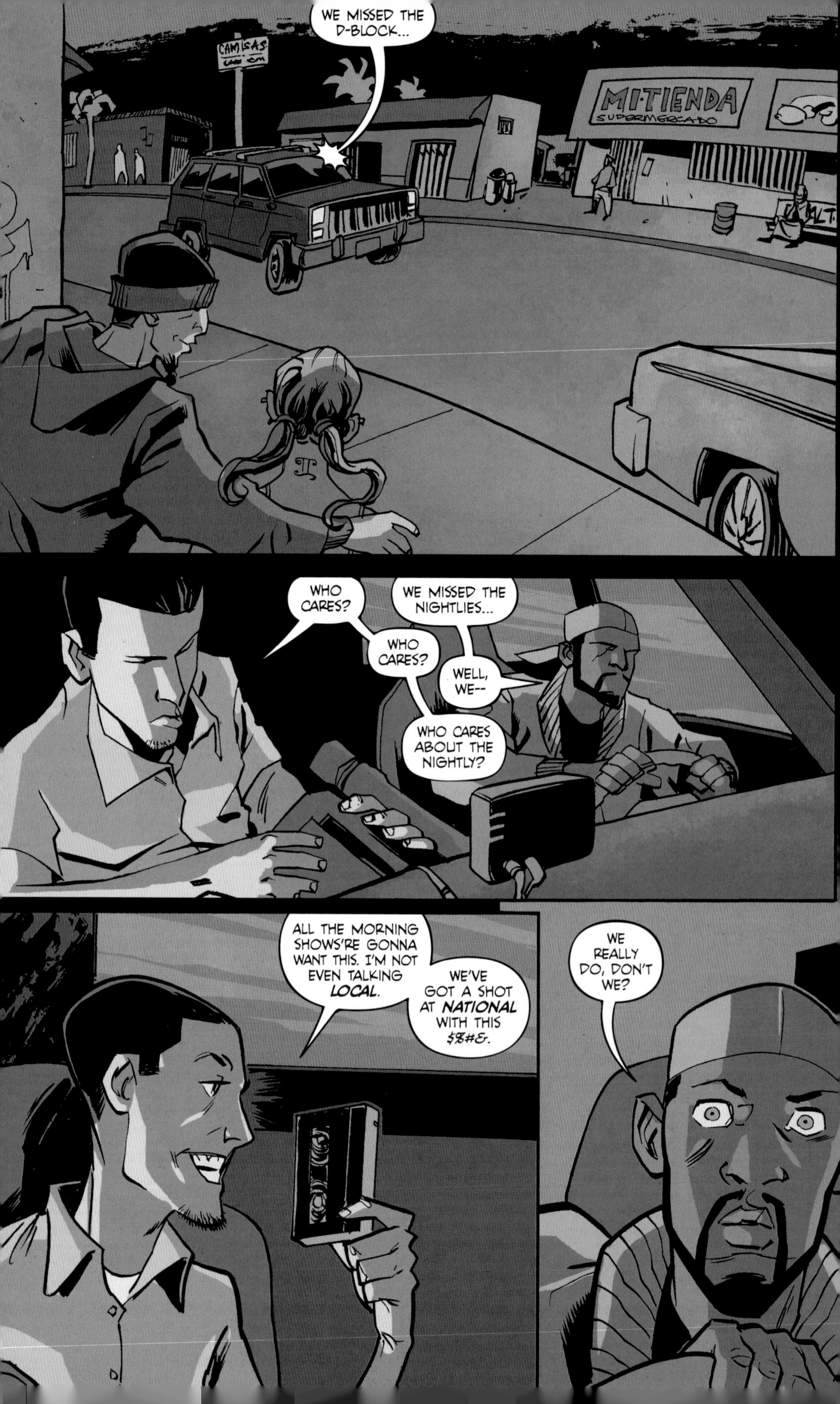
CAMISAS
MI·TIENDA
SUPERMERCADO
WE MISSED THE D-BLOCK...
WHO CARES?
WE MISSED THE NIGHTLIES...
WHO CARES?
WELL, WE--
WHO CARES ABOUT THE NIGHTLY?
ALL THE MORNING SHOWS'RE GONNA WANT THIS. I'M NOT EVEN TALKING *LOCAL*.
WE'VE GOT A SHOT AT ***NATIONAL*** WITH THIS $%#&.
WE REALLY DO, DON'T WE?

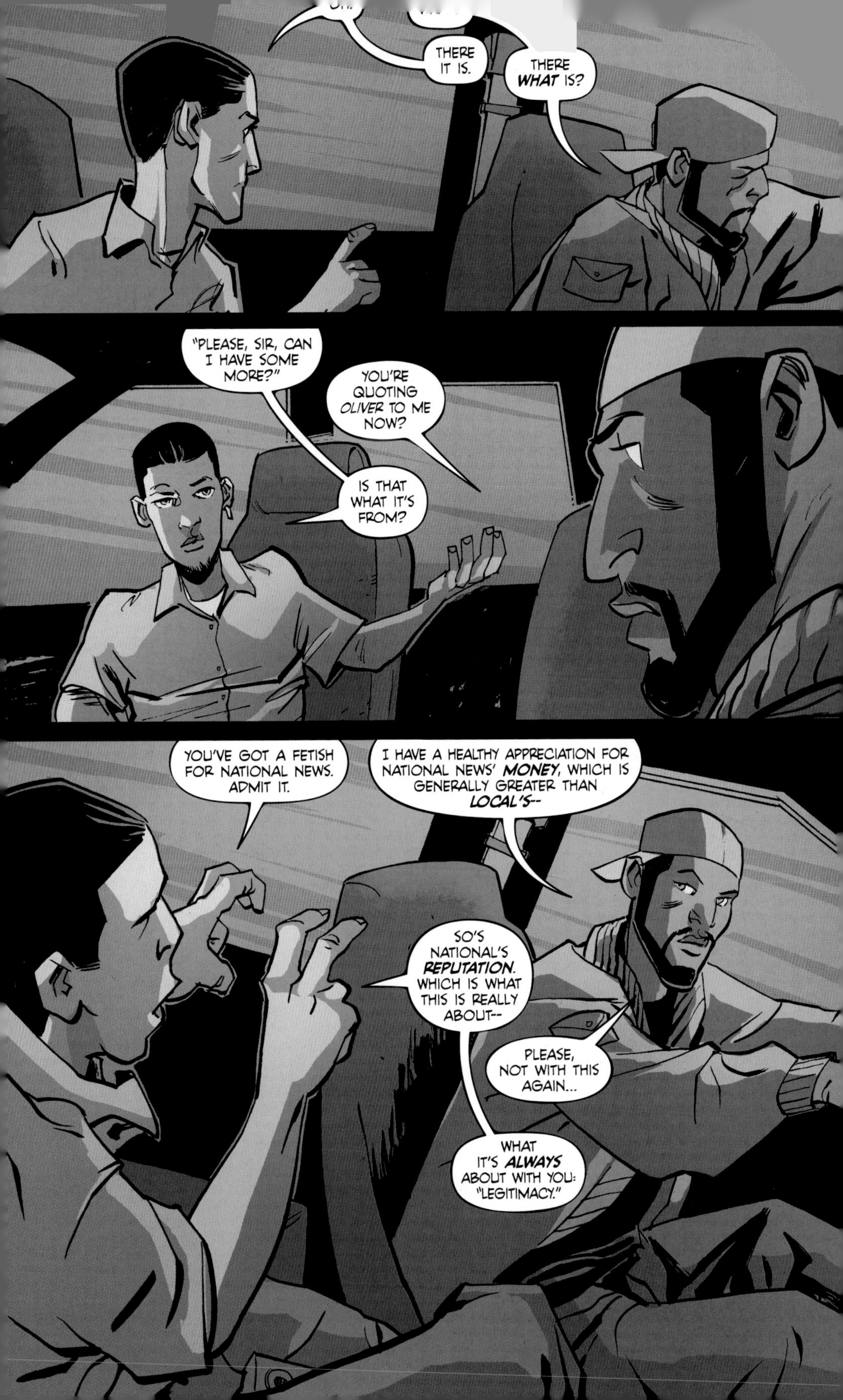
THERE IT IS.
THERE WHAT IS?
"PLEASE, SIR, CAN I HAVE SOME MORE?"
YOU'RE QUOTING OLIVER TO ME NOW?
IS THAT WHAT IT'S FROM?
YOU'VE GOT A FETISH FOR NATIONAL NEWS. ADMIT IT.
I HAVE A HEALTHY APPRECIATION FOR NATIONAL NEWS' MONEY, WHICH IS GENERALLY GREATER THAN LOCAL'S--
SO'S NATIONAL'S REPUTATION. WHICH IS WHAT THIS IS REALLY ABOUT--
PLEASE, NOT WITH THIS AGAIN...
WHAT IT'S ALWAYS ABOUT WITH YOU: "LEGITIMACY."

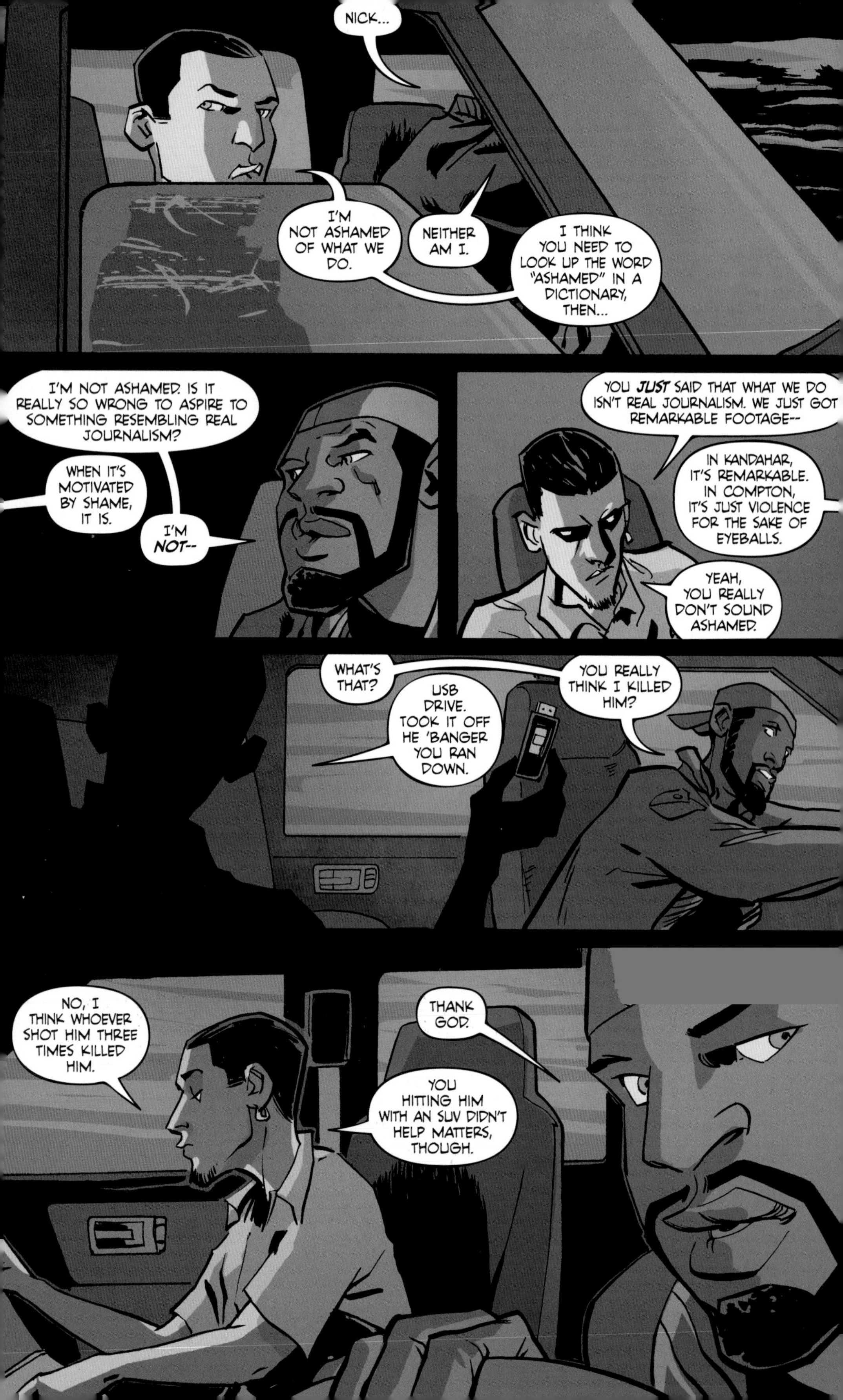
NICK...
I'M NOT ASHAMED OF WHAT WE DO.
NEITHER AM I.
I THINK YOU NEED TO LOOK UP THE WORD "ASHAMED" IN A DICTIONARY, THEN...
I'M NOT ASHAMED. IS IT REALLY SO WRONG TO ASPIRE TO SOMETHING RESEMBLING REAL JOURNALISM?
WHEN IT'S MOTIVATED BY SHAME, IT IS.
I'M *NOT*--
YOU ***JUST*** SAID THAT WHAT WE DO ISN'T REAL JOURNALISM. WE JUST GOT REMARKABLE FOOTAGE--
IN KANDAHAR, IT'S REMARKABLE. IN COMPTON, IT'S JUST VIOLENCE FOR THE SAKE OF EYEBALLS.
YEAH, YOU REALLY DON'T SOUND ASHAMED.
WHAT'S THAT?
USB DRIVE. TOOK IT OFF HE 'BANGER YOU RAN DOWN.
YOU REALLY THINK I KILLED HIM?
NO, I THINK WHOEVER SHOT HIM THREE TIMES KILLED HIM.
THANK GOD.
YOU HITTING HIM WITH AN SUV DIDN'T HELP MATTERS, THOUGH.

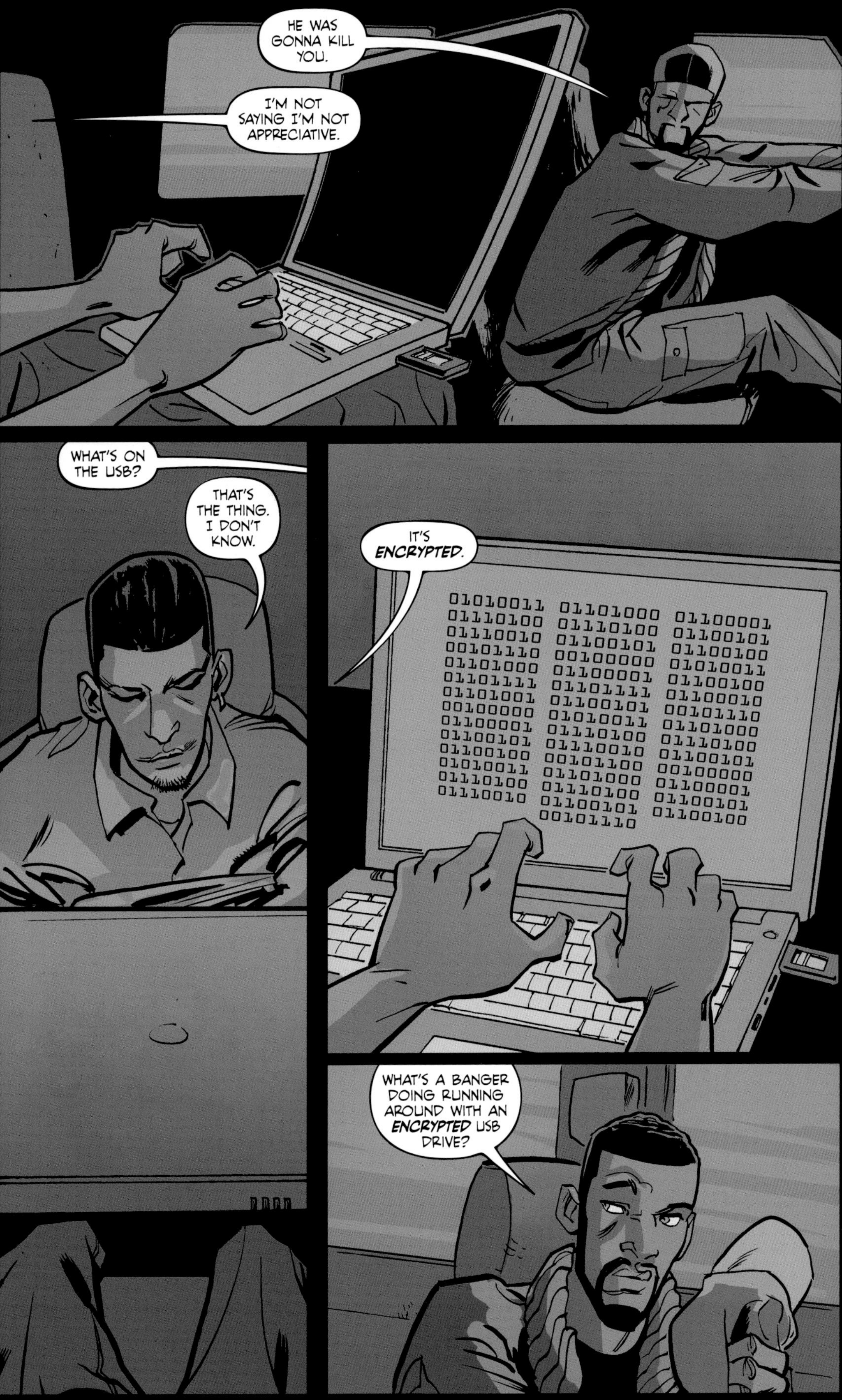
HE WAS GONNA KILL YOU.
I'M NOT SAYING I'M NOT APPRECIATIVE.
WHAT'S ON THE USB?
THAT'S THE THING. I DON'T KNOW.
IT'S *ENCRYPTED*.
01010011
01110100
01110010
00101110
01101000
01101111
01101001
00100000
01100001
01100101
01100100
01010011
01110100
01110010
01101000
01110100
01100101
00100000
01100001
01101111
01100101
01010011
01110100
01110010
00101100
01101000
01110100
01100101
00101110
01100001
01100101
01100100
01010011
01100100
01100010
00101110
01101000
01110100
01100101
00100000
01100001
01100101
01100100
WHAT'S A BANGER DOING RUNNING AROUND WITH AN *ENCRYPTED* USB DRIVE?

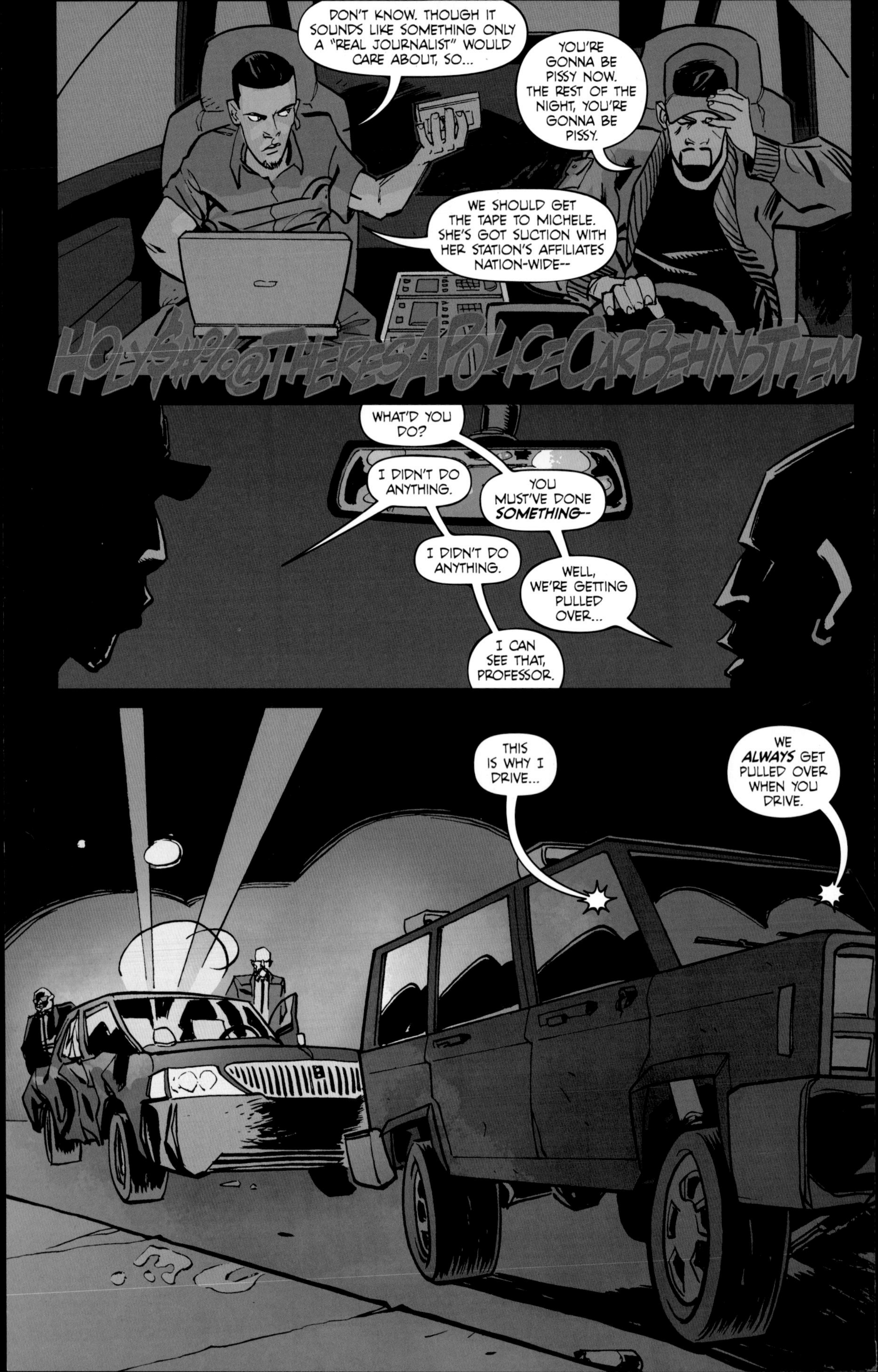
DON'T KNOW. THOUGH IT SOUNDS LIKE SOMETHING ONLY A "REAL JOURNALIST" WOULD CARE ABOUT, SO...
YOU'RE GONNA BE PISSY NOW. THE REST OF THE NIGHT, YOU'RE GONNA BE PISSY.
WE SHOULD GET THE TAPE TO MICHELE. SHE'S GOT SUCTION WITH HER STATION'S AFFILIATES NATION-WIDE--
HOLY$#%@THERESAPOLICECARBEHINDTHEM
WHAT'D YOU DO?
I DIDN'T DO ANYTHING.
YOU MUST'VE DONE SOMETHING--
I DIDN'T DO ANYTHING.
WELL, WE'RE GETTING PULLED OVER...
I CAN SEE THAT, PROFESSOR.
THIS IS WHY I DRIVE...
WE ALWAYS GET PULLED OVER WHEN YOU DRIVE.

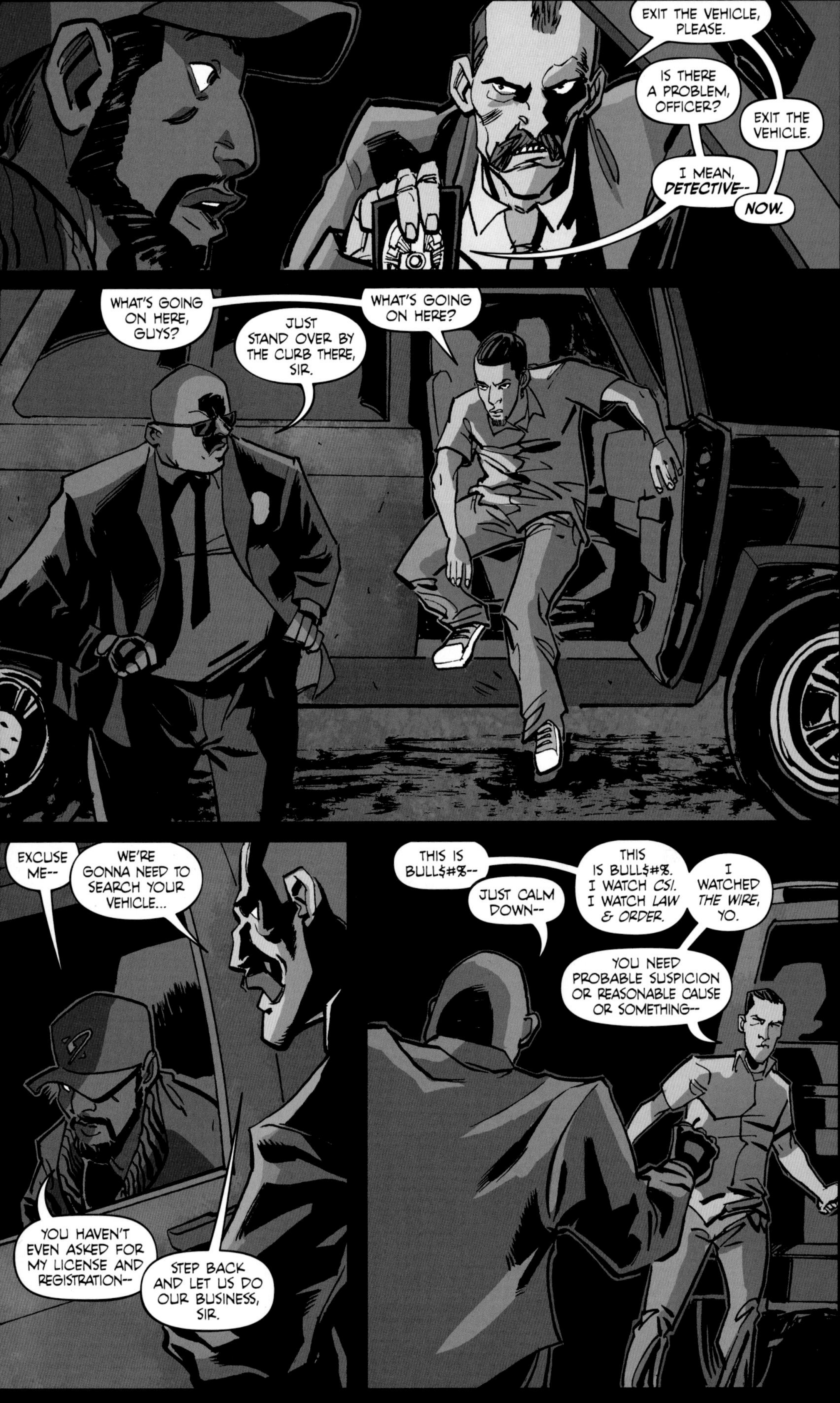
EXIT THE VEHICLE, PLEASE.
IS THERE A PROBLEM, OFFICER?
EXIT THE VEHICLE.
I MEAN, *DETECTIVE*--
NOW.
WHAT'S GOING ON HERE, GUYS?
JUST STAND OVER BY THE CURB THERE, SIR.
WHAT'S GOING ON HERE?
EXCUSE ME--
WE'RE GONNA NEED TO SEARCH YOUR VEHICLE...
YOU HAVEN'T EVEN ASKED FOR MY LICENSE AND REGISTRATION--
STEP BACK AND LET US DO OUR BUSINESS, SIR.
THIS IS BULL$#%--
JUST CALM DOWN--
THIS IS BULL$#%. I WATCH *CSI*. I WATCH *LAW & ORDER*.
I WATCHED *THE WIRE*, YO.
YOU NEED PROBABLE SUSPICION OR REASONABLE CAUSE OR SOMETHING--

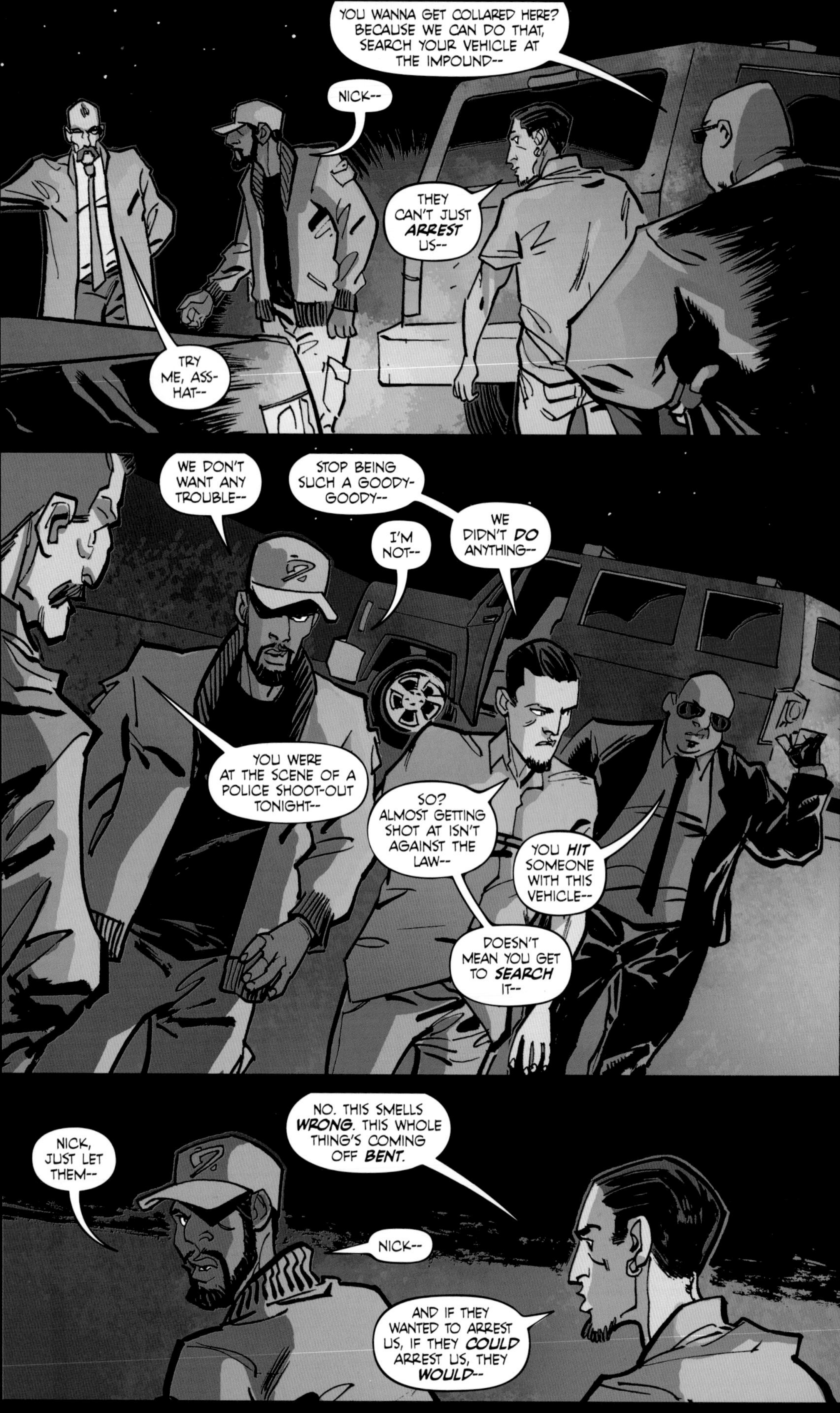
YOU WANNA GET COLLARED HERE? BECAUSE WE CAN DO THAT, SEARCH YOUR VEHICLE AT THE IMPOUND--
NICK--
THEY CAN'T JUST ARREST US--
TRY ME, ASS-HAT--
WE DON'T WANT ANY TROUBLE--
STOP BEING SUCH A GOODY-GOODY--
I'M NOT--
WE DIDN'T DO ANYTHING--
YOU WERE AT THE SCENE OF A POLICE SHOOT-OUT TONIGHT--
SO? ALMOST GETTING SHOT AT ISN'T AGAINST THE LAW--
YOU HIT SOMEONE WITH THIS VEHICLE--
DOESN'T MEAN YOU GET TO SEARCH IT--
NICK, JUST LET THEM--
NO. THIS SMELLS WRONG. THIS WHOLE THING'S COMING OFF BENT.
NICK--
AND IF THEY WANTED TO ARREST US, IF THEY COULD ARREST US, THEY WOULD--

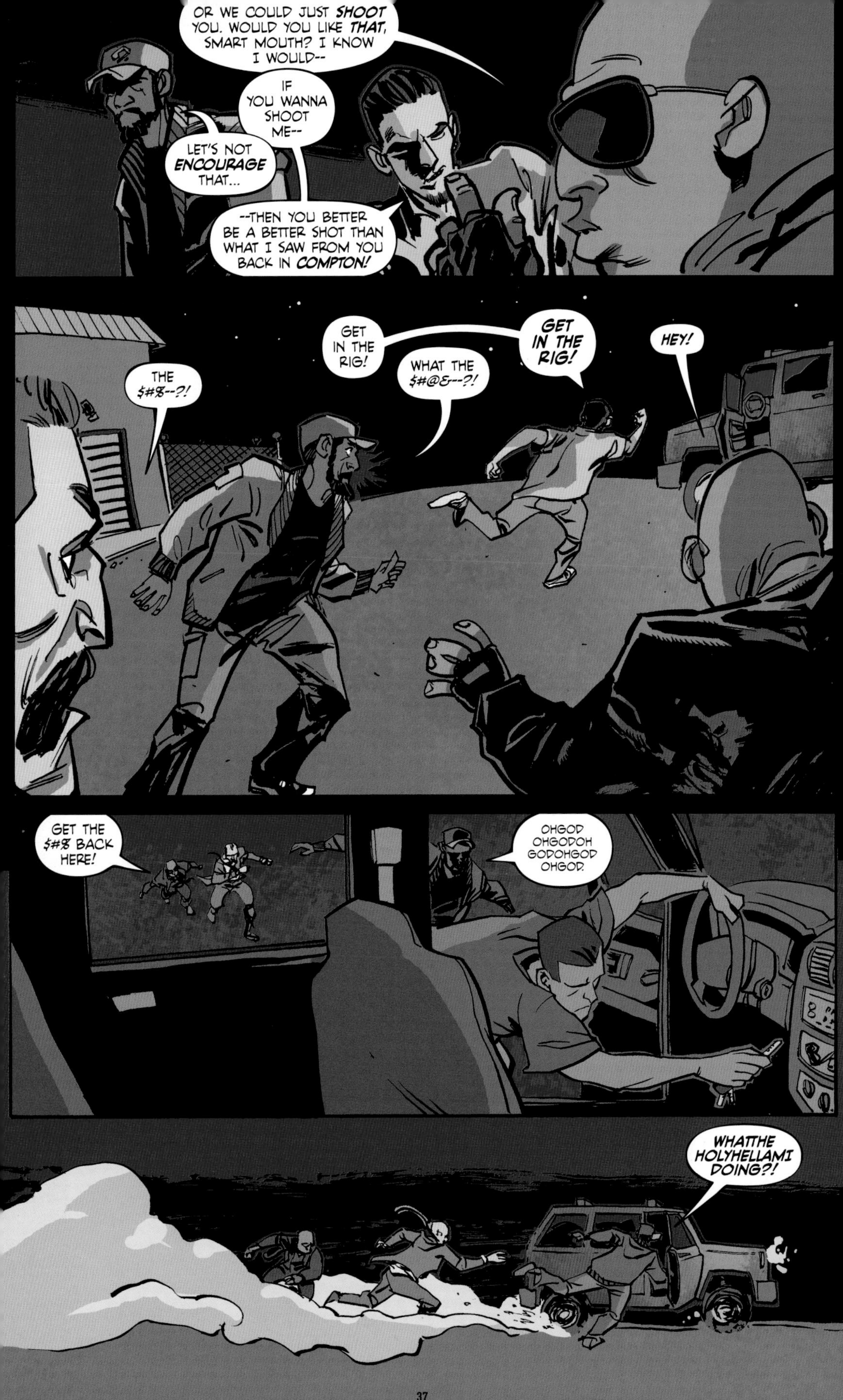
OR WE COULD JUST SHOOT YOU. WOULD YOU LIKE THAT, SMART MOUTH? I KNOW I WOULD--
IF YOU WANNA SHOOT ME--
LET'S NOT ENCOURAGE THAT...
--THEN YOU BETTER BE A BETTER SHOT THAN WHAT I SAW FROM YOU BACK IN COMPTON!
THE $#%--?!
GET IN THE RIG!
WHAT THE $#@&--?!
GET IN THE RIG!
HEY!
GET THE $#% BACK HERE!
OHGOD OHGODOH GODOHGOD OHGOD.
WHATTHE HOLYHELLAMI DOING?!

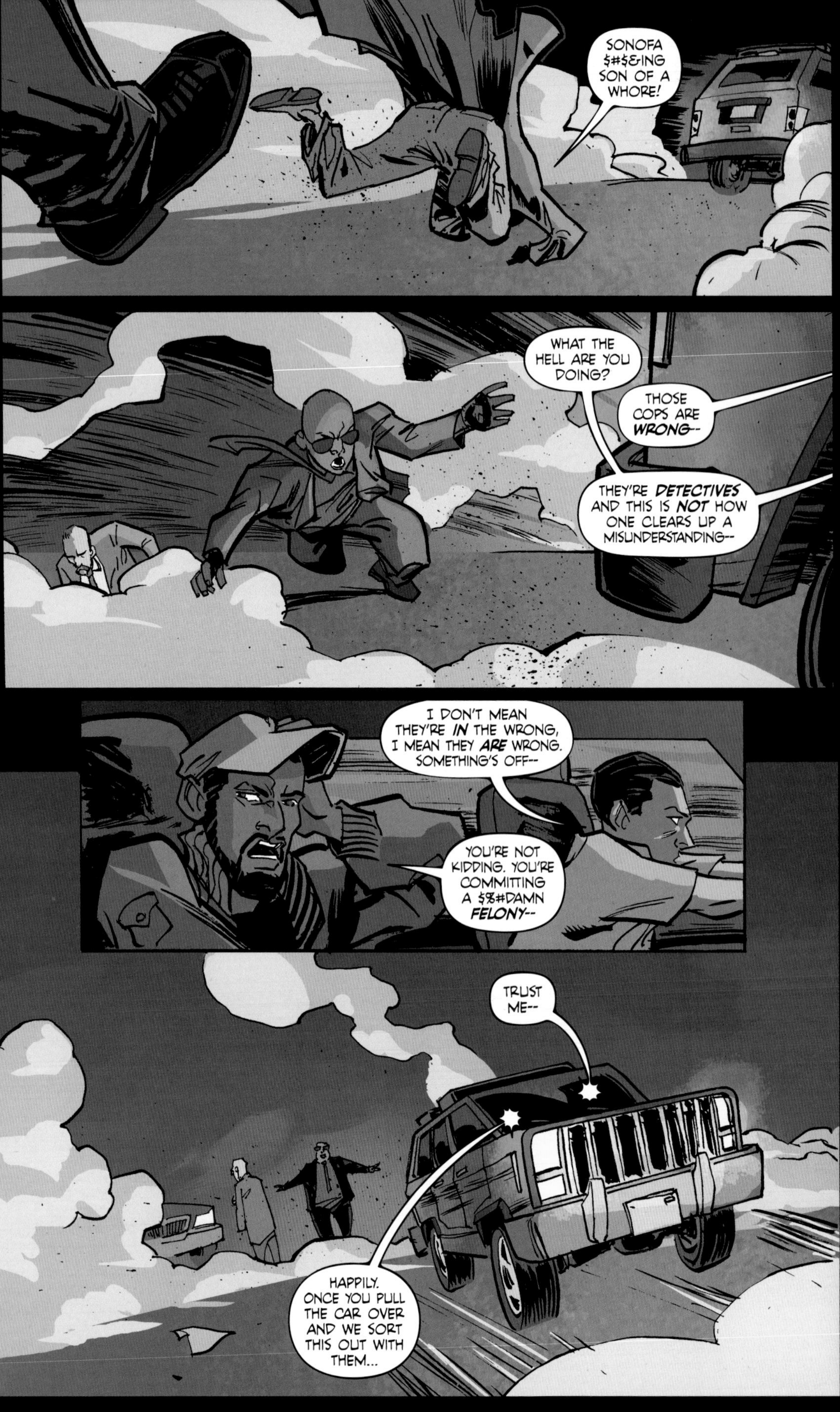

SONOFA $#$&ING SON OF A WHORE!
WHAT THE HELL ARE YOU DOING?
THOSE COPS ARE **WRONG**--
THEY'RE **DETECTIVES** AND THIS IS **NOT** HOW ONE CLEARS UP A MISUNDERSTANDING--
I DON'T MEAN THEY'RE **IN** THE WRONG, I MEAN THEY **ARE** WRONG. SOMETHING'S OFF--
YOU'RE NOT KIDDING. YOU'RE COMMITTING A $%#DAMN **FELONY**--
TRUST ME--
HAPPILY. ONCE YOU PULL THE CAR OVER AND WE SORT THIS OUT WITH THEM...

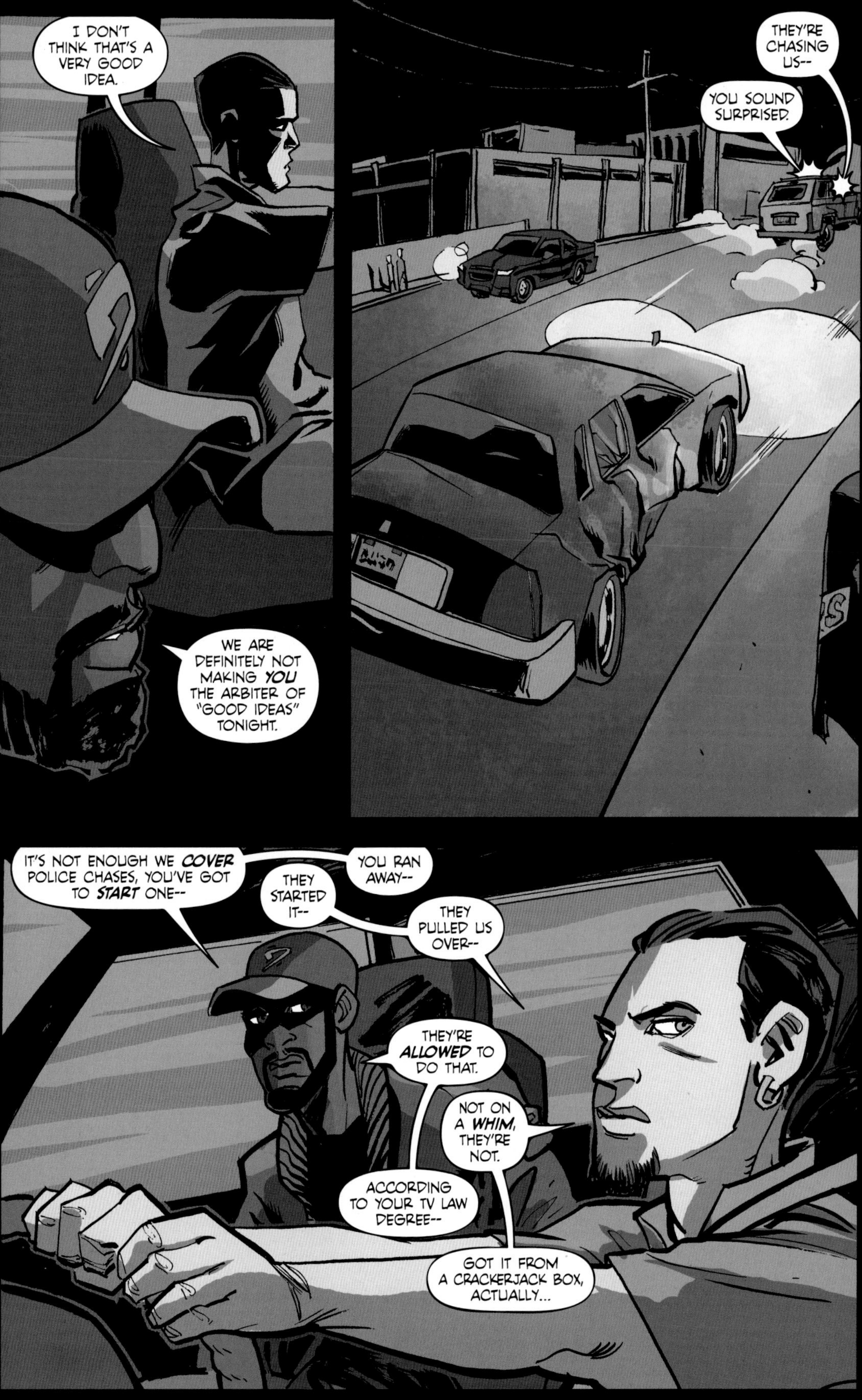
I DON'T THINK THAT'S A VERY GOOD IDEA.
WE ARE DEFINITELY NOT MAKING *YOU* THE ARBITER OF "GOOD IDEAS" TONIGHT.
THEY'RE CHASING US--
YOU SOUND SURPRISED.
IT'S NOT ENOUGH WE *COVER* POLICE CHASES, YOU'VE GOT TO *START* ONE--
YOU RAN AWAY--
THEY STARTED IT--
THEY PULLED US OVER--
THEY'RE *ALLOWED* TO DO THAT.
NOT ON A *WHIM*, THEY'RE NOT.
ACCORDING TO YOUR TV LAW DEGREE--
GOT IT FROM A CRACKERJACK BOX, ACTUALLY...

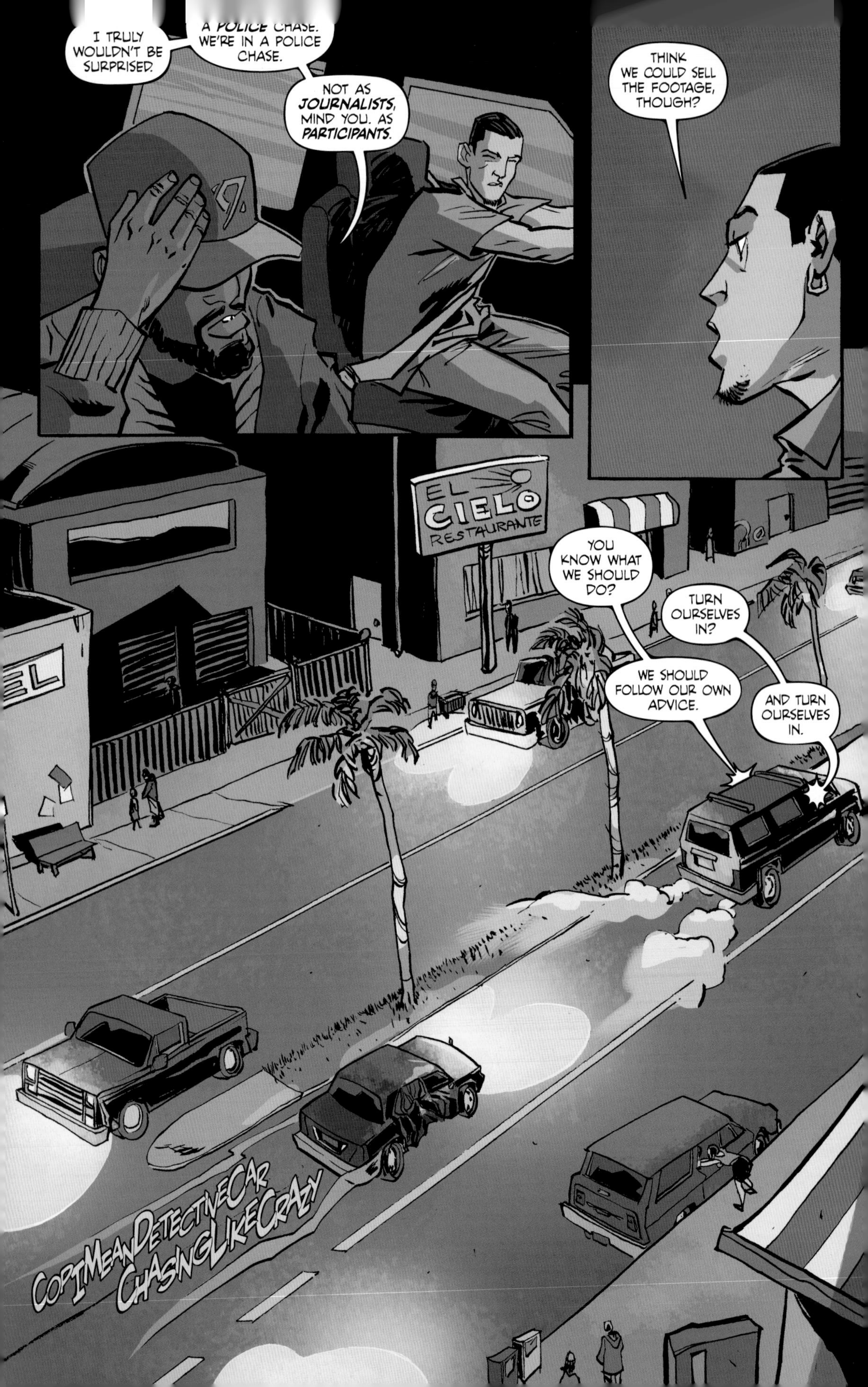
I TRULY WOULDN'T BE SURPRISED.
A POLICE CHASE. WE'RE IN A POLICE CHASE.
NOT AS JOURNALISTS, MIND YOU. AS PARTICIPANTS.
THINK WE COULD SELL THE FOOTAGE, THOUGH?
EL CIELO RESTAURANTE
YOU KNOW WHAT WE SHOULD DO?
TURN OURSELVES IN?
WE SHOULD FOLLOW OUR OWN ADVICE.
AND TURN OURSELVES IN.
COPIMEANDETECTIVECAR CHASINGLIKECRAZY

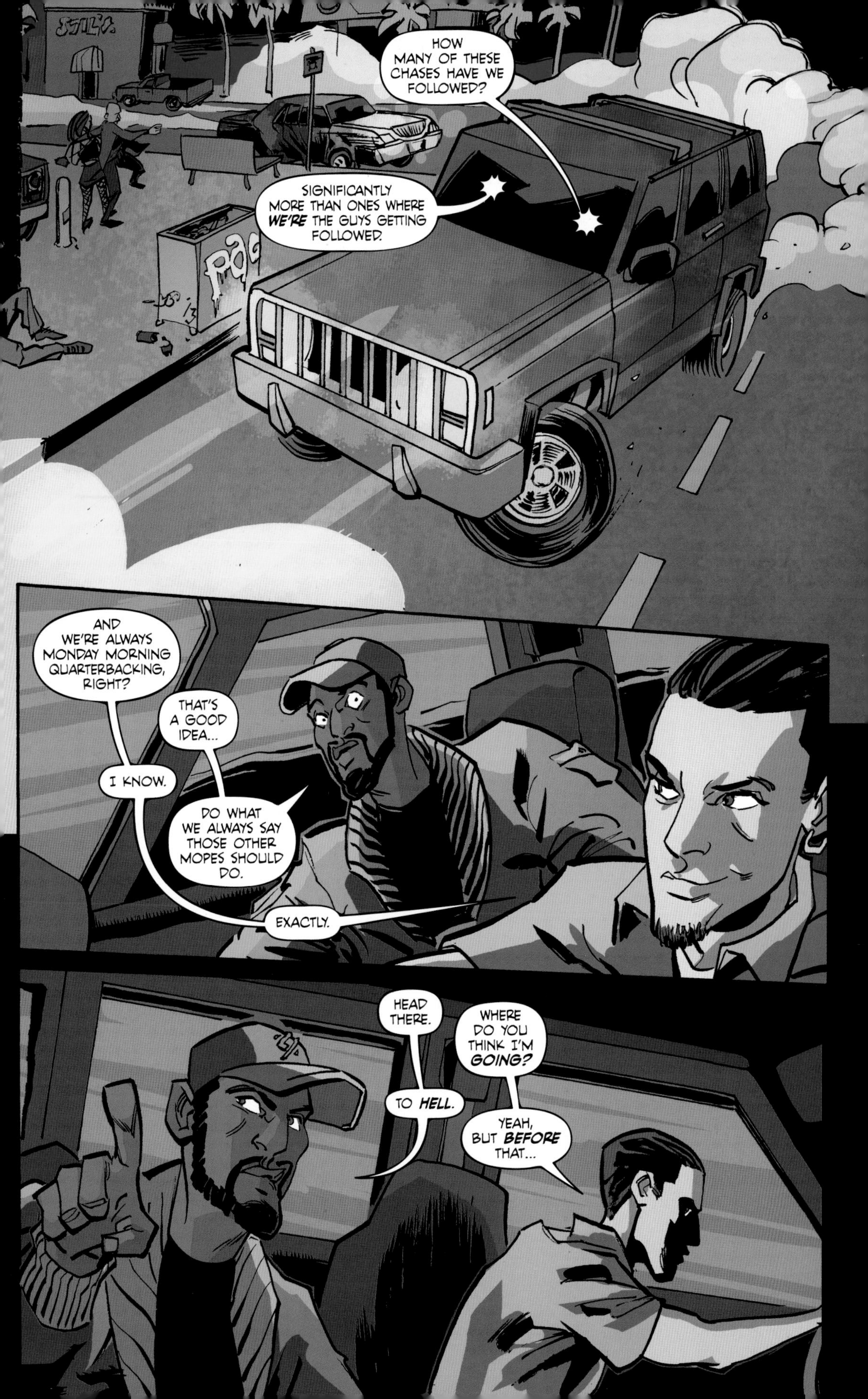
HOW MANY OF THESE CHASES HAVE WE FOLLOWED?
SIGNIFICANTLY MORE THAN ONES WHERE WE'RE THE GUYS GETTING FOLLOWED.
AND WE'RE ALWAYS MONDAY MORNING QUARTERBACKING, RIGHT?
THAT'S A GOOD IDEA...
I KNOW.
DO WHAT WE ALWAYS SAY THOSE OTHER MOPES SHOULD DO.
EXACTLY.
HEAD THERE.
WHERE DO YOU THINK I'M GOING?
TO HELL.
YEAH, BUT BEFORE THAT...

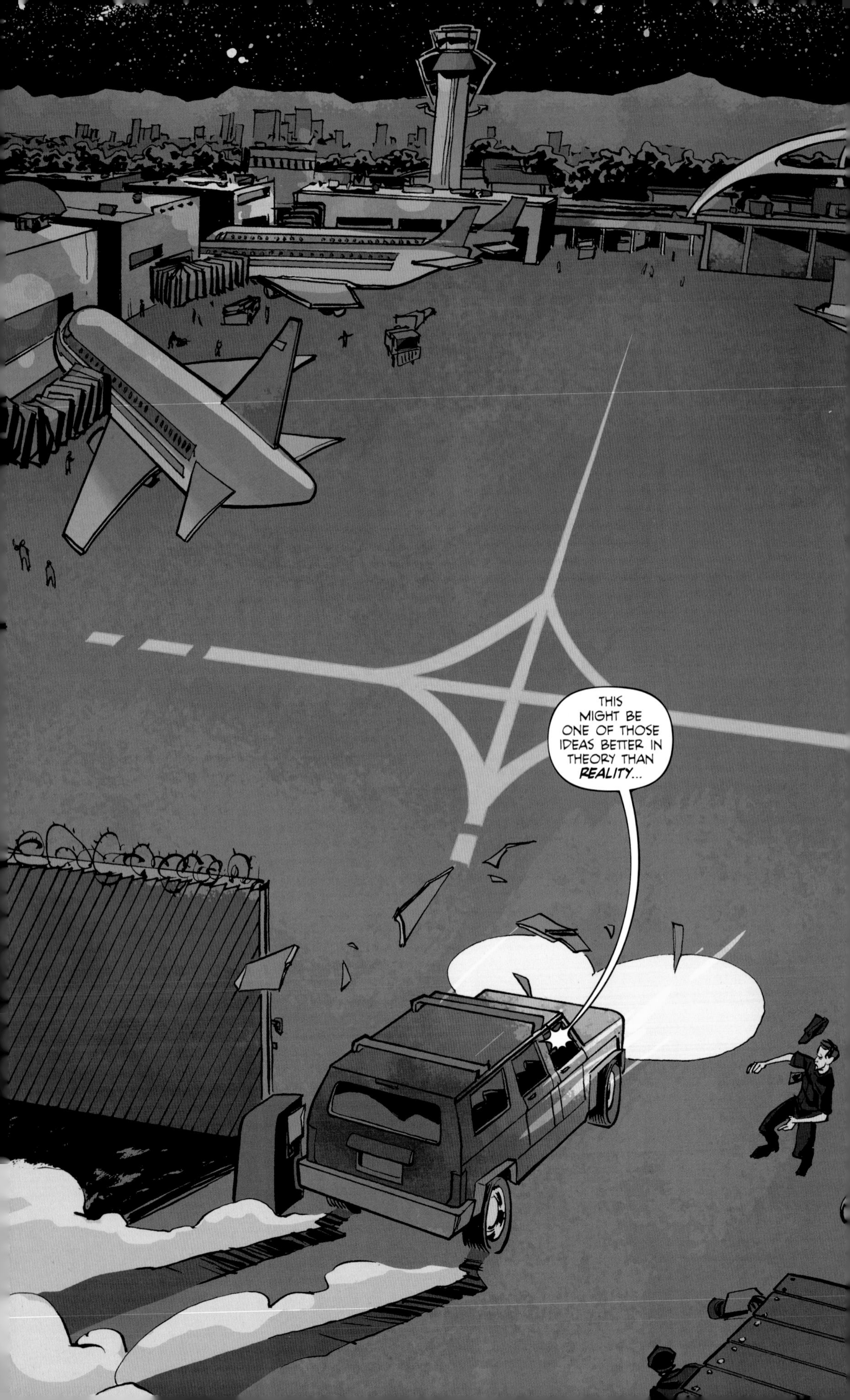
THIS MIGHT BE ONE OF THOSE IDEAS BETTER IN THEORY THAN REALITY...

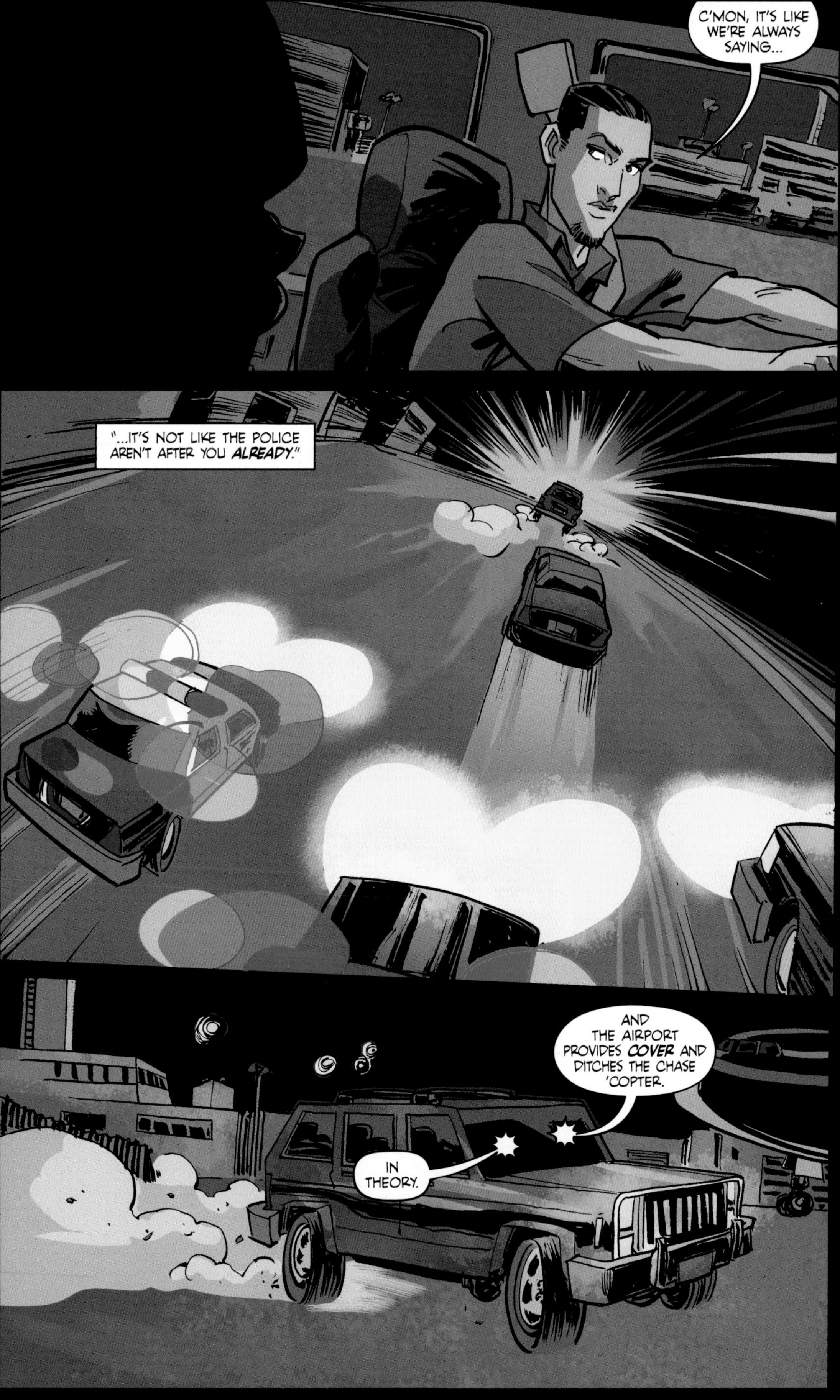
C'MON, IT'S LIKE WE'RE ALWAYS SAYING...
"...IT'S NOT LIKE THE POLICE AREN'T AFTER YOU ALREADY."
AND THE AIRPORT PROVIDES COVER AND DITCHES THE CHASE 'COPTER.
IN THEORY.

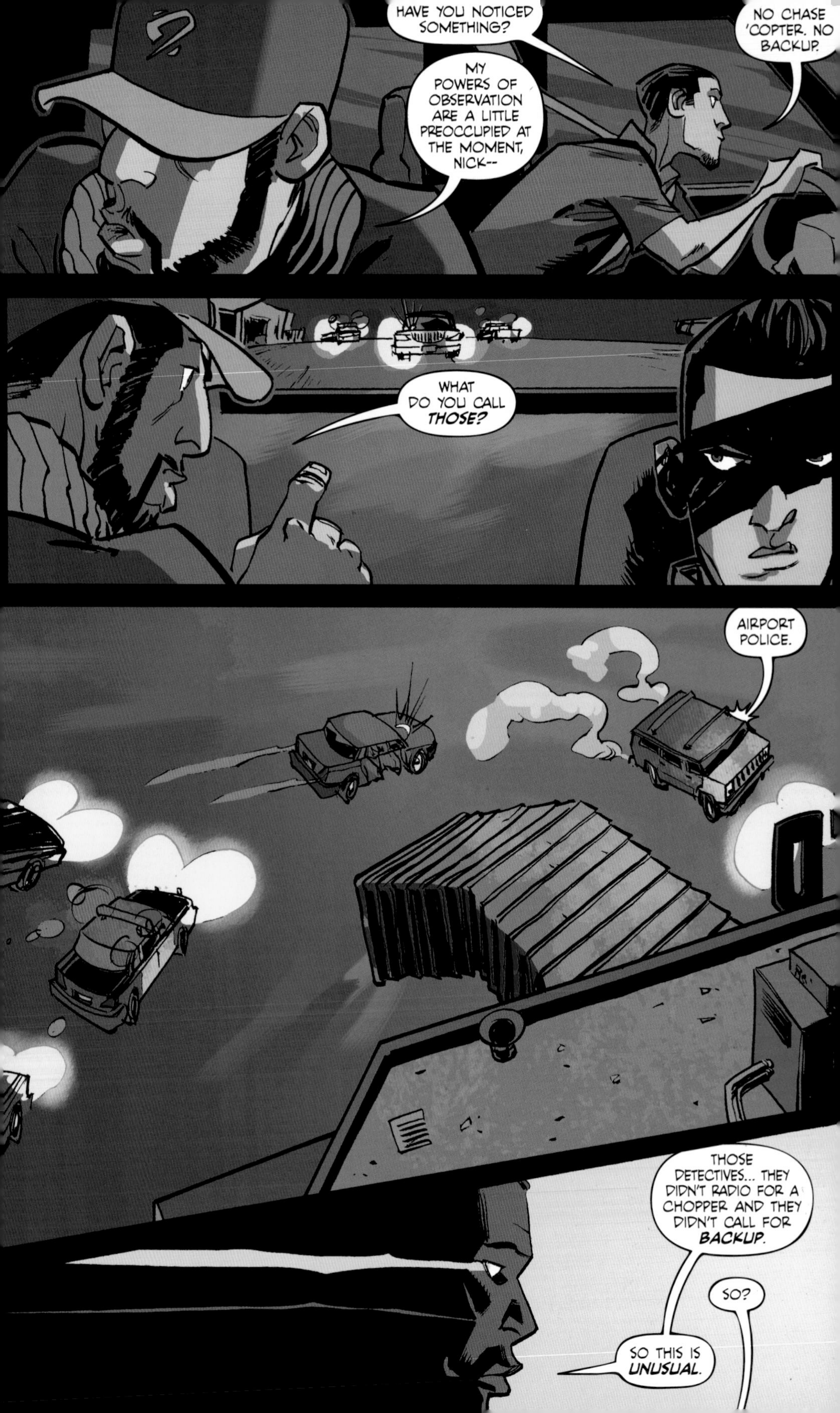
HAVE YOU NOTICED SOMETHING?
NO CHASE 'COPTER. NO BACKUP.
MY POWERS OF OBSERVATION ARE A LITTLE PREOCCUPIED AT THE MOMENT, NICK--
WHAT DO YOU CALL *THOSE?*
AIRPORT POLICE.
THOSE DETECTIVES... THEY DIDN'T RADIO FOR A CHOPPER AND THEY DIDN'T CALL FOR *BACKUP*.
SO?
SO THIS IS *UNUSUAL*.

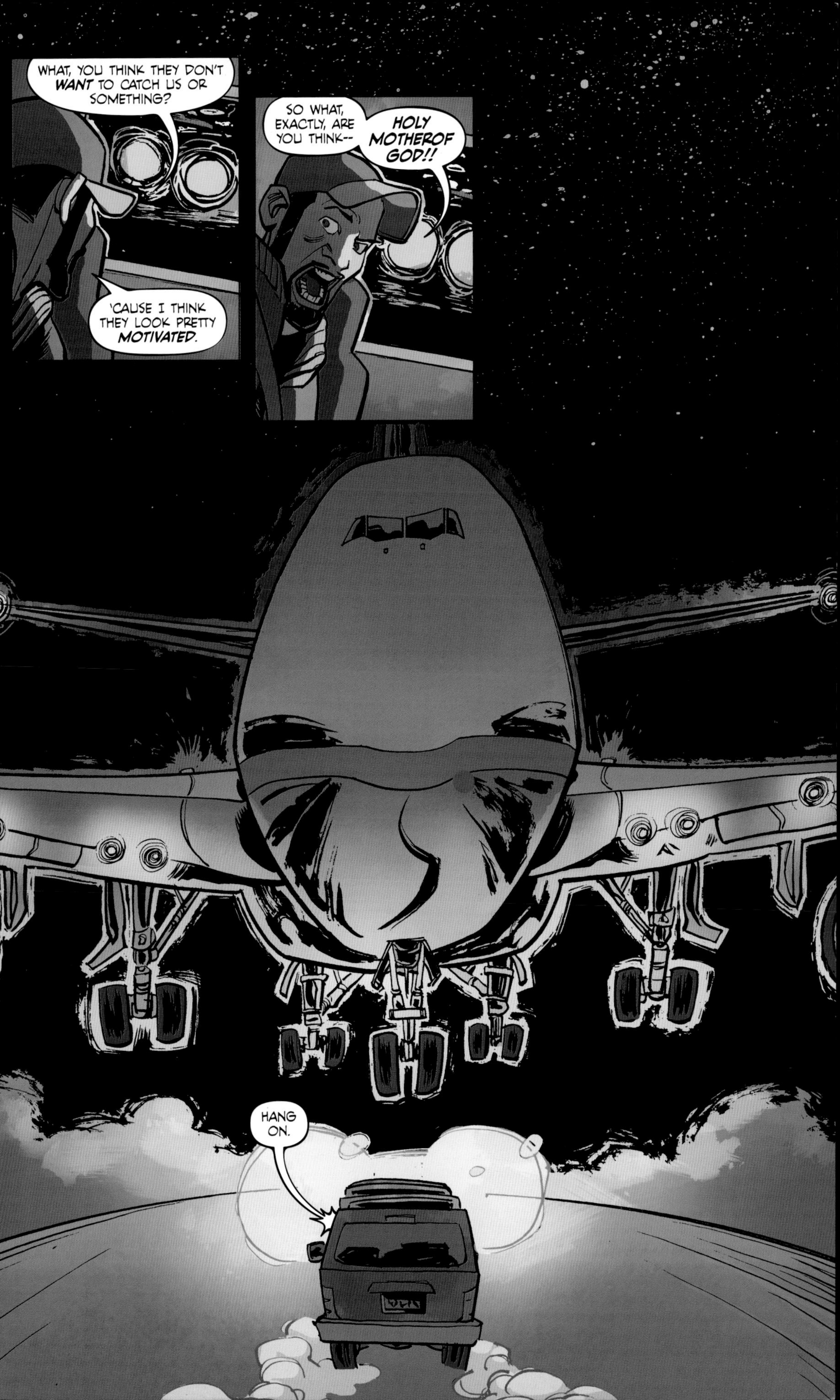
WHAT, YOU THINK THEY DON'T *WANT* TO CATCH US OR SOMETHING?
'CAUSE I THINK THEY LOOK PRETTY *MOTIVATED*.
SO WHAT, EXACTLY, ARE YOU THINK--
HOLY MOTHEROF GOD!!
HANG ON.

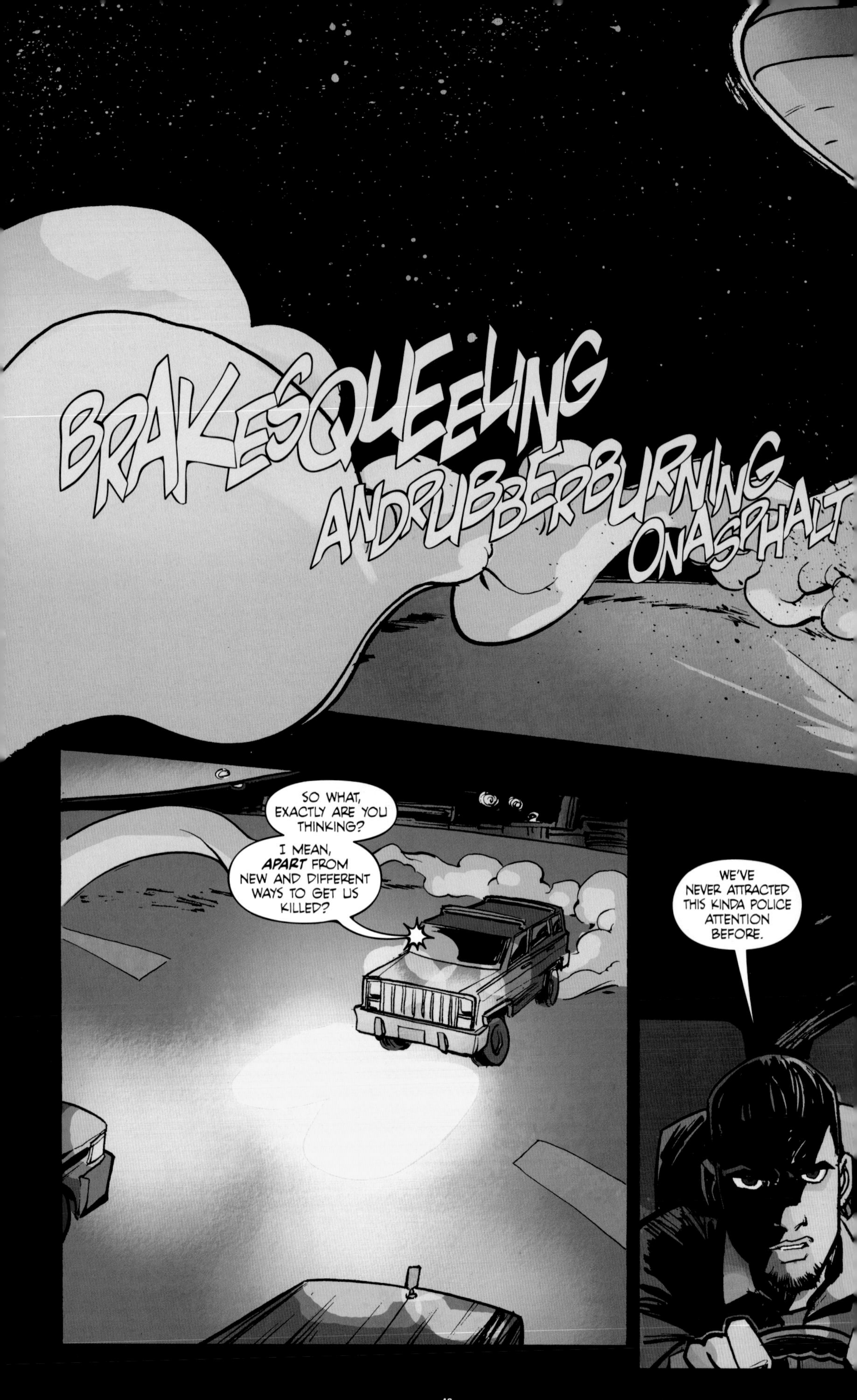

BRAKESQUEEELING ANDRUBBERBURNING ONASPHALT
SO WHAT, EXACTLY ARE YOU THINKING?
I MEAN, *APART* FROM NEW AND DIFFERENT WAYS TO GET US KILLED?
WE'VE NEVER ATTRACTED THIS KINDA POLICE ATTENTION BEFORE.

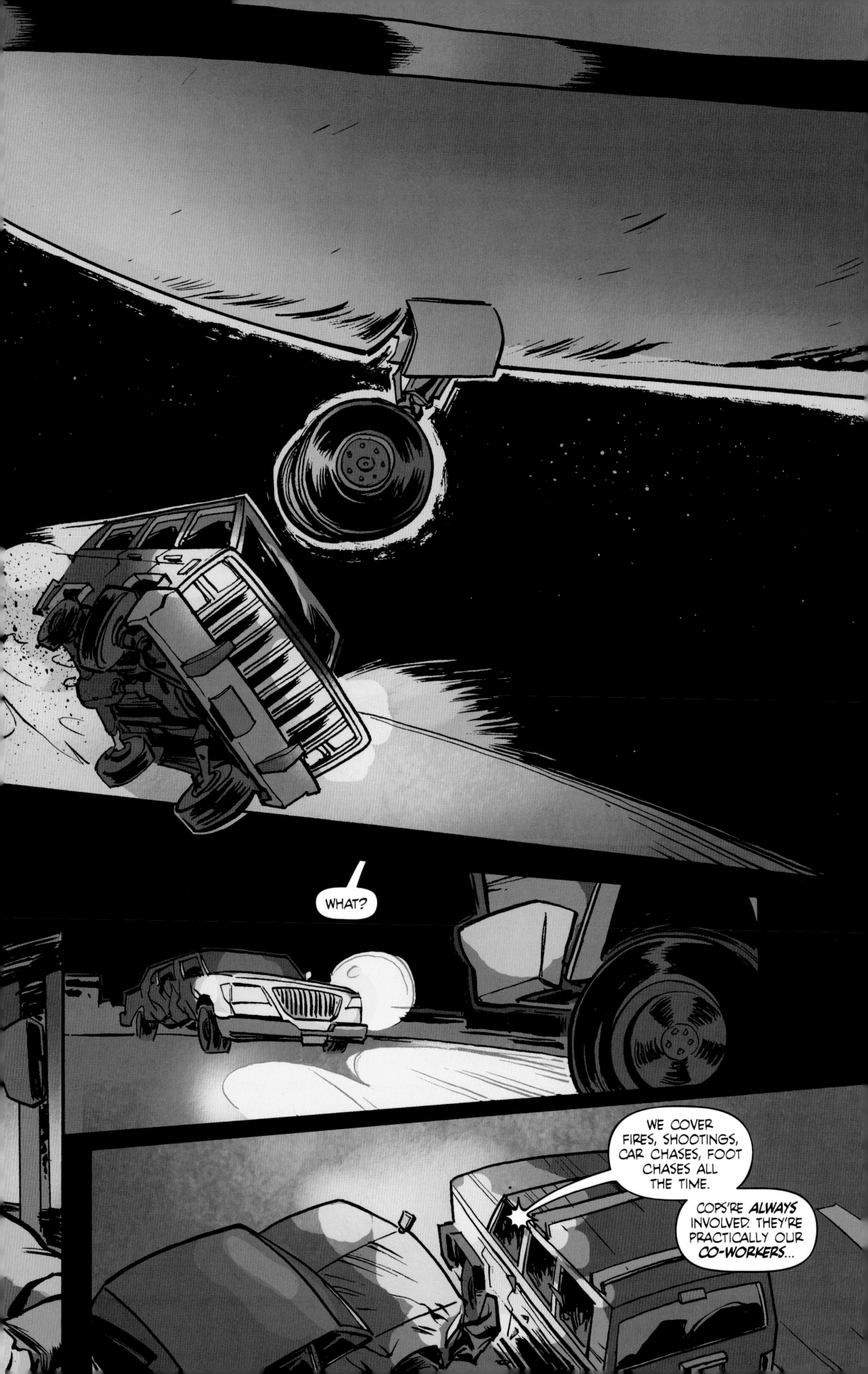
WHAT?
WE COVER FIRES, SHOOTINGS, CAR CHASES, FOOT CHASES ALL THE TIME.
COPS'RE ALWAYS INVOLVED. THEY'RE PRACTICALLY OUR CO-WORKERS...

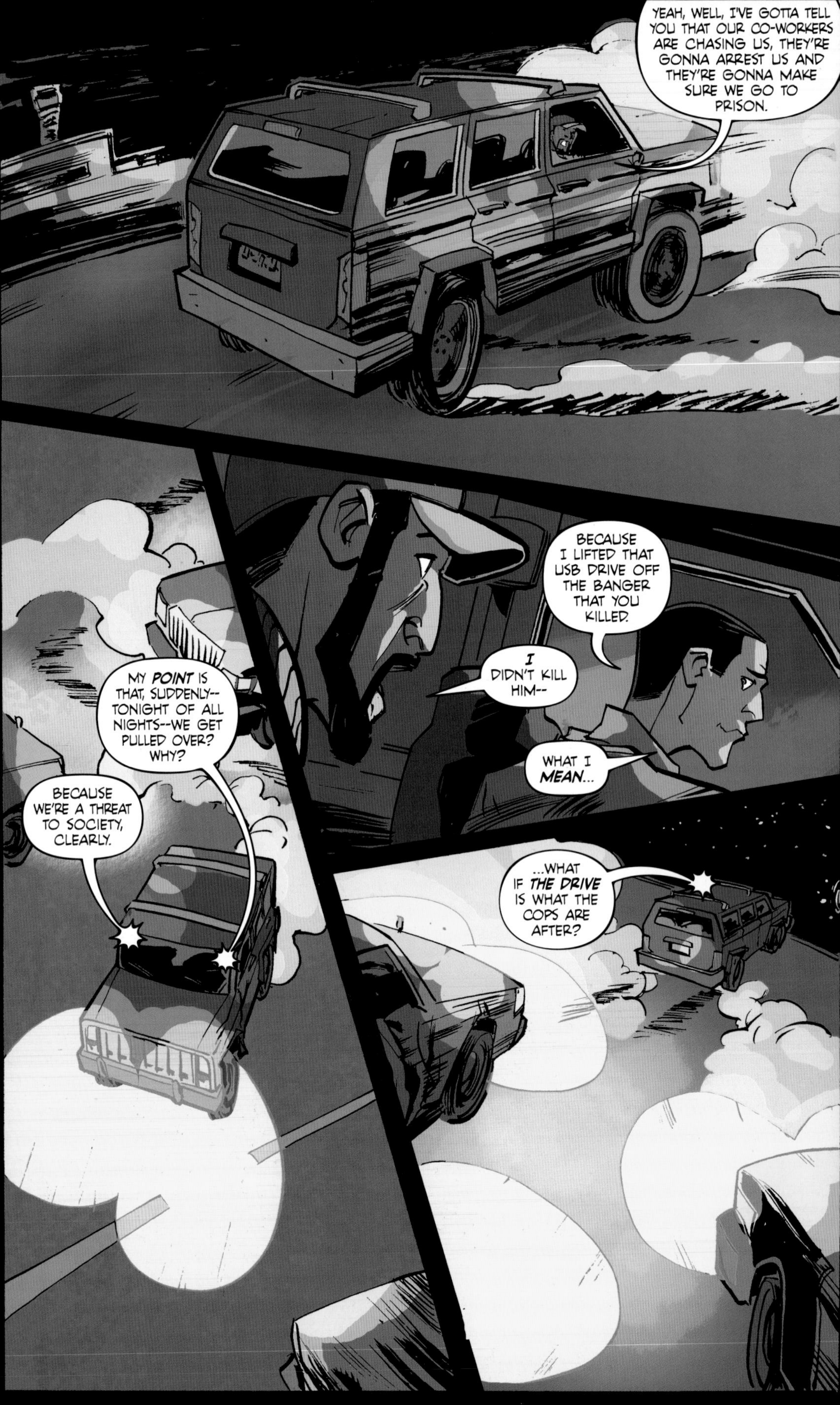

YEAH, WELL, I'VE GOTTA TELL YOU THAT OUR CO-WORKERS ARE CHASING US, THEY'RE GONNA ARREST US AND THEY'RE GONNA MAKE SURE WE GO TO PRISON.
MY *POINT* IS THAT, SUDDENLY-- TONIGHT OF ALL NIGHTS--WE GET PULLED OVER? WHY?
BECAUSE WE'RE A THREAT TO SOCIETY, CLEARLY.
BECAUSE I LIFTED THAT USB DRIVE OFF THE BANGER THAT YOU KILLED.
I DIDN'T KILL HIM--
WHAT I *MEAN*...
...WHAT IF *THE DRIVE* IS WHAT THE COPS ARE AFTER?

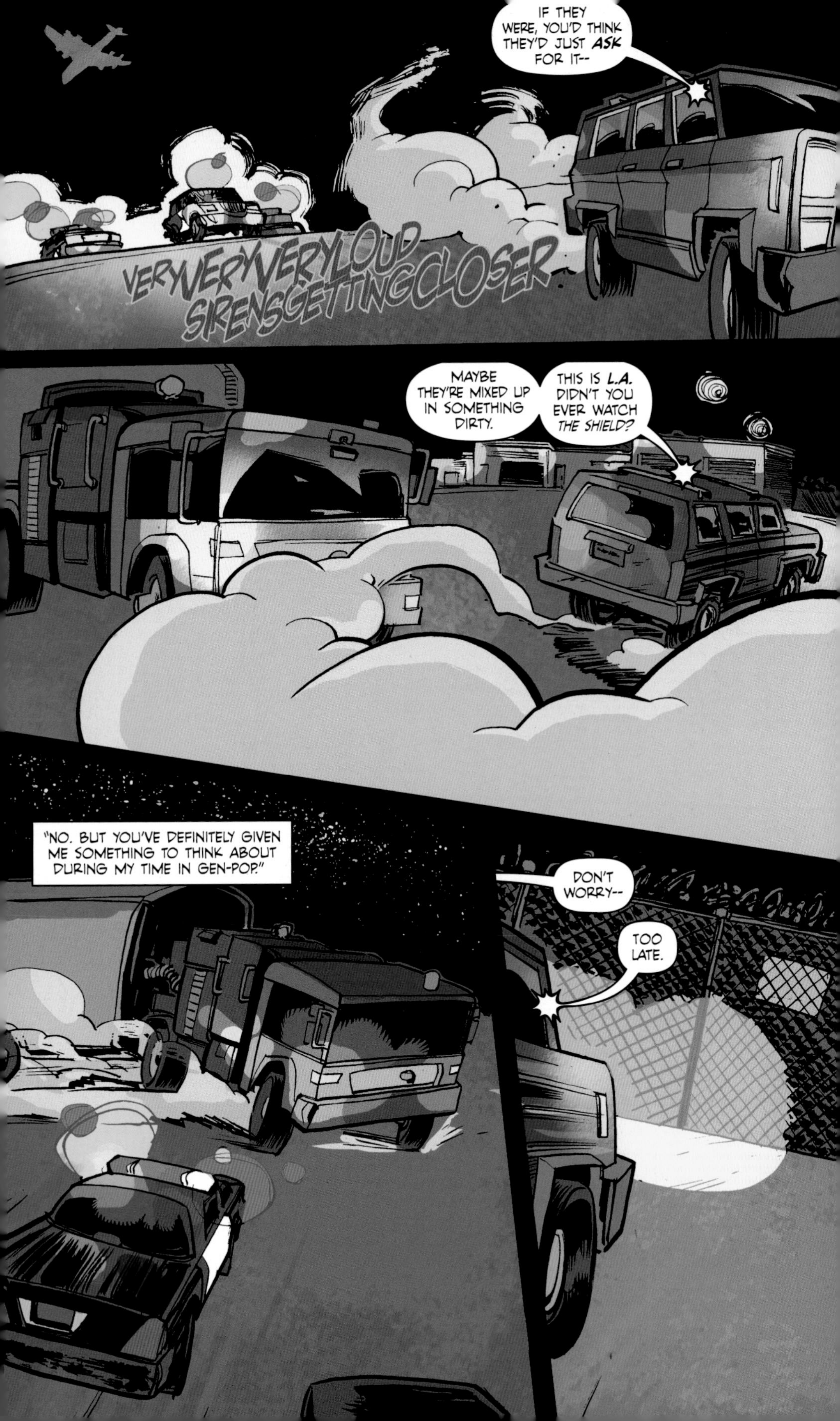
IF THEY WERE, YOU'D THINK THEY'D JUST ASK FOR IT--
VERYVERYVERYLOUD SIRENSGETTINGCLOSER
MAYBE THEY'RE MIXED UP IN SOMETHING DIRTY.
THIS IS L.A. DIDN'T YOU EVER WATCH THE SHIELD?
"NO. BUT YOU'VE DEFINITELY GIVEN ME SOMETHING TO THINK ABOUT DURING MY TIME IN GEN-POP."
DON'T WORRY--
TOO LATE.

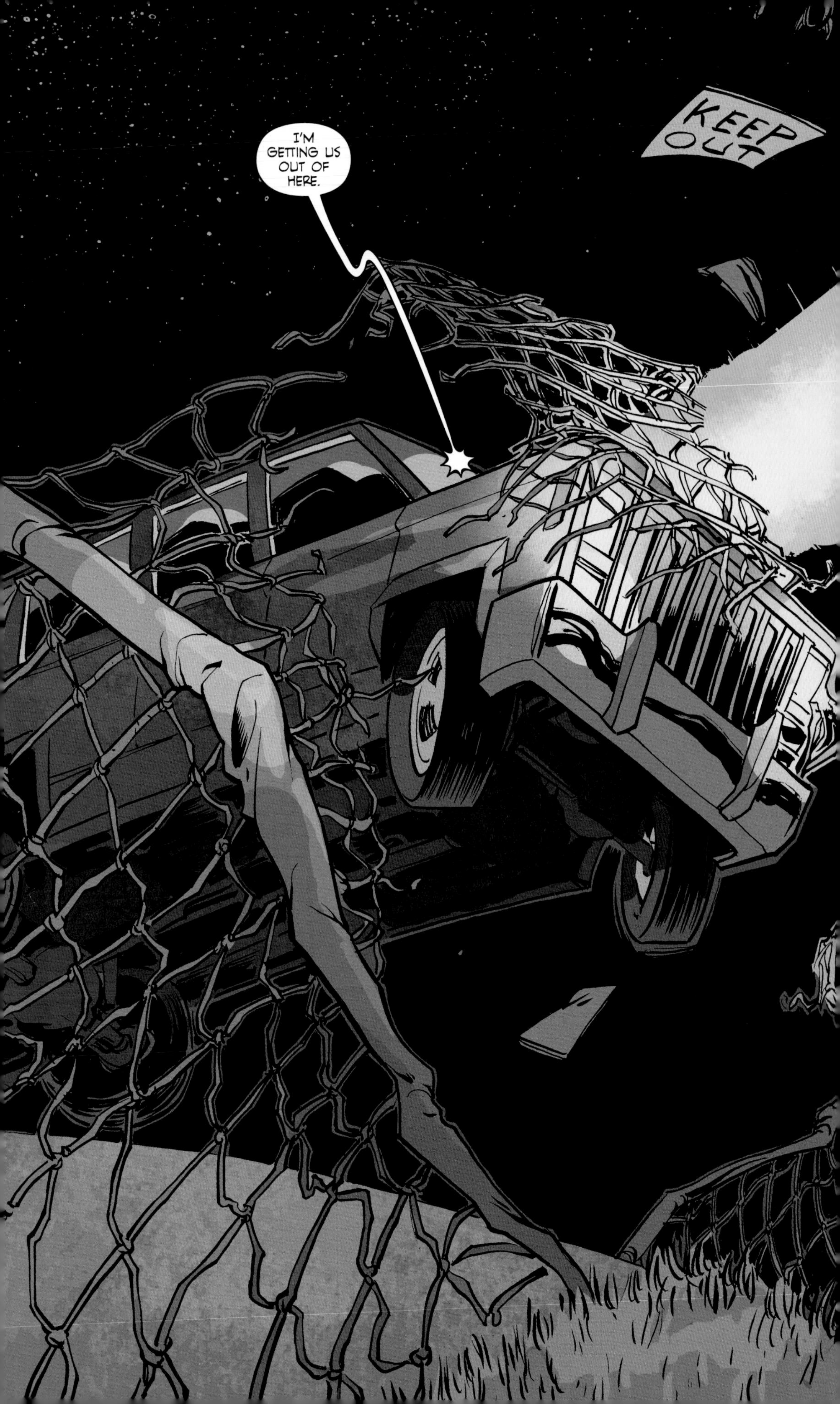
KEEP OUT
I'M GETTING US OUT OF HERE.

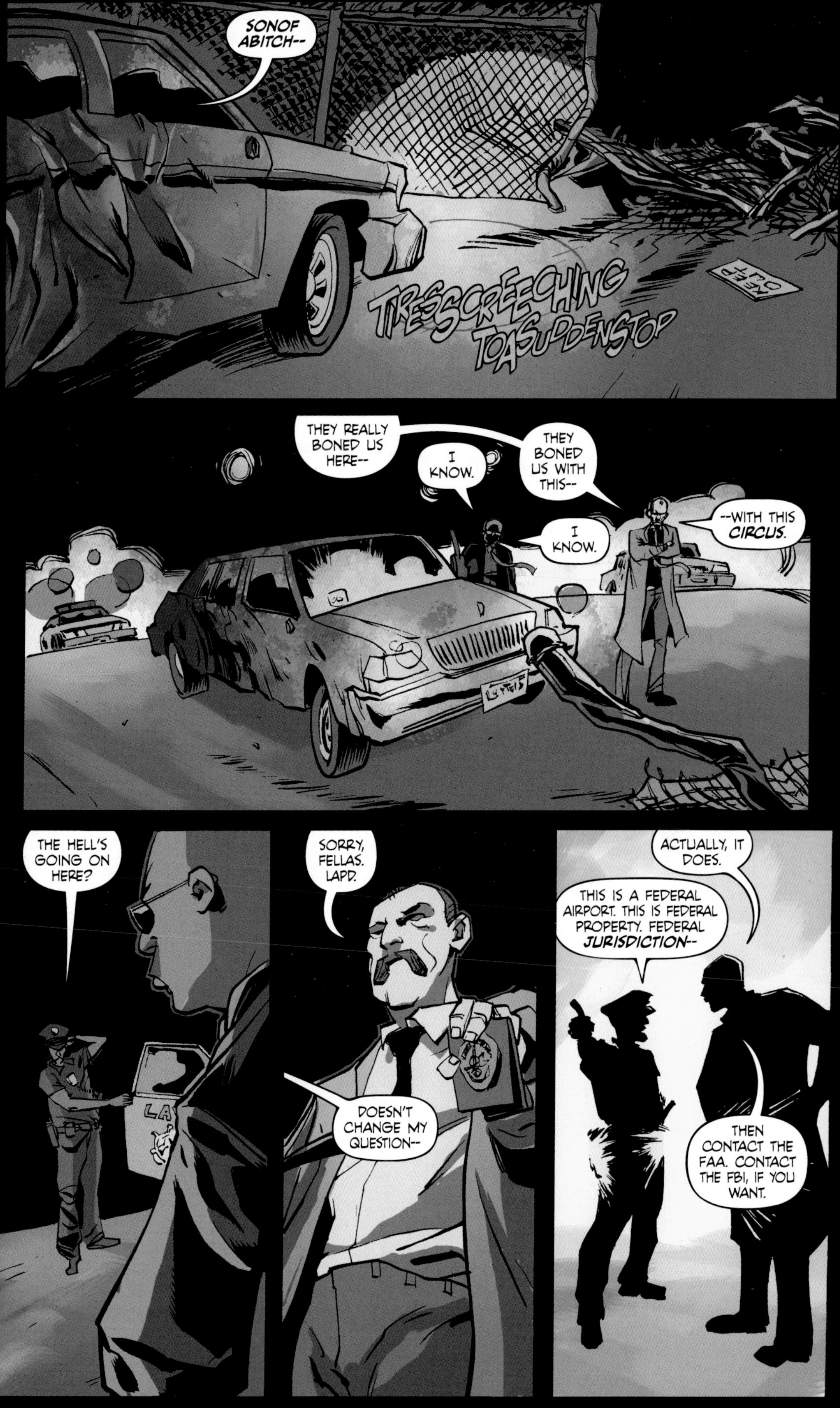
SONOF ABITCH--
TIRESSCREECHING TOASUDDENSTOP
KEEP OUT
THEY REALLY BONED US HERE--
I KNOW.
THEY BONED US WITH THIS--
I KNOW.
--WITH THIS *CIRCUS*.
THE HELL'S GOING ON HERE?
SORRY, FELLAS. LAPD.
DOESN'T CHANGE MY QUESTION--
ACTUALLY, IT DOES.
THIS IS A FEDERAL AIRPORT. THIS IS FEDERAL PROPERTY. FEDERAL *JURISDICTION*--
THEN CONTACT THE FAA. CONTACT THE FBI, IF YOU WANT.

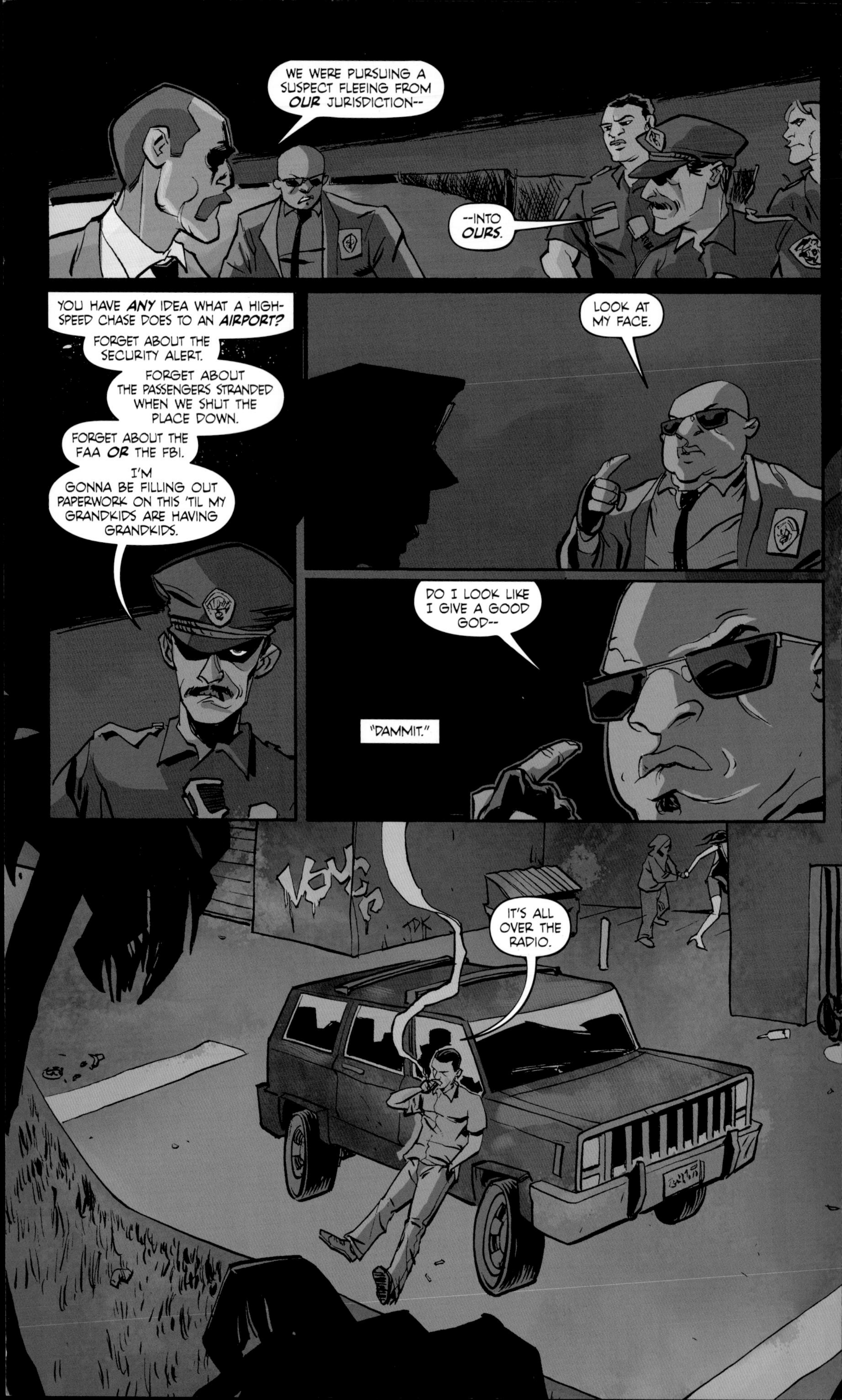

WE WERE PURSUING A SUSPECT FLEEING FROM *OUR* JURISDICTION--
--INTO *OURS*.
YOU HAVE *ANY* IDEA WHAT A HIGH-SPEED CHASE DOES TO AN *AIRPORT?*
FORGET ABOUT THE SECURITY ALERT.
FORGET ABOUT THE PASSENGERS STRANDED WHEN WE SHUT THE PLACE DOWN.
FORGET ABOUT THE FAA *OR* THE FBI.
I'M GONNA BE FILLING OUT PAPERWORK ON THIS 'TIL MY GRANDKIDS ARE HAVING GRANDKIDS.
LOOK AT MY FACE.
DO I LOOK LIKE I GIVE A GOOD GOD--
"DAMMIT."
IT'S ALL OVER THE RADIO.

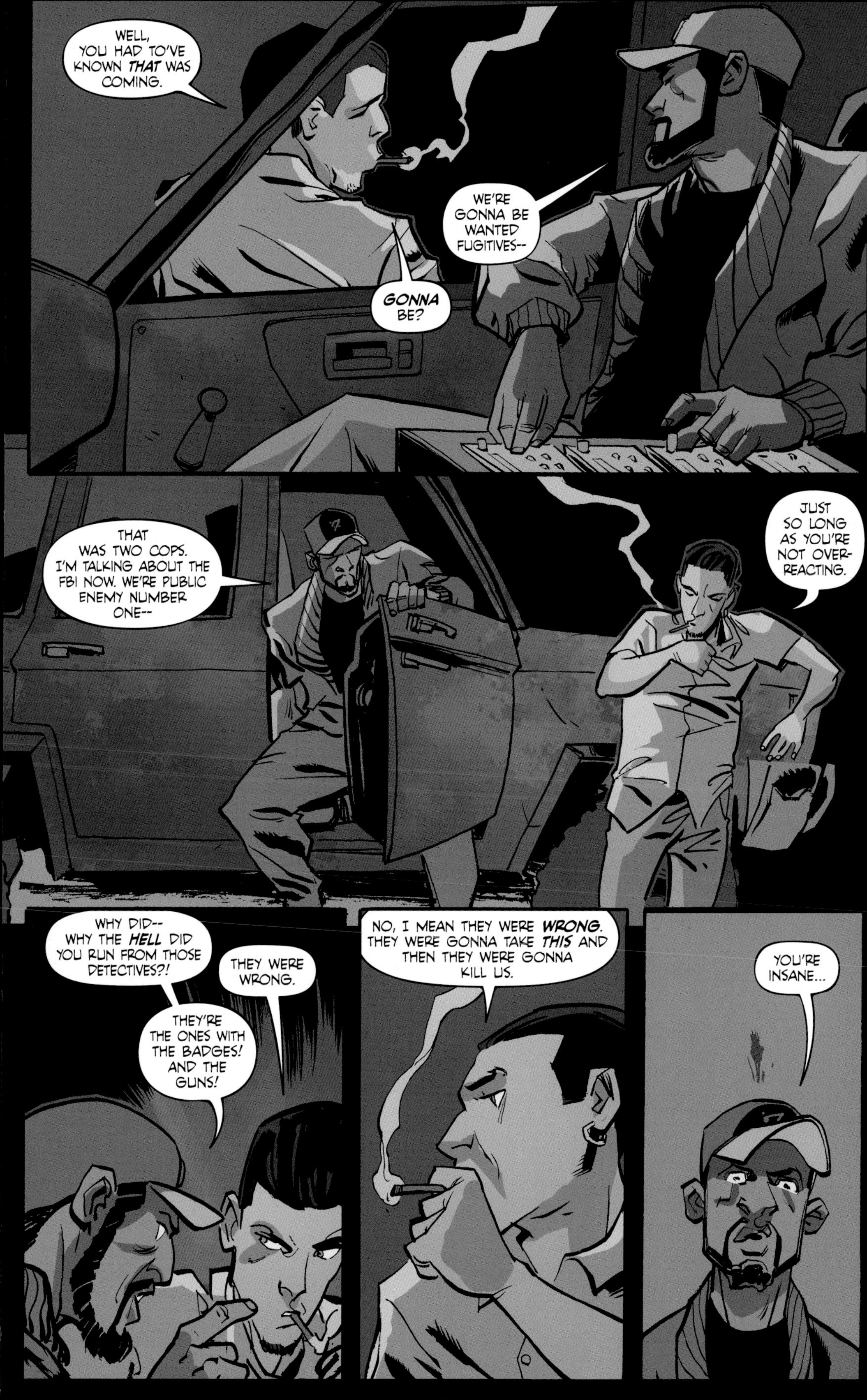
WELL, YOU HAD TO'VE KNOWN *THAT* WAS COMING.
WE'RE GONNA BE WANTED FUGITIVES--
GONNA BE?
THAT WAS TWO COPS. I'M TALKING ABOUT THE FBI NOW. WE'RE PUBLIC ENEMY NUMBER ONE--
JUST SO LONG AS YOU'RE NOT OVER-REACTING.
WHY DID-- WHY THE *HELL* DID YOU RUN FROM THOSE DETECTIVES?!
THEY WERE WRONG.
THEY'RE THE ONES WITH THE BADGES! AND THE GUNS!
NO, I MEAN THEY WERE *WRONG*. THEY WERE GONNA TAKE *THIS* AND THEN THEY WERE GONNA KILL US.
YOU'RE INSANE...

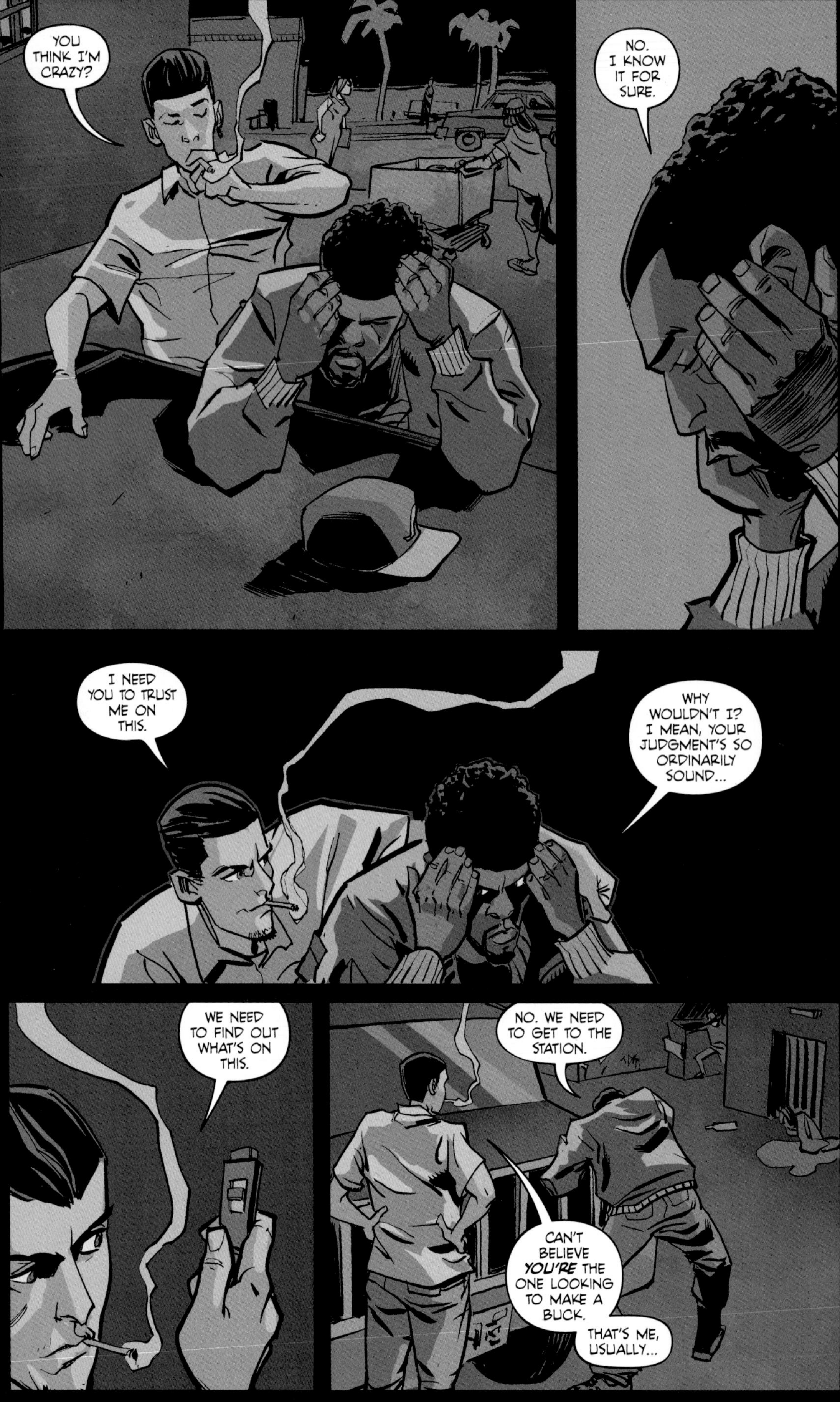
YOU THINK I'M CRAZY?
NO. I KNOW IT FOR SURE.
I NEED YOU TO TRUST ME ON THIS.
WHY WOULDN'T I? I MEAN, YOUR JUDGMENT'S SO ORDINARILY SOUND...
WE NEED TO FIND OUT WHAT'S ON THIS.
NO. WE NEED TO GET TO THE STATION.
CAN'T BELIEVE *YOU'RE* THE ONE LOOKING TO MAKE A BUCK.
THAT'S ME, USUALLY...

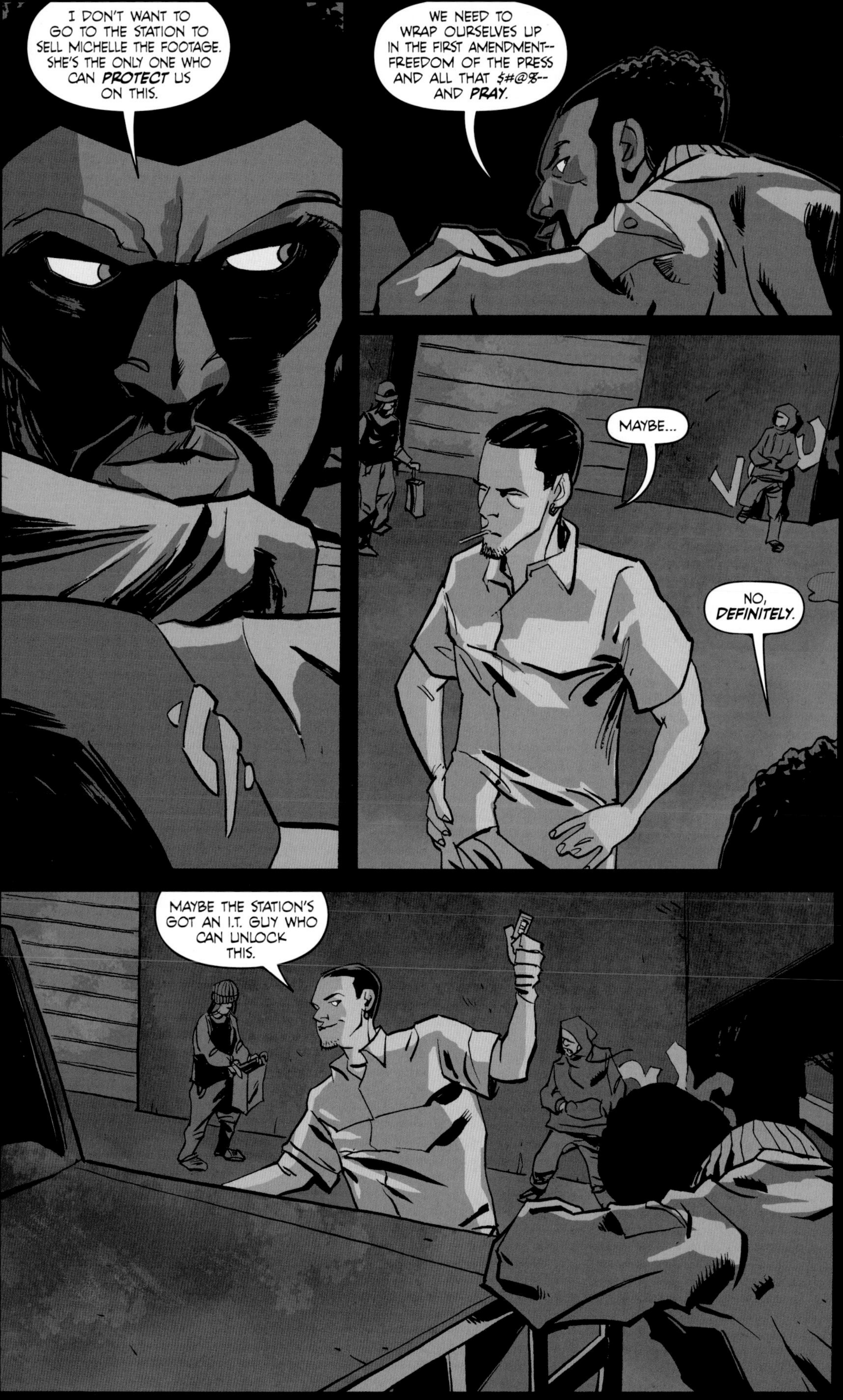

I DON'T WANT TO GO TO THE STATION TO SELL MICHELLE THE FOOTAGE. SHE'S THE ONLY ONE WHO CAN *PROTECT* US ON THIS.
WE NEED TO WRAP OURSELVES UP IN THE FIRST AMENDMENT-- FREEDOM OF THE PRESS AND ALL THAT $#@%-- AND *PRAY*.
MAYBE...
NO, *DEFINITELY*.
MAYBE THE STATION'S GOT AN I.T. GUY WHO CAN UNLOCK THIS.

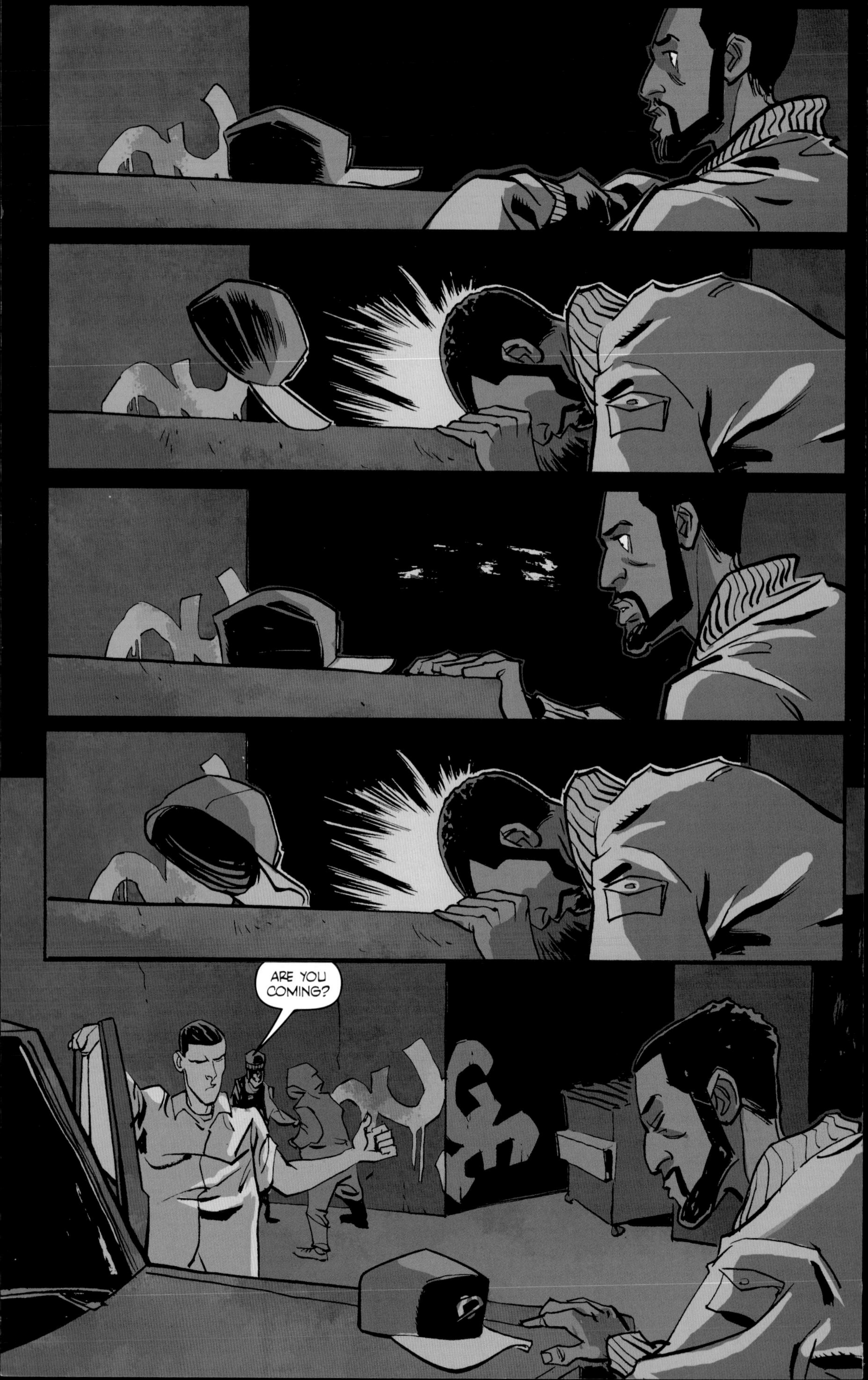
ARE YOU COMING?

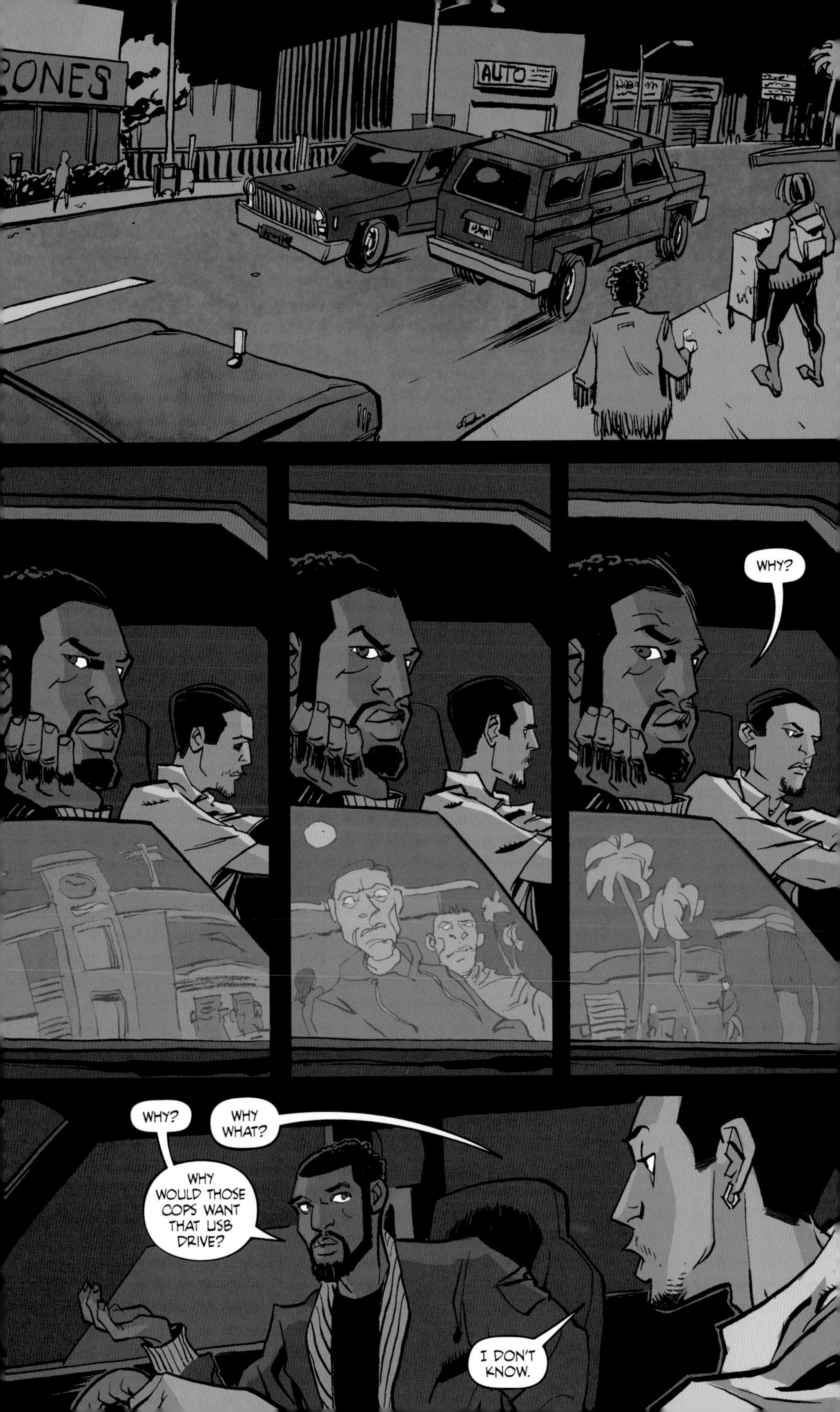
RONES
AUTO
WHY?
WHY?
WHY WHAT?
WHY WOULD THOSE COPS WANT THAT USB DRIVE?
I DON'T KNOW.

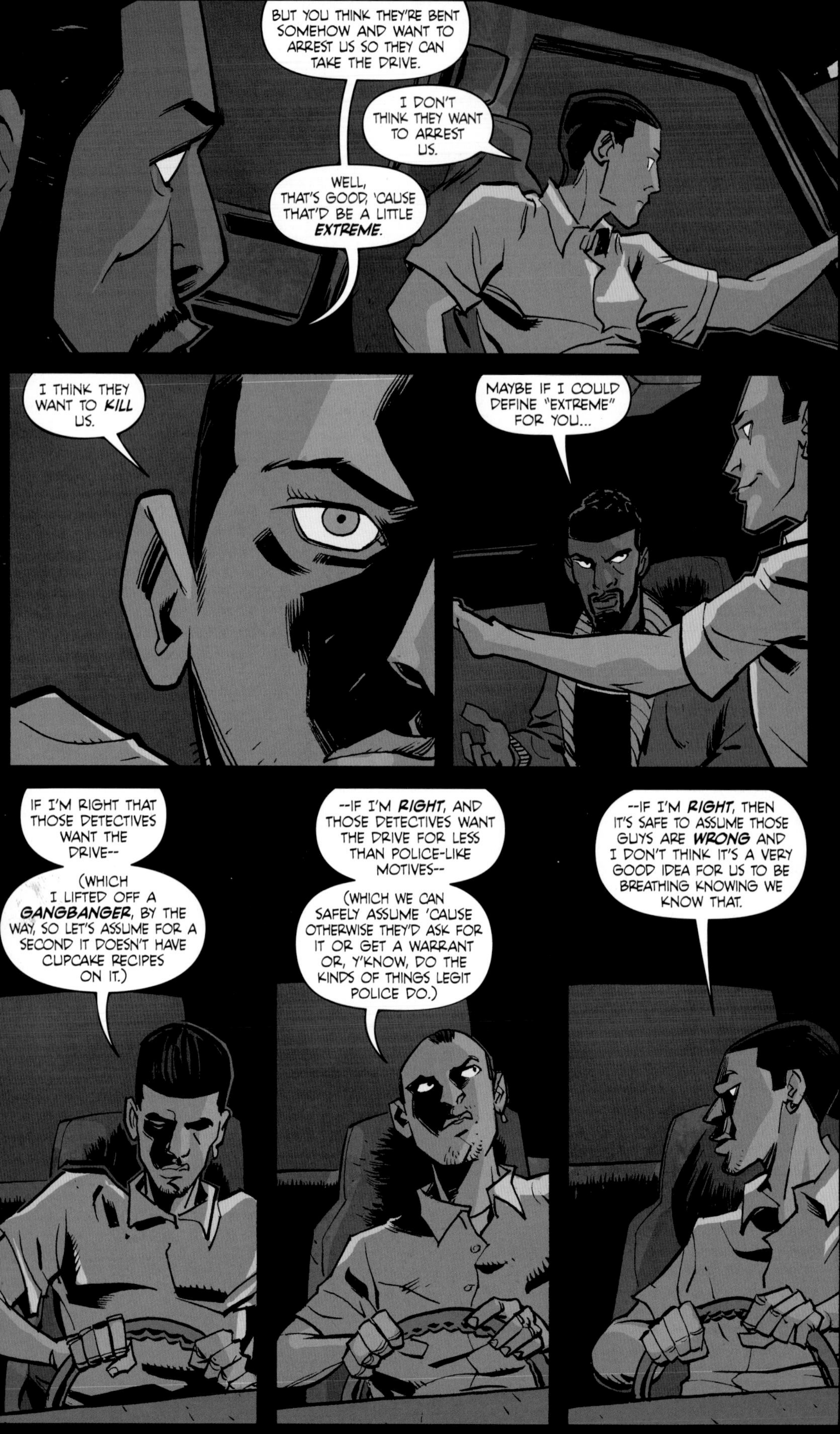
BUT YOU THINK THEY'RE BENT SOMEHOW AND WANT TO ARREST US SO THEY CAN TAKE THE DRIVE.
I DON'T THINK THEY WANT TO ARREST US.
WELL, THAT'S GOOD, 'CAUSE THAT'D BE A LITTLE EXTREME.
I THINK THEY WANT TO KILL US.
MAYBE IF I COULD DEFINE "EXTREME" FOR YOU...
IF I'M RIGHT THAT THOSE DETECTIVES WANT THE DRIVE--
(WHICH I LIFTED OFF A GANGBANGER, BY THE WAY, SO LET'S ASSUME FOR A SECOND IT DOESN'T HAVE CUPCAKE RECIPES ON IT.)
--IF I'M RIGHT, AND THOSE DETECTIVES WANT THE DRIVE FOR LESS THAN POLICE-LIKE MOTIVES--
(WHICH WE CAN SAFELY ASSUME 'CAUSE OTHERWISE THEY'D ASK FOR IT OR GET A WARRANT OR, Y'KNOW, DO THE KINDS OF THINGS LEGIT POLICE DO.)
--IF I'M RIGHT, THEN IT'S SAFE TO ASSUME THOSE GUYS ARE WRONG AND I DON'T THINK IT'S A VERY GOOD IDEA FOR US TO BE BREATHING KNOWING WE KNOW THAT.

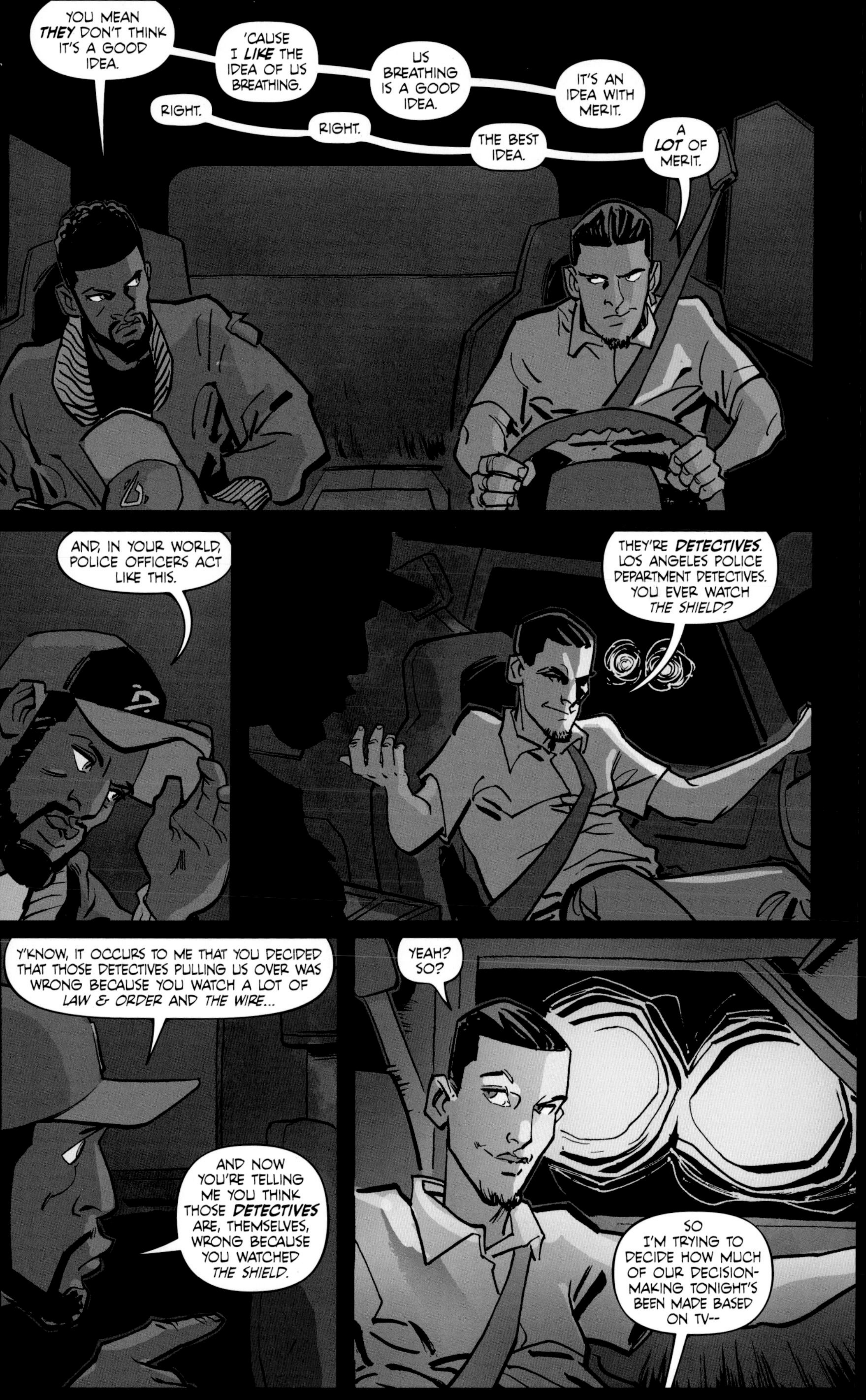
YOU MEAN *THEY* DON'T THINK IT'S A GOOD IDEA.
'CAUSE I *LIKE* THE IDEA OF US BREATHING.
US BREATHING IS A GOOD IDEA.
IT'S AN IDEA WITH MERIT.
RIGHT.
RIGHT.
THE BEST IDEA.
A *LOT* OF MERIT.
AND, IN YOUR WORLD, POLICE OFFICERS ACT LIKE THIS.
THEY'RE *DETECTIVES*. LOS ANGELES POLICE DEPARTMENT DETECTIVES. YOU EVER WATCH *THE SHIELD?*
Y'KNOW, IT OCCURS TO ME THAT YOU DECIDED THAT THOSE DETECTIVES PULLING US OVER WAS WRONG BECAUSE YOU WATCH A LOT OF *LAW & ORDER* AND *THE WIRE*...
AND NOW YOU'RE TELLING ME YOU THINK THOSE *DETECTIVES* ARE, THEMSELVES, WRONG BECAUSE YOU WATCHED *THE SHIELD.*
YEAH? SO?
SO I'M TRYING TO DECIDE HOW MUCH OF OUR DECISION-MAKING TONIGHT'S BEEN MADE BASED ON TV--

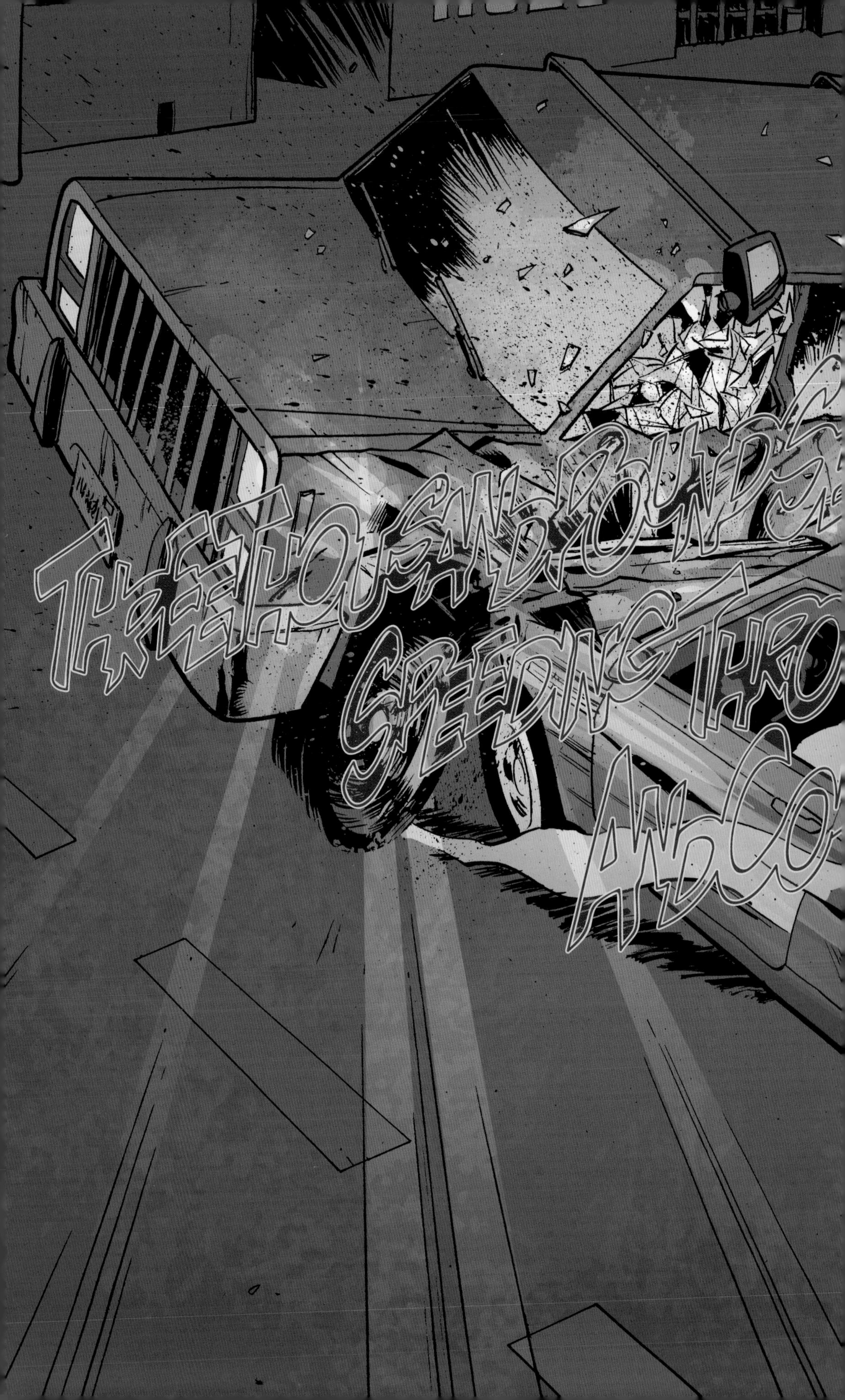
THREE THOUSAND POUNDS
SPEEDING THRO
AND CO

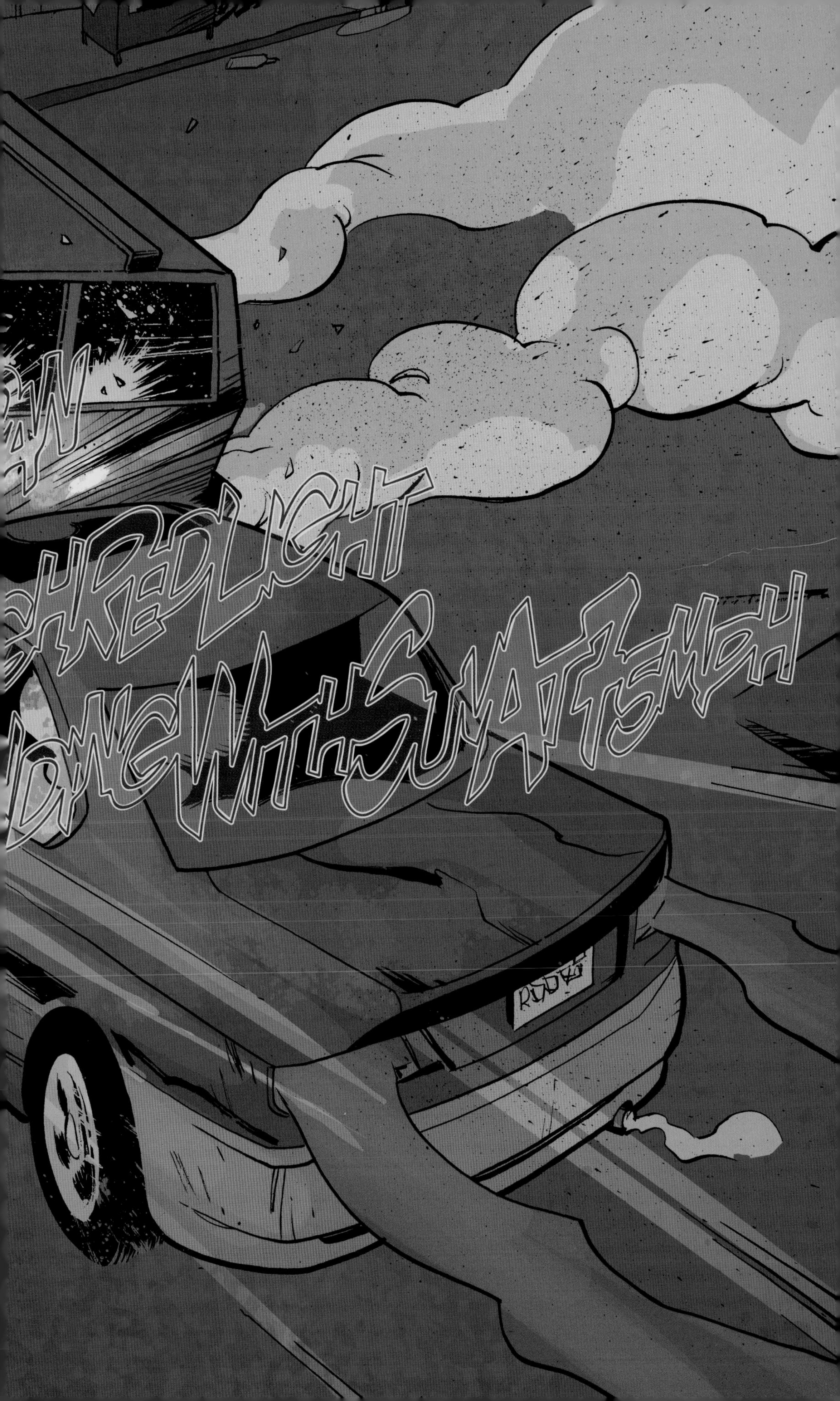

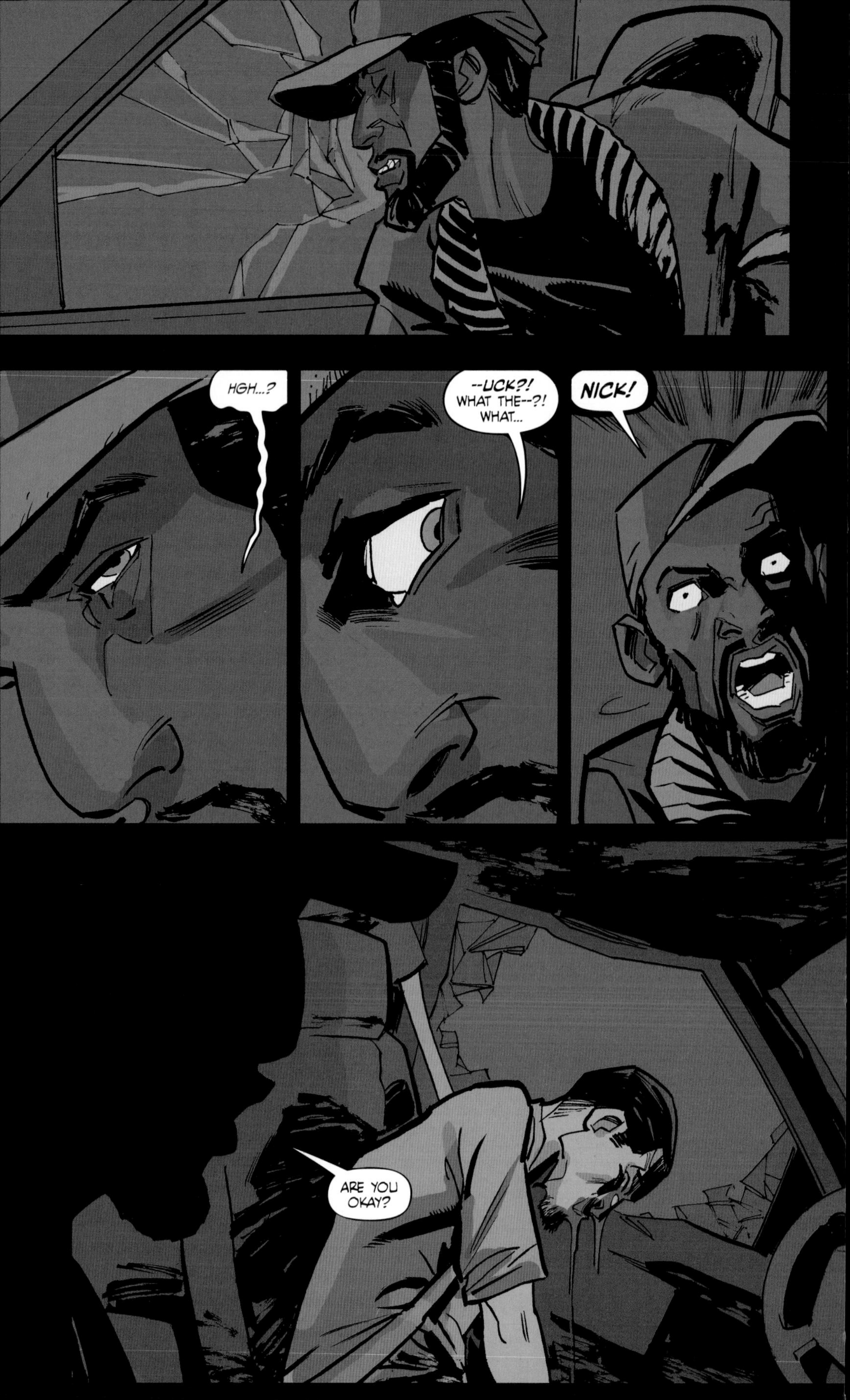
HGH...?
--UCK?! WHAT THE--?! WHAT...
NICK!
ARE YOU OKAY?

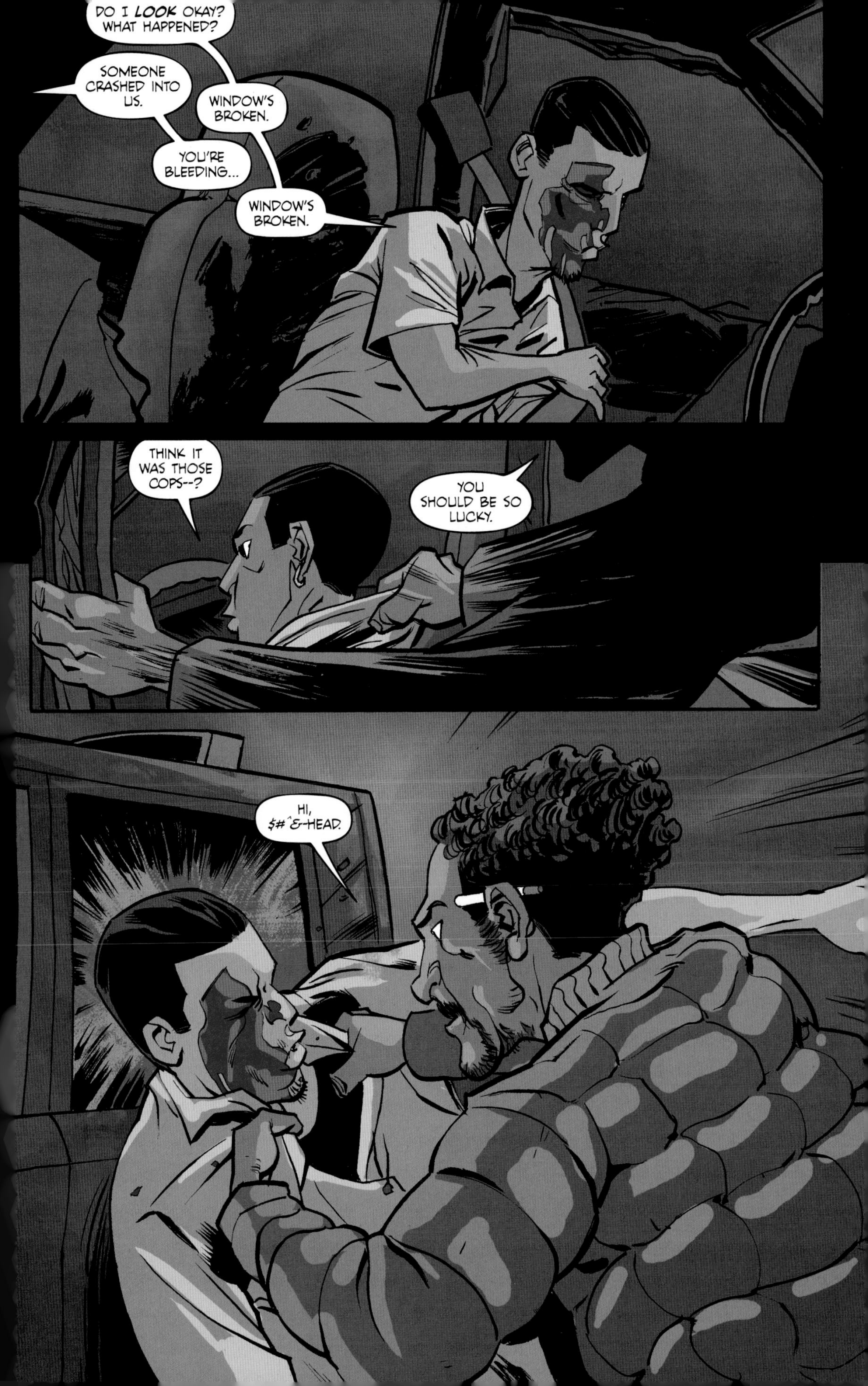
DO I LOOK OKAY? WHAT HAPPENED?
SOMEONE CRASHED INTO US.
WINDOW'S BROKEN.
YOU'RE BLEEDING...
WINDOW'S BROKEN.
THINK IT WAS THOSE COPS--?
YOU SHOULD BE SO LUCKY.
HI, $#^&-HEAD.

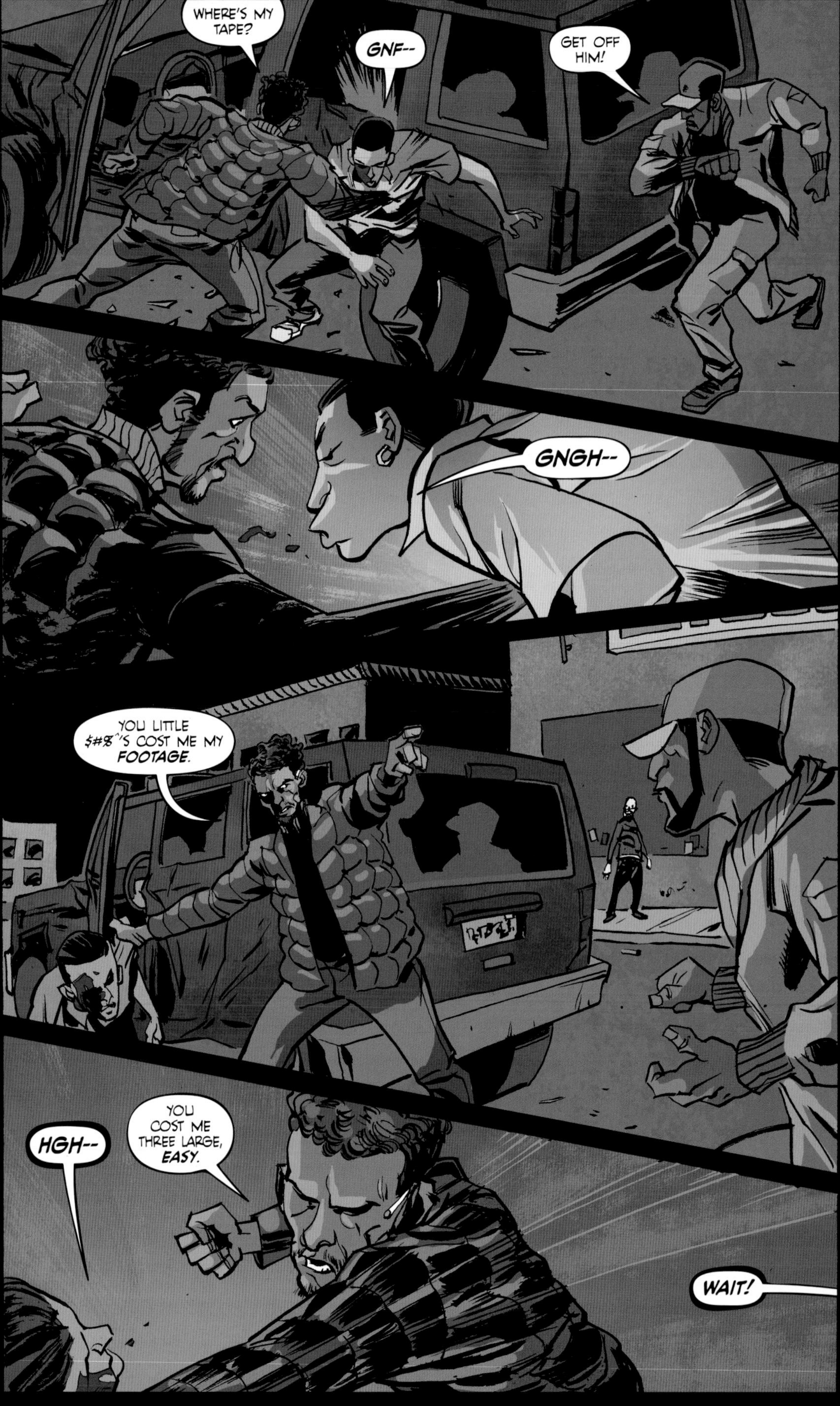
WHERE'S MY TAPE?
GNF--
GET OFF HIM!
GNGH--
YOU LITTLE $#%^'S COST ME MY FOOTAGE.
HGH--
YOU COST ME THREE LARGE, EASY.
WAIT!

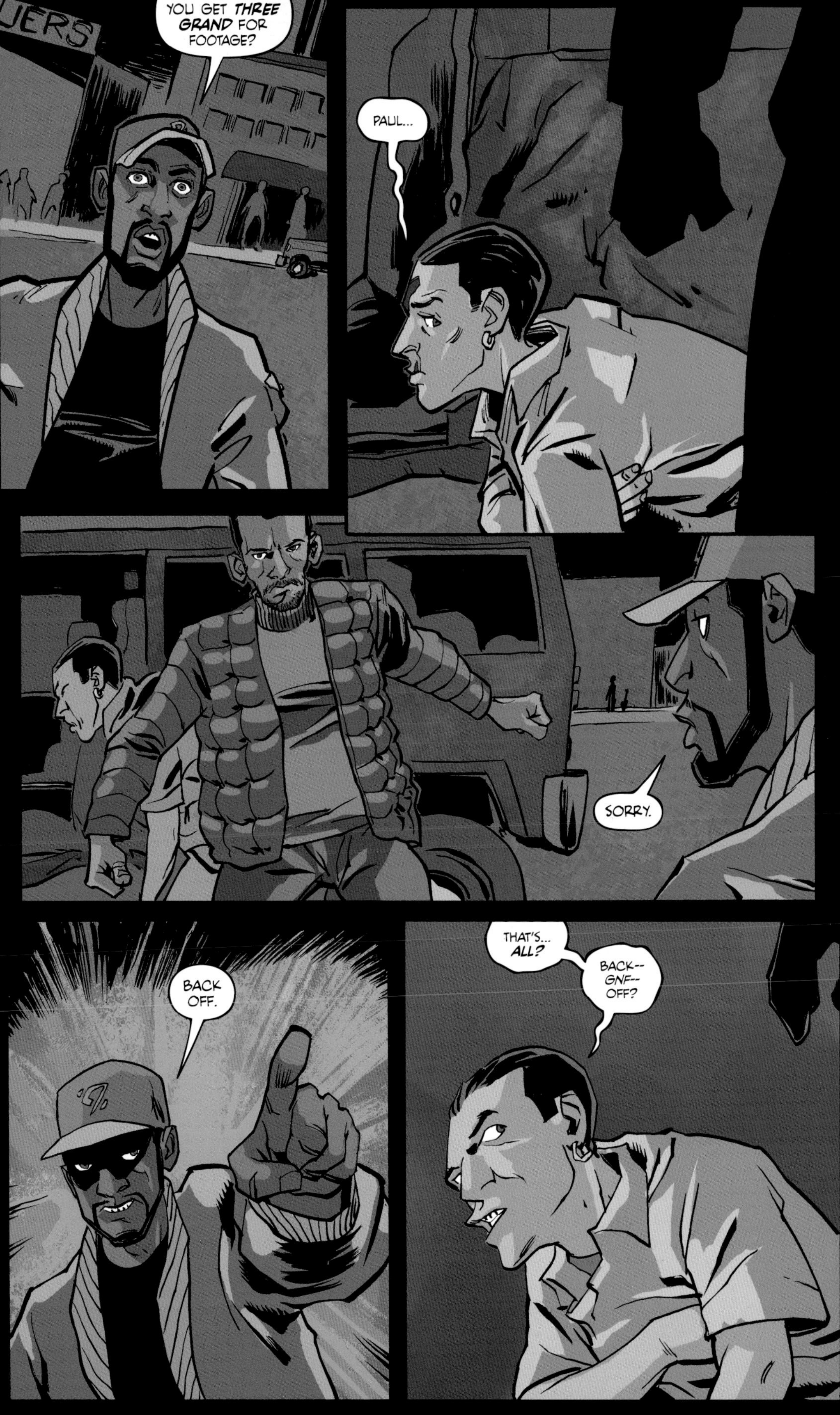
YOU GET THREE GRAND FOR FOOTAGE?
PAUL...
SORRY.
BACK OFF.
THAT'S... ALL?
BACK-- GNF-- OFF?

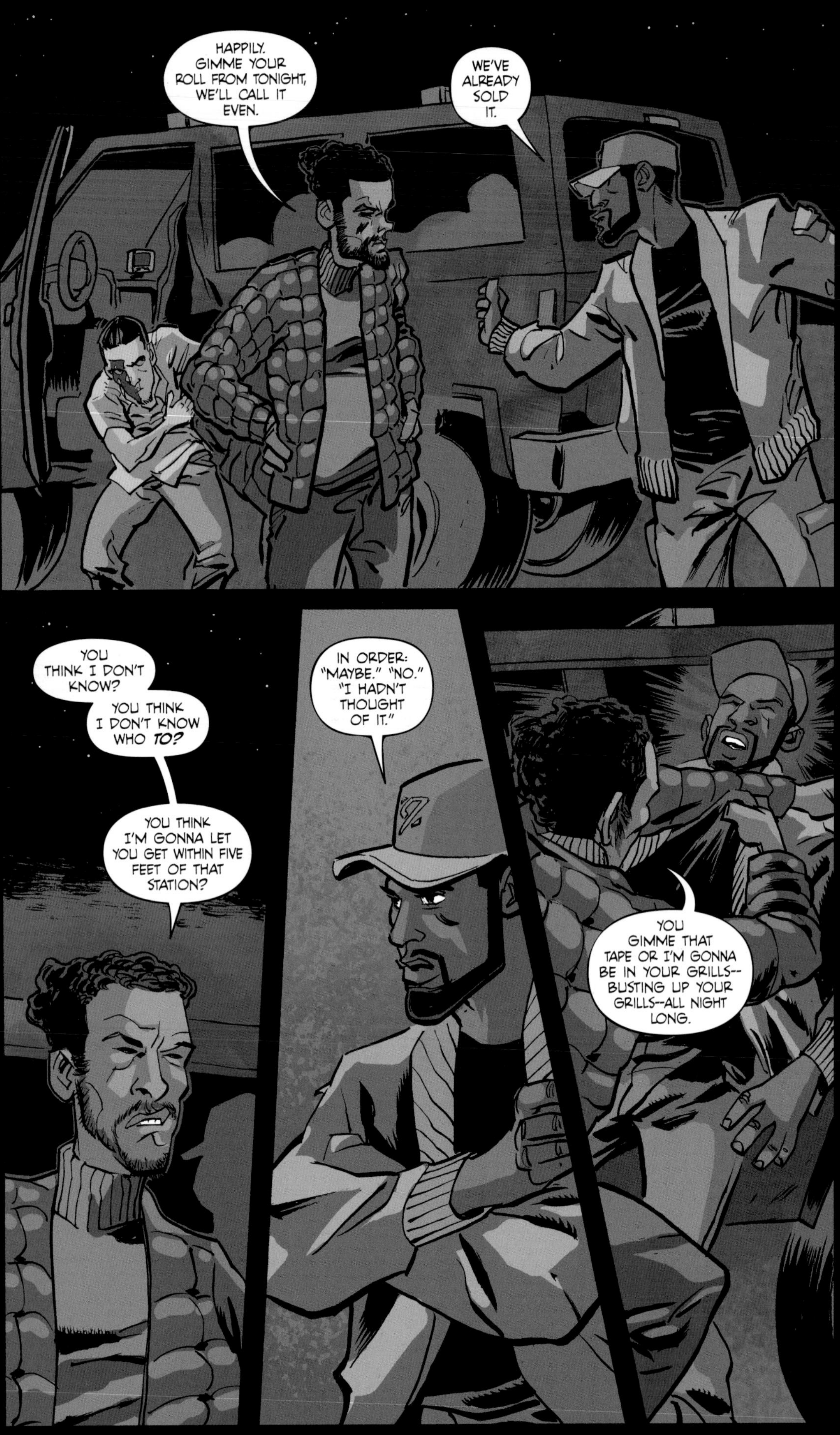
HAPPILY. GIMME YOUR ROLL FROM TONIGHT, WE'LL CALL IT EVEN.
WE'VE ALREADY SOLD IT.
YOU THINK I DON'T KNOW?
YOU THINK I DON'T KNOW WHO *TO?*
YOU THINK I'M GONNA LET YOU GET WITHIN FIVE FEET OF THAT STATION?
IN ORDER: "MAYBE." "NO." "I HADN'T THOUGHT OF IT."
YOU GIMME THAT TAPE OR I'M GONNA BE IN YOUR GRILLS-- BUSTING UP YOUR GRILLS--ALL NIGHT LONG.

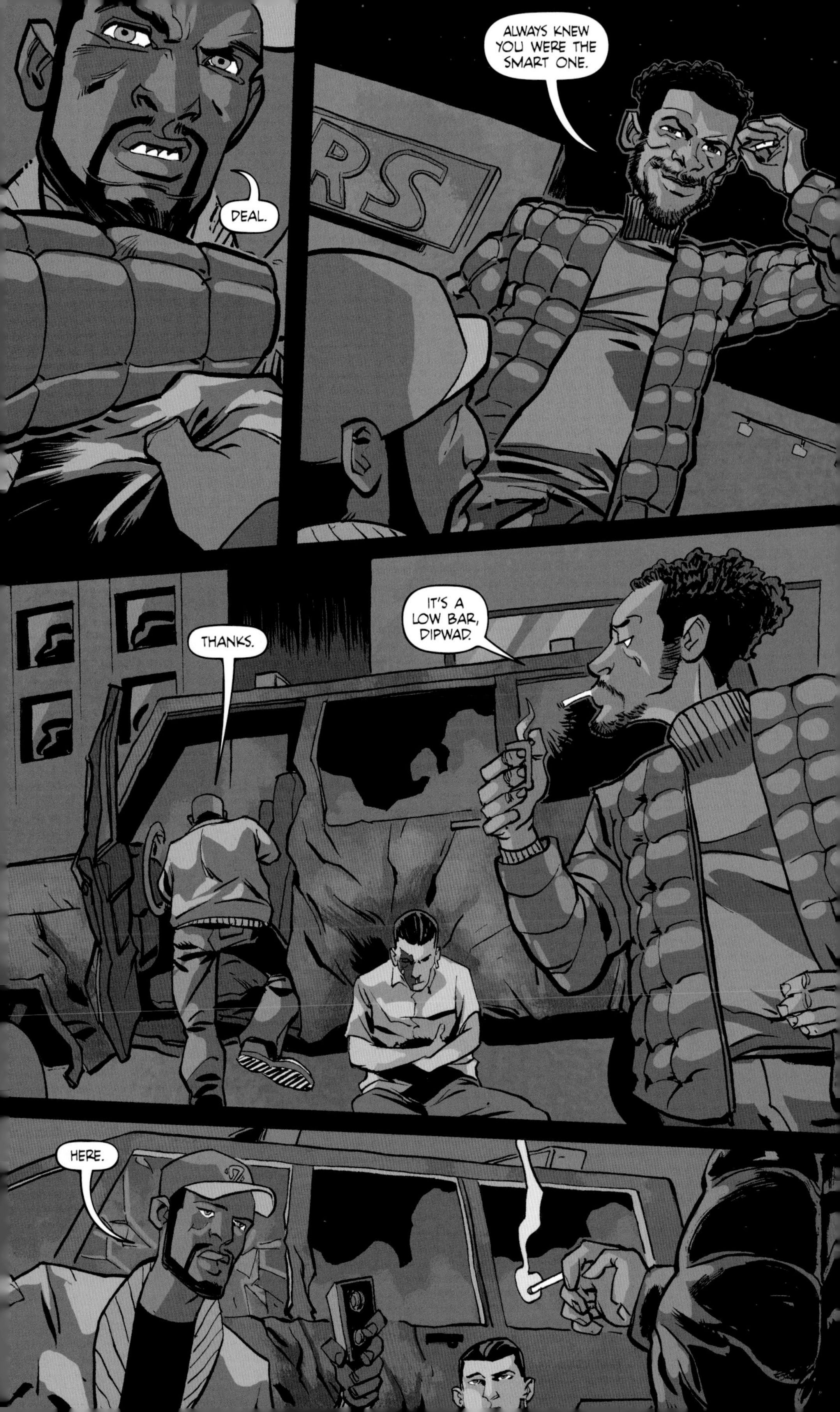
DEAL.
ALWAYS KNEW YOU WERE THE SMART ONE.
THANKS.
IT'S A LOW BAR, DIPWAD.
HERE.

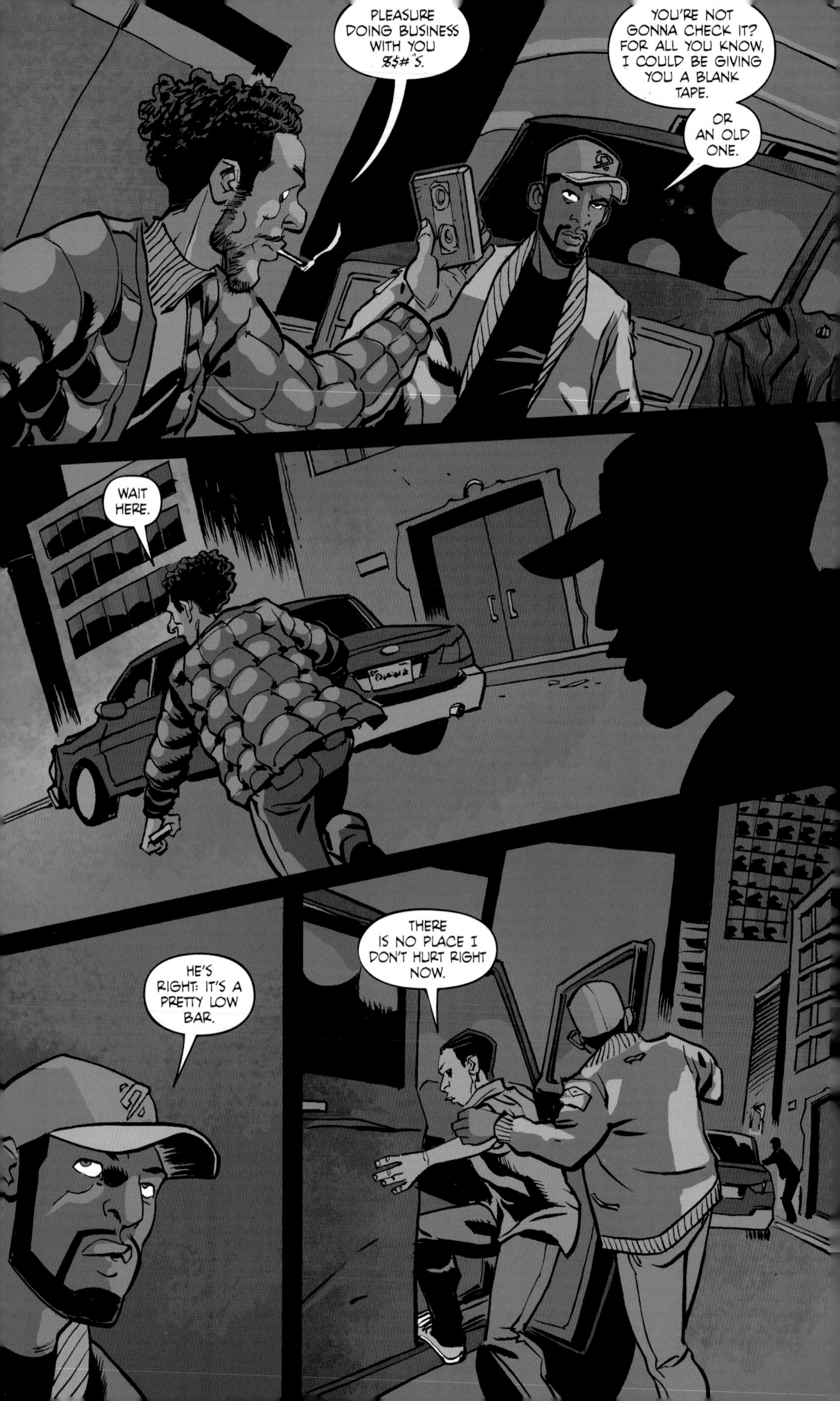
PLEASURE DOING BUSINESS WITH YOU %$#^S.
YOU'RE NOT GONNA CHECK IT? FOR ALL YOU KNOW, I COULD BE GIVING YOU A BLANK TAPE.
OR AN OLD ONE.
WAIT HERE.
HE'S RIGHT: IT'S A PRETTY LOW BAR.
THERE IS NO PLACE I DON'T HURT RIGHT NOW.

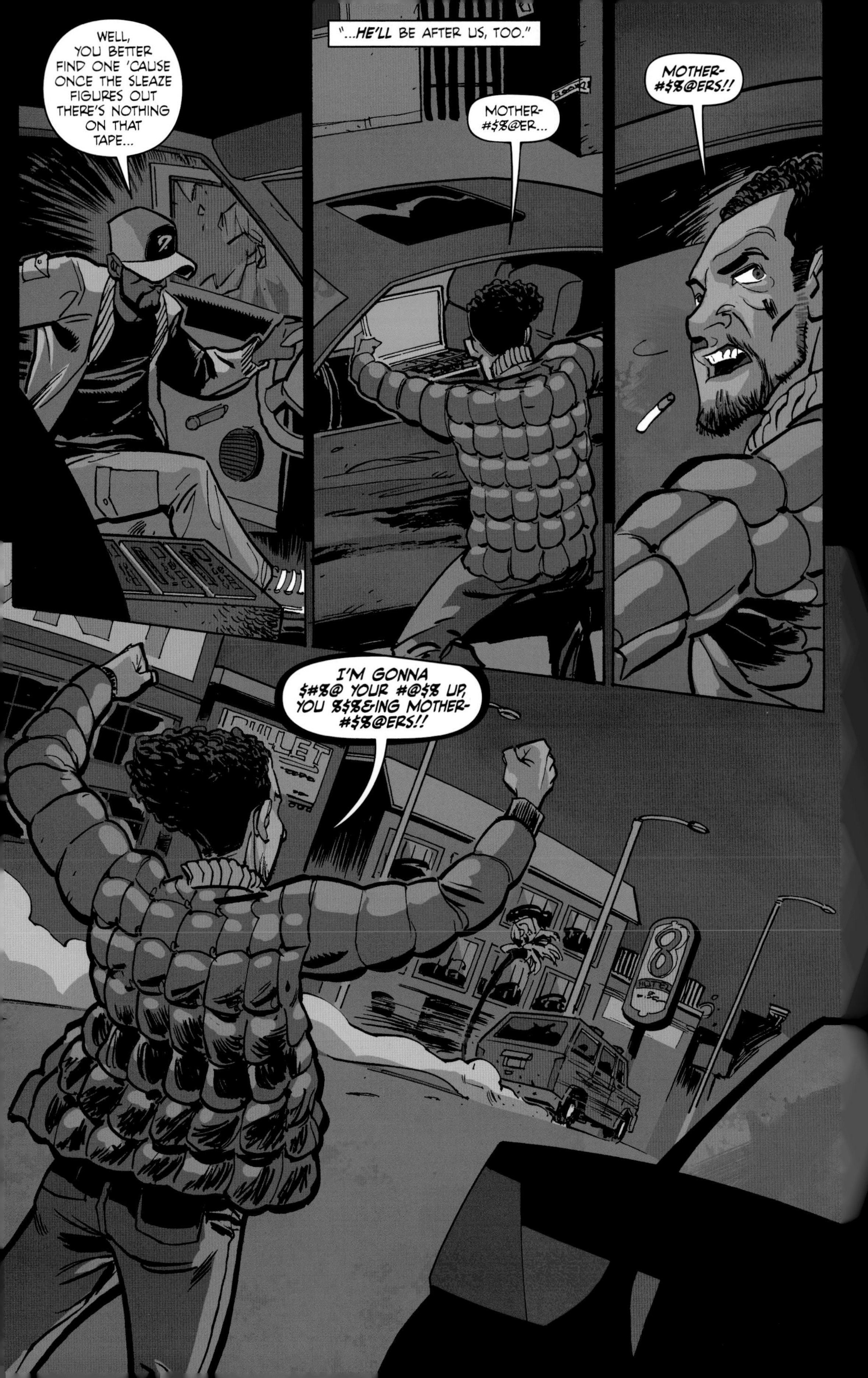
WELL, YOU BETTER FIND ONE 'CAUSE ONCE THE SLEAZE FIGURES OUT THERE'S NOTHING ON THAT TAPE...
"...HE'LL BE AFTER US, TOO."
MOTHER-#$%@ER...
MOTHER-#$%@ERS!!
I'M GONNA $#%@ YOUR #@$% UP, YOU %$%&ING MOTHER-#$%@ERS!!

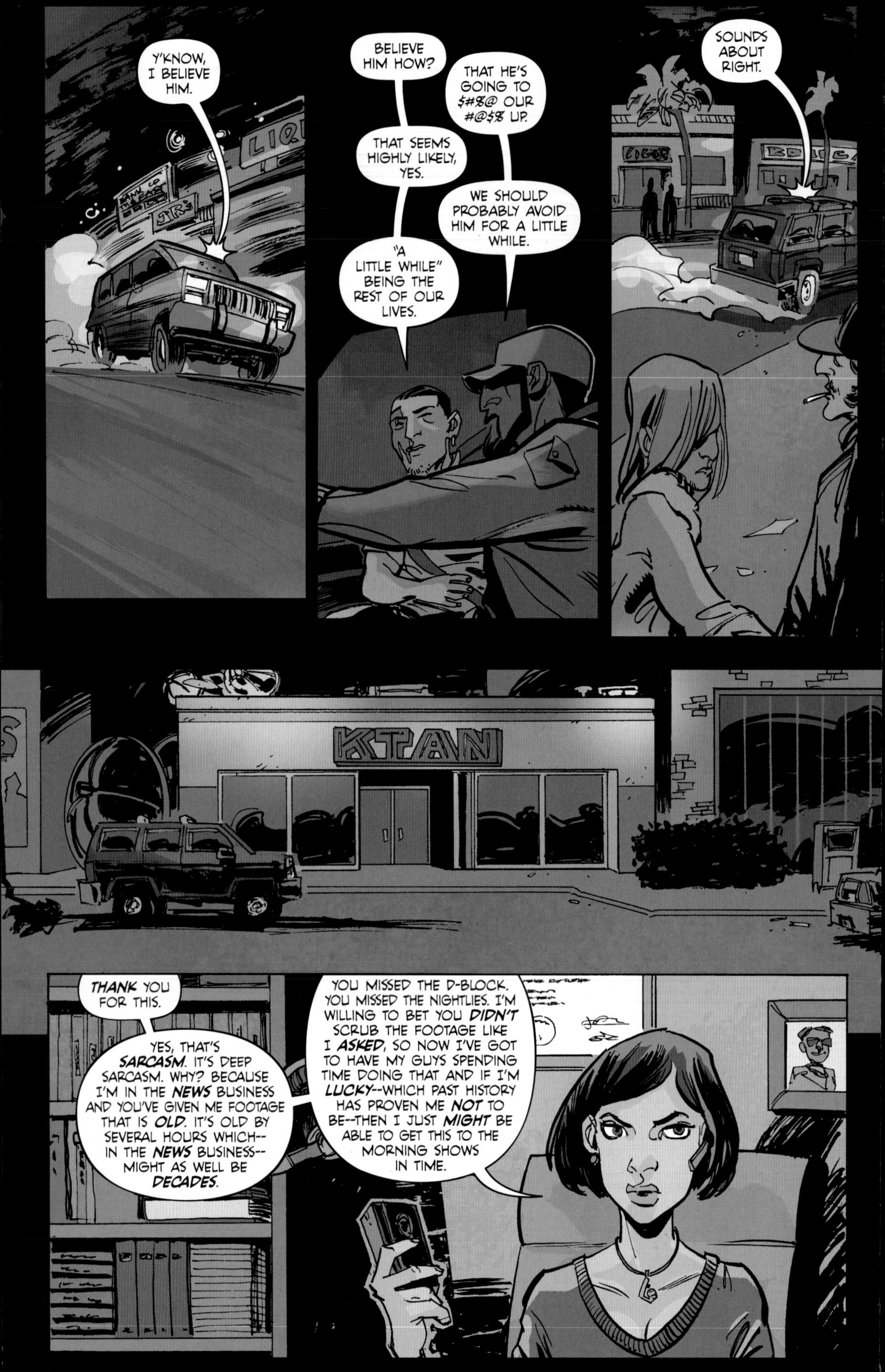

Y'KNOW, I BELIEVE HIM.
BELIEVE HIM HOW?
THAT HE'S GOING TO $#%@ OUR #@$% UP.
THAT SEEMS HIGHLY LIKELY, YES.
WE SHOULD PROBABLY AVOID HIM FOR A LITTLE WHILE.
"A LITTLE WHILE" BEING THE REST OF OUR LIVES.
SOUNDS ABOUT RIGHT.
KTAN
THANK YOU FOR THIS.
YES, THAT'S SARCASM. IT'S DEEP SARCASM. WHY? BECAUSE I'M IN THE NEWS BUSINESS AND YOU'VE GIVEN ME FOOTAGE THAT IS OLD. IT'S OLD BY SEVERAL HOURS WHICH-- IN THE NEWS BUSINESS-- MIGHT AS WELL BE DECADES.
YOU MISSED THE D-BLOCK. YOU MISSED THE NIGHTLIES. I'M WILLING TO BET YOU DIDN'T SCRUB THE FOOTAGE LIKE I ASKED, SO NOW I'VE GOT TO HAVE MY GUYS SPENDING TIME DOING THAT AND IF I'M LUCKY--WHICH PAST HISTORY HAS PROVEN ME NOT TO BE--THEN I JUST MIGHT BE ABLE TO GET THIS TO THE MORNING SHOWS IN TIME.

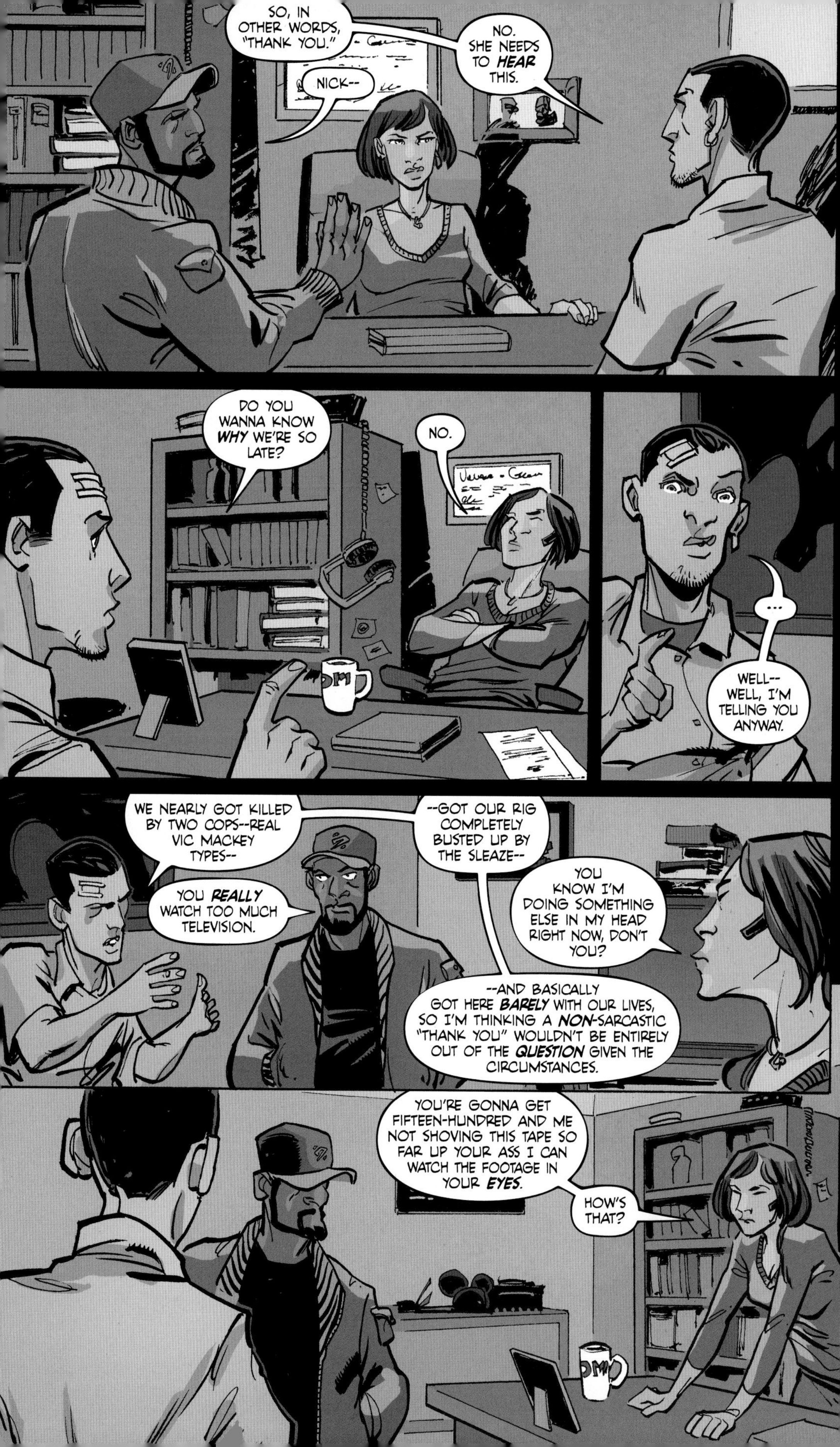
SO, IN OTHER WORDS, "THANK YOU."
NO. SHE NEEDS TO HEAR THIS.
NICK--
DO YOU WANNA KNOW WHY WE'RE SO LATE?
NO.
...
WELL-- WELL, I'M TELLING YOU ANYWAY.
WE NEARLY GOT KILLED BY TWO COPS--REAL VIC MACKEY TYPES--
--GOT OUR RIG COMPLETELY BUSTED UP BY THE SLEAZE--
YOU REALLY WATCH TOO MUCH TELEVISION.
YOU KNOW I'M DOING SOMETHING ELSE IN MY HEAD RIGHT NOW, DON'T YOU?
--AND BASICALLY GOT HERE BARELY WITH OUR LIVES, SO I'M THINKING A NON-SARCASTIC "THANK YOU" WOULDN'T BE ENTIRELY OUT OF THE QUESTION GIVEN THE CIRCUMSTANCES.
YOU'RE GONNA GET FIFTEEN-HUNDRED AND ME NOT SHOVING THIS TAPE SO FAR UP YOUR ASS I CAN WATCH THE FOOTAGE IN YOUR EYES.
HOW'S THAT?

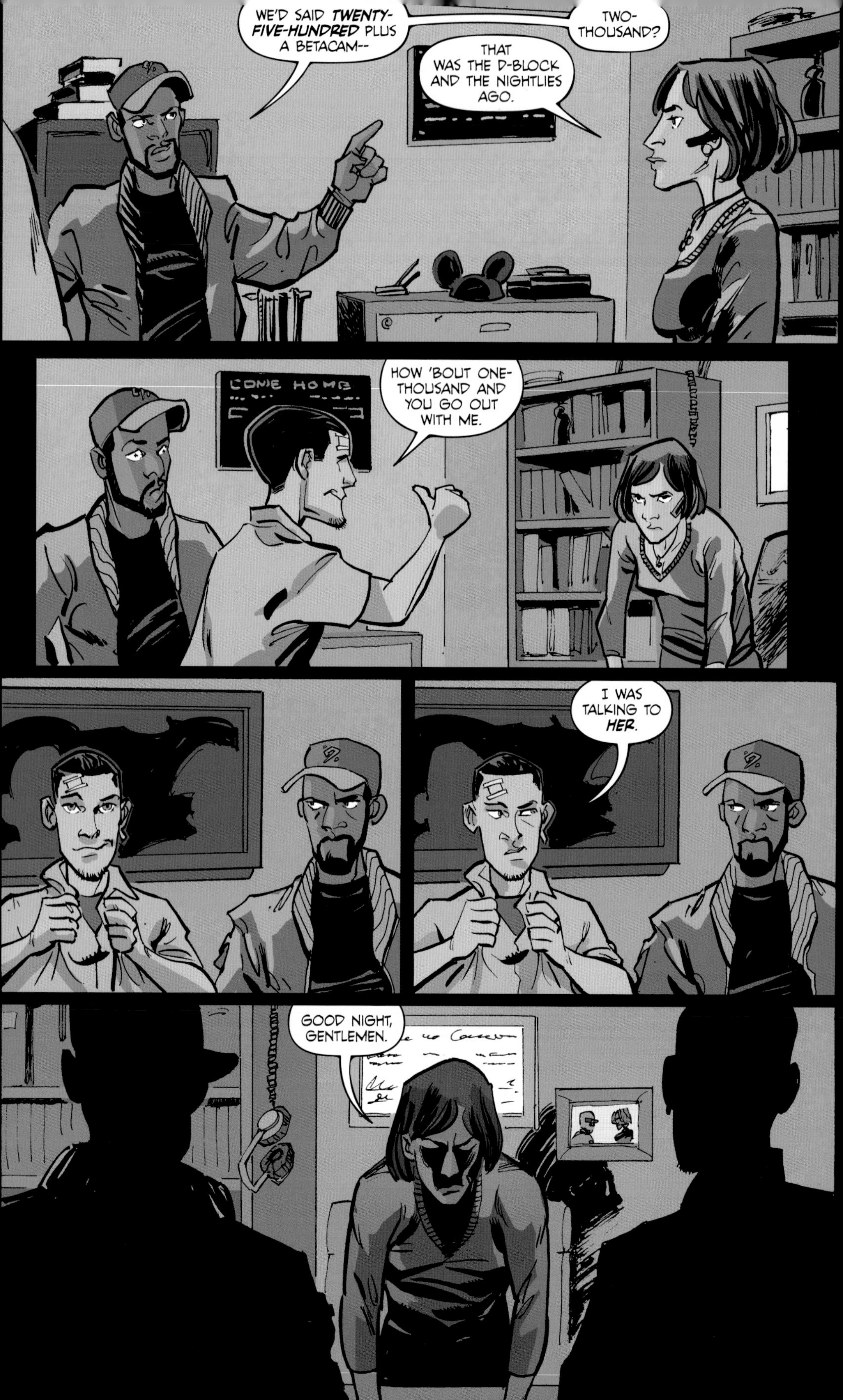
WE'D SAID **TWENTY-FIVE-HUNDRED** PLUS A BETACAM--
TWO-THOUSAND?
THAT WAS THE D-BLOCK AND THE NIGHTLIES AGO.
HOW 'BOUT ONE-THOUSAND AND YOU GO OUT WITH ME.
I WAS TALKING TO **HER**.
GOOD NIGHT, GENTLEMEN.

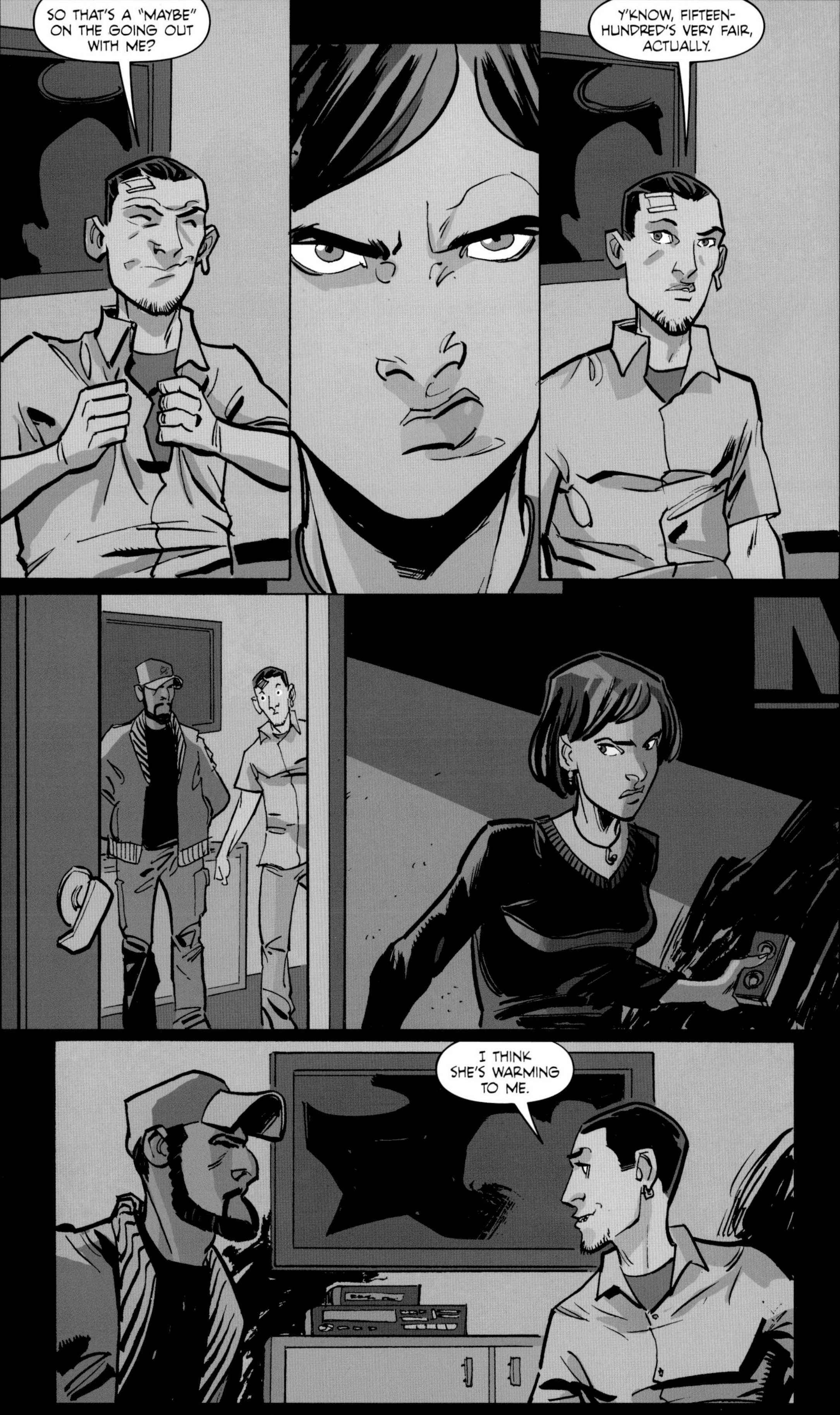
SO THAT'S A "MAYBE" ON THE GOING OUT WITH ME?
Y'KNOW, FIFTEEN-HUNDRED'S VERY FAIR, ACTUALLY.
I THINK SHE'S WARMING TO ME.

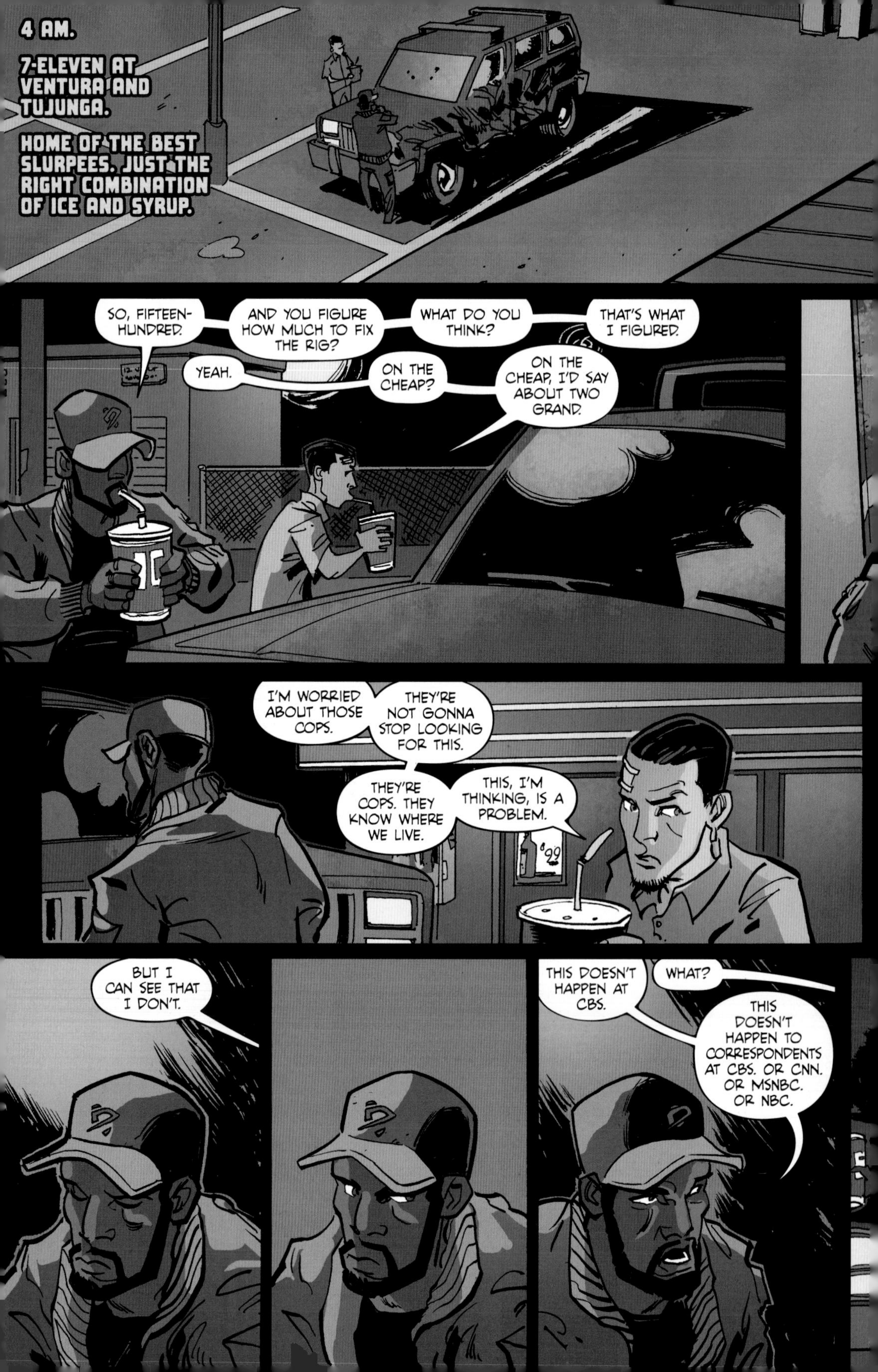
4 AM.
7-ELEVEN AT VENTURA AND TUJUNGA.
HOME OF THE BEST SLURPEES. JUST THE RIGHT COMBINATION OF ICE AND SYRUP.
SO, FIFTEEN-HUNDRED.
YEAH.
AND YOU FIGURE HOW MUCH TO FIX THE RIG?
ON THE CHEAP?
WHAT DO YOU THINK?
ON THE CHEAP, I'D SAY ABOUT TWO GRAND.
THAT'S WHAT I FIGURED.
I'M WORRIED ABOUT THOSE COPS.
THEY'RE NOT GONNA STOP LOOKING FOR THIS.
THEY'RE COPS. THEY KNOW WHERE WE LIVE.
THIS, I'M THINKING, IS A PROBLEM.
BUT I CAN SEE THAT I DON'T.
THIS DOESN'T HAPPEN AT CBS.
WHAT?
THIS DOESN'T HAPPEN TO CORRESPONDENTS AT CBS. OR CNN. OR MSNBC. OR NBC.

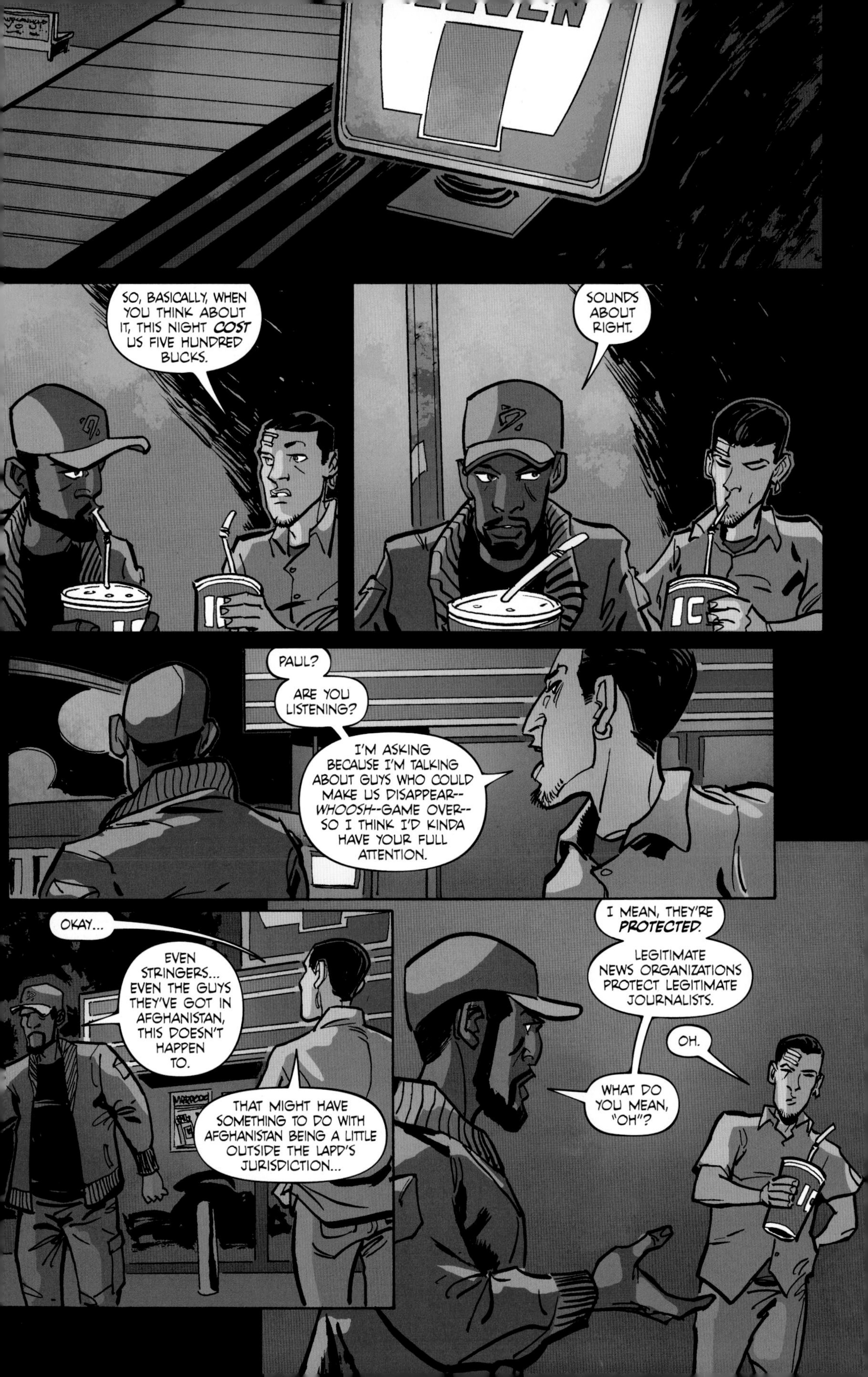
SO, BASICALLY, WHEN YOU THINK ABOUT IT, THIS NIGHT COST US FIVE HUNDRED BUCKS.
SOUNDS ABOUT RIGHT.
PAUL?
ARE YOU LISTENING?
I'M ASKING BECAUSE I'M TALKING ABOUT GUYS WHO COULD MAKE US DISAPPEAR-- WHOOSH--GAME OVER-- SO I THINK I'D KINDA HAVE YOUR FULL ATTENTION.
OKAY...
EVEN STRINGERS... EVEN THE GUYS THEY'VE GOT IN AFGHANISTAN, THIS DOESN'T HAPPEN TO.
THAT MIGHT HAVE SOMETHING TO DO WITH AFGHANISTAN BEING A LITTLE OUTSIDE THE LAPD'S JURISDICTION...
I MEAN, THEY'RE PROTECTED.
LEGITIMATE NEWS ORGANIZATIONS PROTECT LEGITIMATE JOURNALISTS.
OH.
WHAT DO YOU MEAN, "OH"?

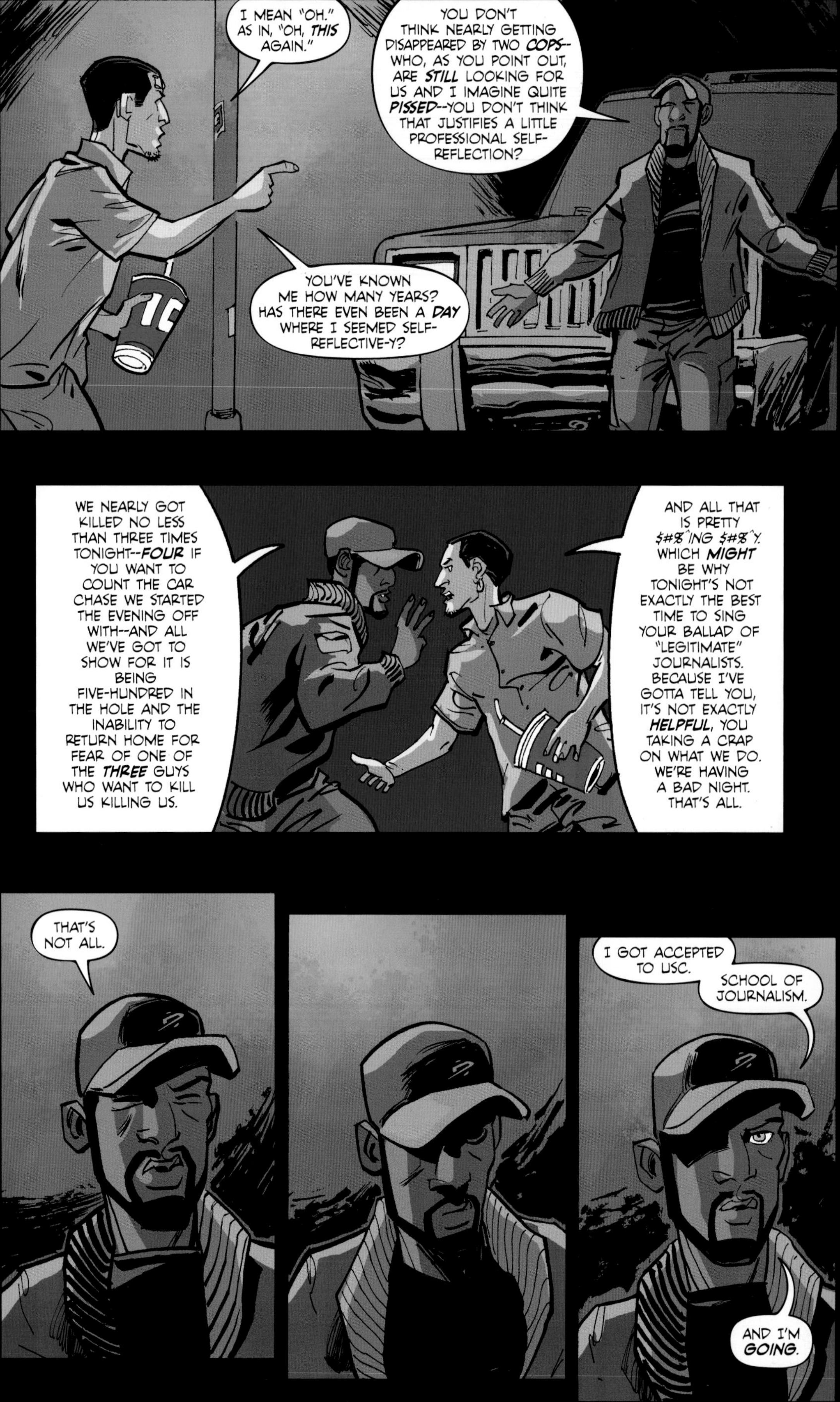

I MEAN "OH." AS IN, "OH, THIS AGAIN."
YOU DON'T THINK NEARLY GETTING DISAPPEARED BY TWO COPS--WHO, AS YOU POINT OUT, ARE STILL LOOKING FOR US AND I IMAGINE QUITE PISSED--YOU DON'T THINK THAT JUSTIFIES A LITTLE PROFESSIONAL SELF-REFLECTION?
YOU'VE KNOWN ME HOW MANY YEARS? HAS THERE EVEN BEEN A DAY WHERE I SEEMED SELF-REFLECTIVE-Y?
WE NEARLY GOT KILLED NO LESS THAN THREE TIMES TONIGHT--FOUR IF YOU WANT TO COUNT THE CAR CHASE WE STARTED THE EVENING OFF WITH--AND ALL WE'VE GOT TO SHOW FOR IT IS BEING FIVE-HUNDRED IN THE HOLE AND THE INABILITY TO RETURN HOME FOR FEAR OF ONE OF THE THREE GUYS WHO WANT TO KILL US KILLING US.
AND ALL THAT IS PRETTY $#%^ING $#%^Y. WHICH MIGHT BE WHY TONIGHT'S NOT EXACTLY THE BEST TIME TO SING YOUR BALLAD OF "LEGITIMATE" JOURNALISTS. BECAUSE I'VE GOTTA TELL YOU, IT'S NOT EXACTLY HELPFUL, YOU TAKING A CRAP ON WHAT WE DO. WE'RE HAVING A BAD NIGHT. THAT'S ALL.
THAT'S NOT ALL.
I GOT ACCEPTED TO USC.
SCHOOL OF JOURNALISM.
AND I'M GOING.

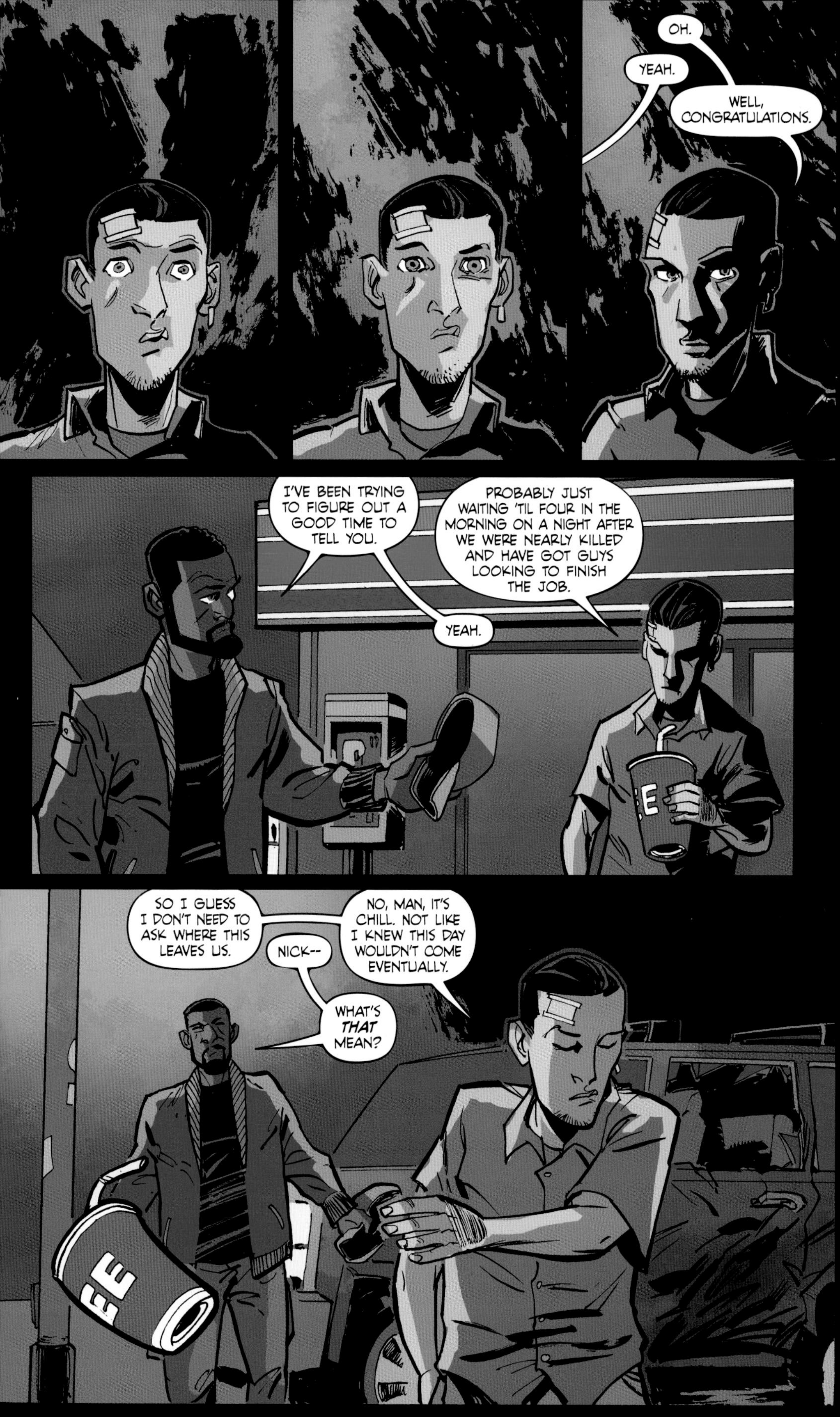
OH.
YEAH.
WELL, CONGRATULATIONS.
I'VE BEEN TRYING TO FIGURE OUT A GOOD TIME TO TELL YOU.
YEAH.
PROBABLY JUST WAITING 'TIL FOUR IN THE MORNING ON A NIGHT AFTER WE WERE NEARLY KILLED AND HAVE GOT GUYS LOOKING TO FINISH THE JOB.
SO I GUESS I DON'T NEED TO ASK WHERE THIS LEAVES US.
NICK--
NO, MAN, IT'S CHILL. NOT LIKE I KNEW THIS DAY WOULDN'T COME EVENTUALLY.
WHAT'S *THAT* MEAN?

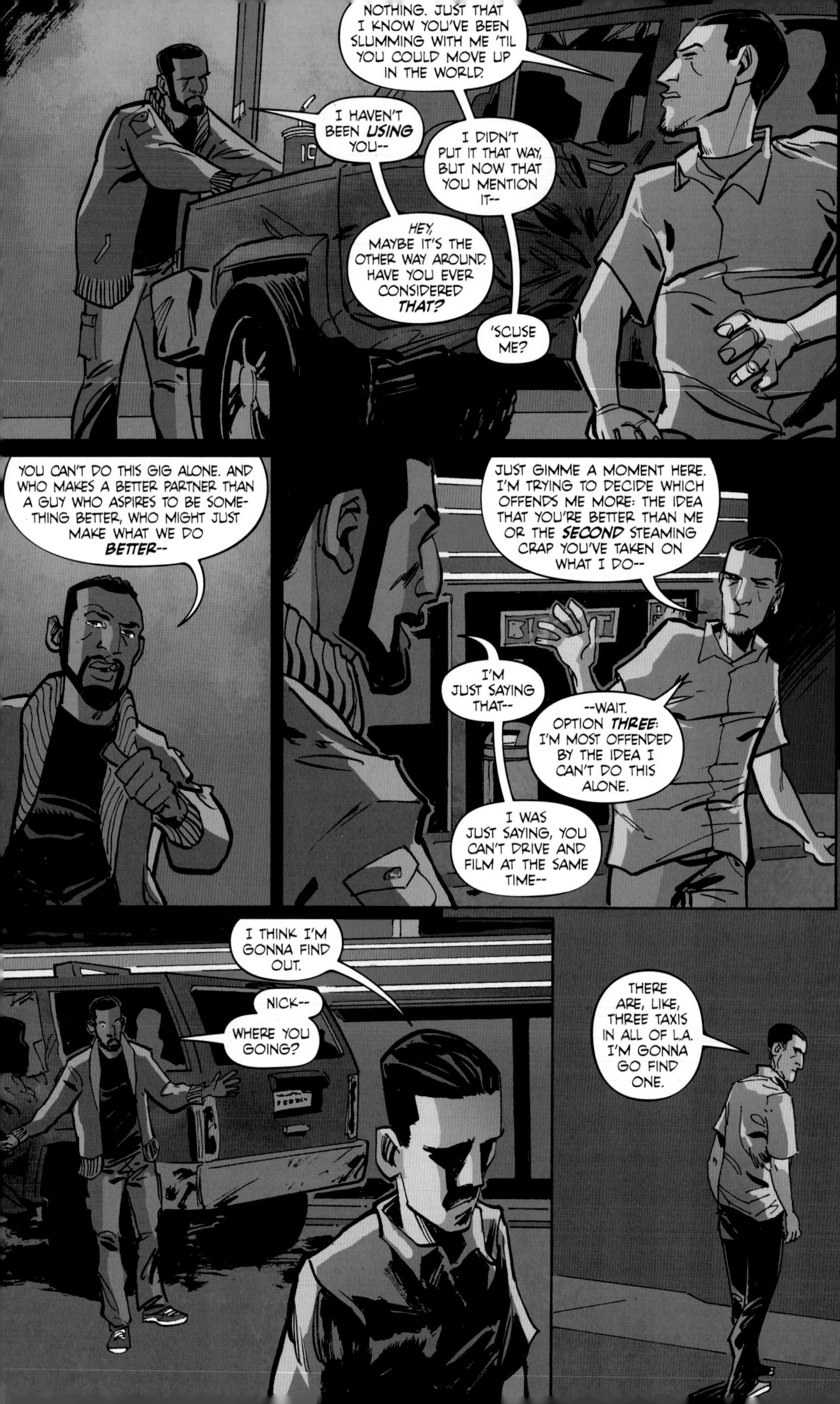
NOTHING. JUST THAT I KNOW YOU'VE BEEN SLUMMING WITH ME 'TIL YOU COULD MOVE UP IN THE WORLD.
I HAVEN'T BEEN *USING* YOU--
I DIDN'T PUT IT THAT WAY, BUT NOW THAT YOU MENTION IT--
HEY, MAYBE IT'S THE OTHER WAY AROUND. HAVE YOU EVER CONSIDERED *THAT?*
'SCUSE ME?
YOU CAN'T DO THIS GIG ALONE. AND WHO MAKES A BETTER PARTNER THAN A GUY WHO ASPIRES TO BE SOMETHING BETTER, WHO MIGHT JUST MAKE WHAT WE DO *BETTER*--
JUST GIMME A MOMENT HERE. I'M TRYING TO DECIDE WHICH OFFENDS ME MORE: THE IDEA THAT YOU'RE BETTER THAN ME OR THE *SECOND* STEAMING CRAP YOU'VE TAKEN ON WHAT I DO--
I'M JUST SAYING THAT--
--WAIT. OPTION *THREE*: I'M MOST OFFENDED BY THE IDEA I CAN'T DO THIS ALONE.
I WAS JUST SAYING, YOU CAN'T DRIVE AND FILM AT THE SAME TIME--
I THINK I'M GONNA FIND OUT.
NICK--
WHERE YOU GOING?
THERE ARE, LIKE, THREE TAXIS IN ALL OF L.A. I'M GONNA GO FIND ONE.

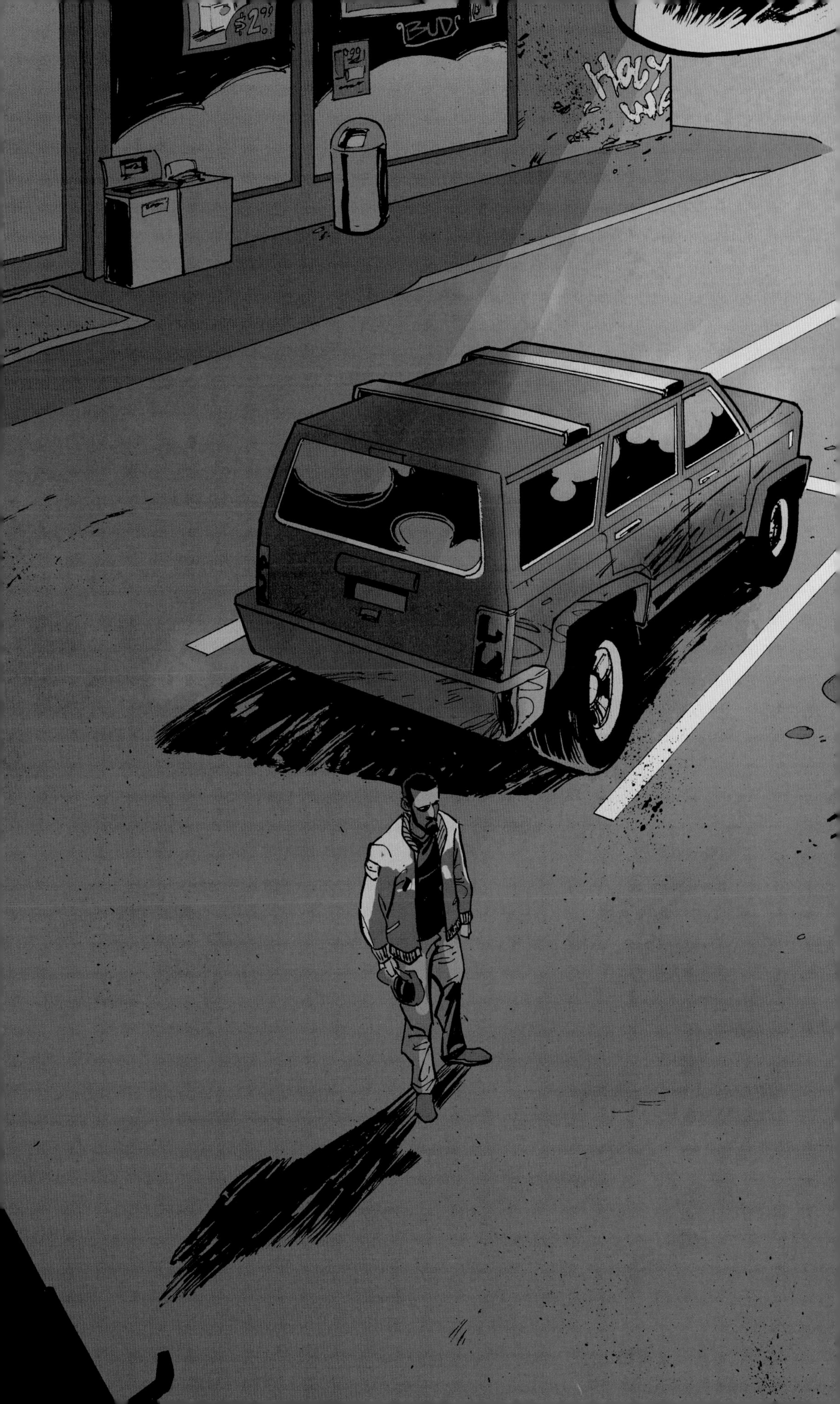
$2.99
BUD

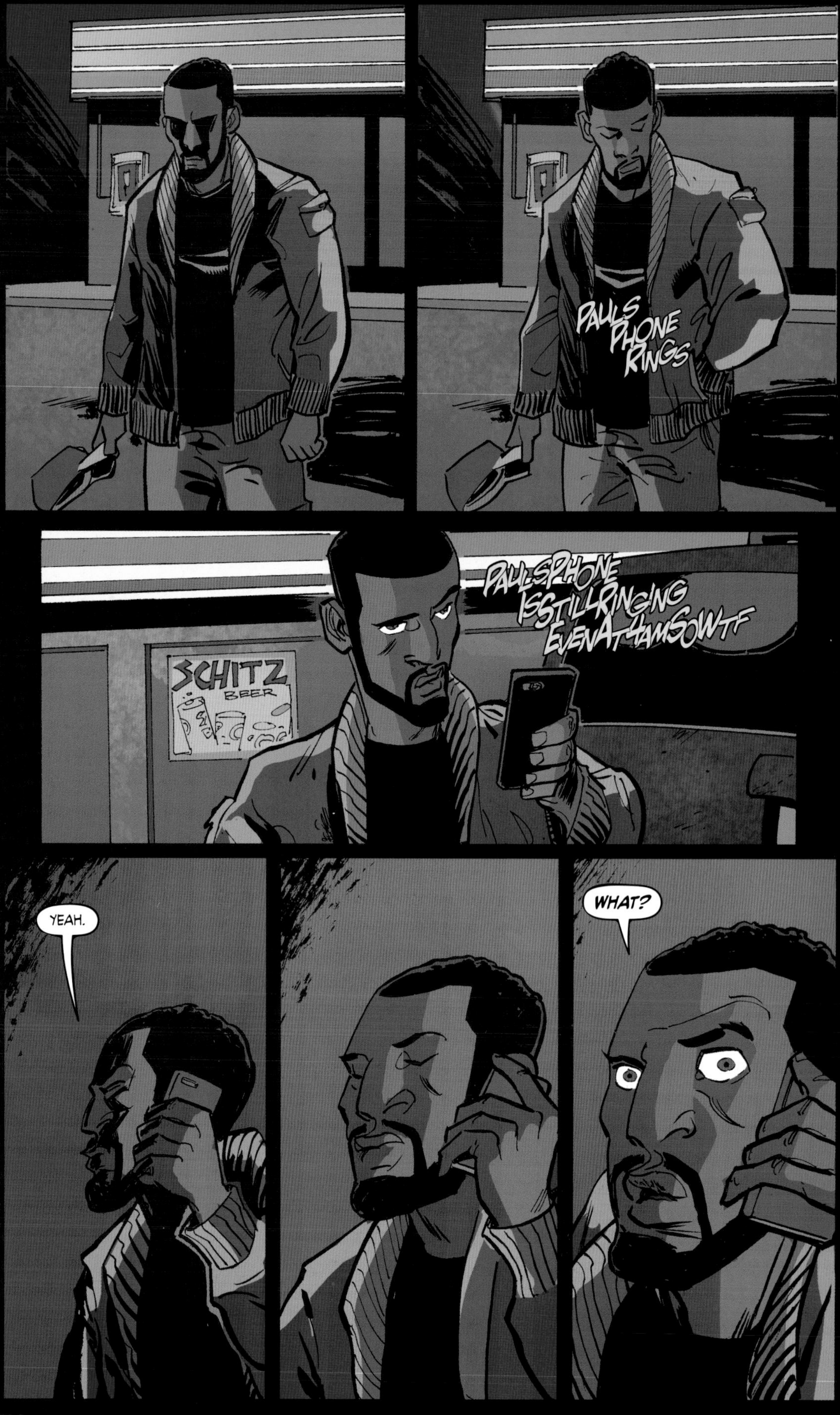
PAULS PHONE RINGS
PAULS PHONE IS STILL RINGING EVEN AT 4AM SO WTF
SCHITZ BEER
YEAH.
WHAT?

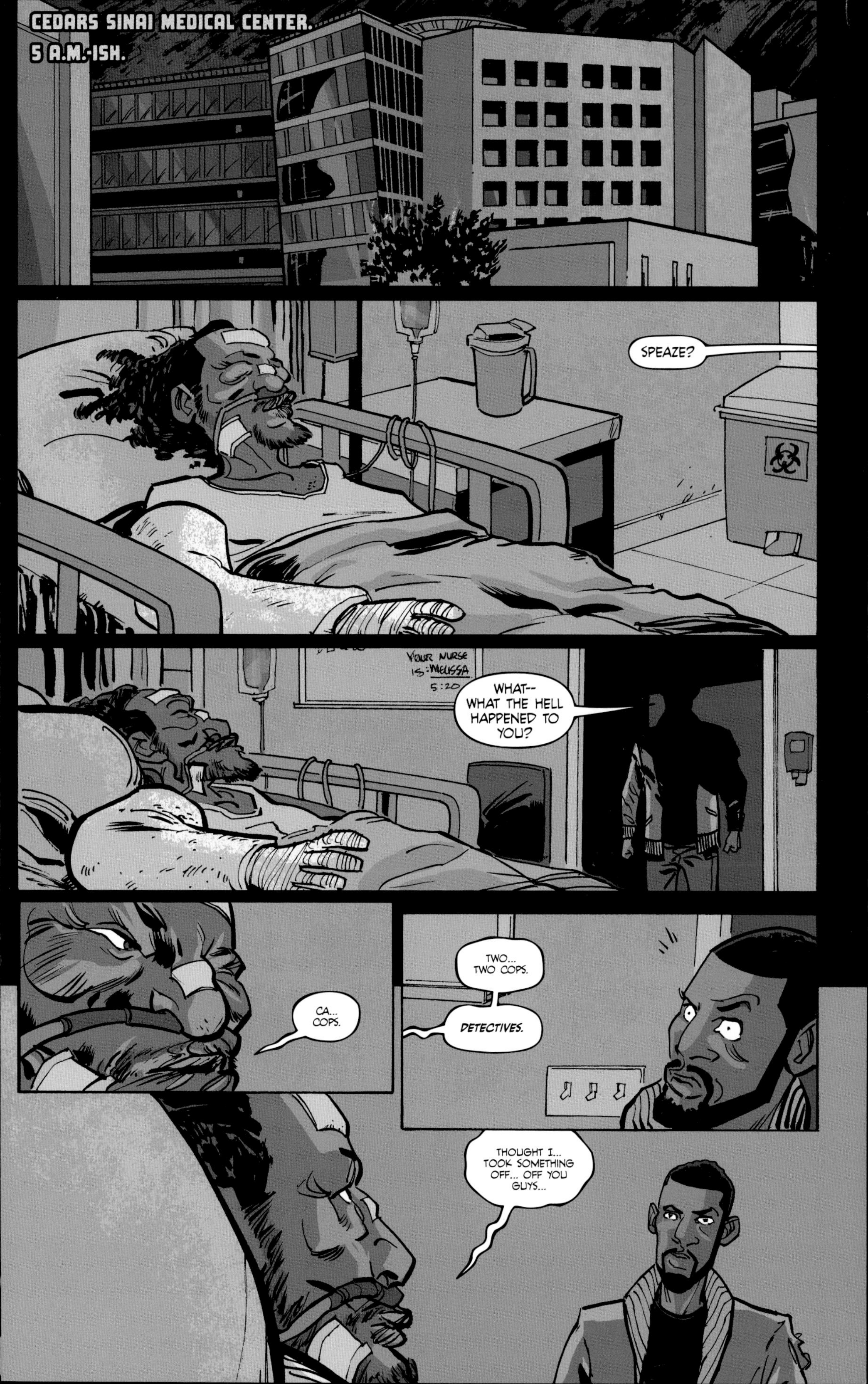
CEDARS SINAI MEDICAL CENTER.
5 A.M.-ISH.
SPEAZE?
YOUR NURSE IS: MELISSA
5:20
WHAT-- WHAT THE HELL HAPPENED TO YOU?
CA... COPS.
TWO... TWO COPS.
DETECTIVES.
THOUGHT I... TOOK SOMETHING OFF... OFF YOU GUYS...

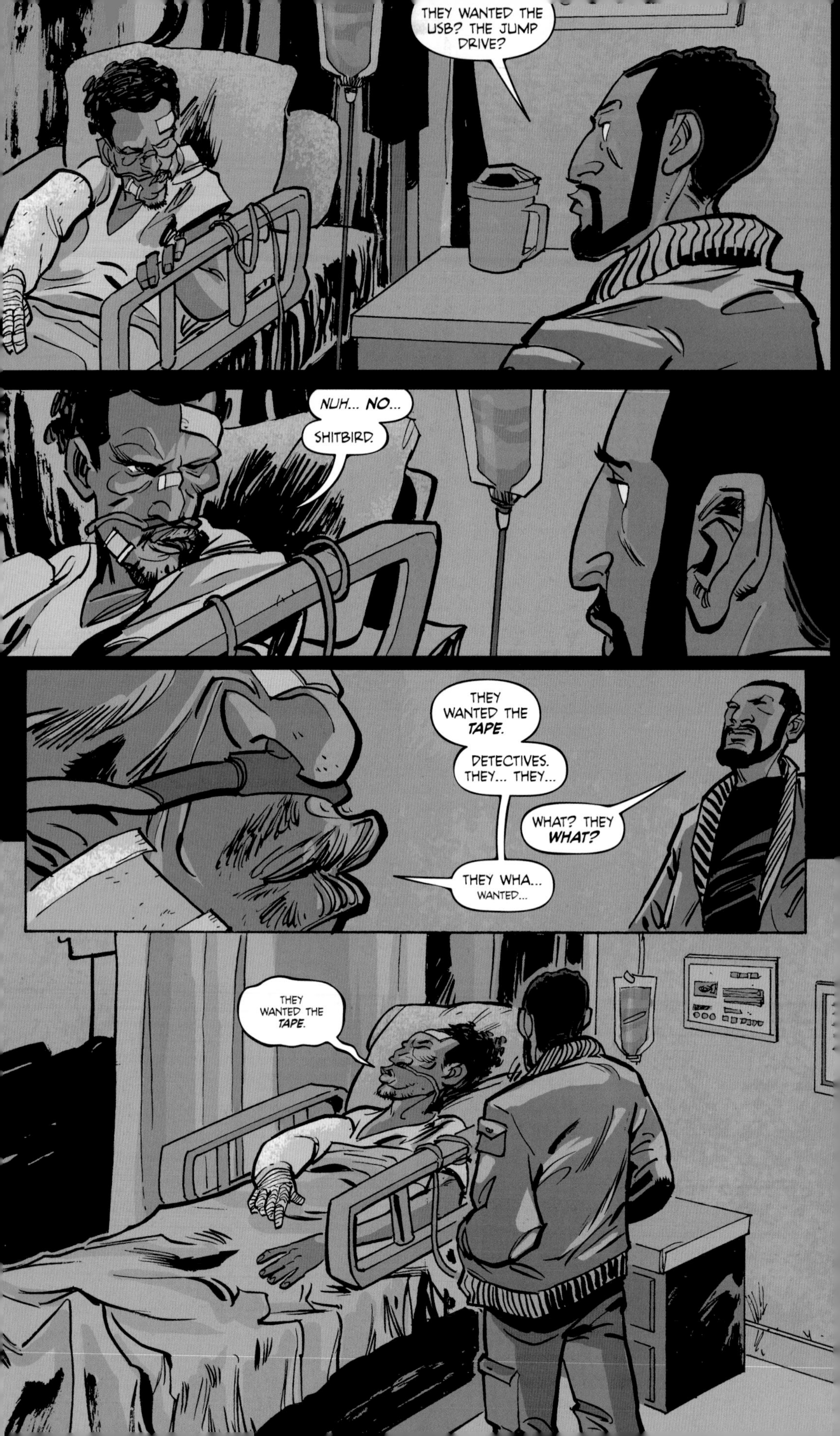
THEY WANTED THE USB? THE JUMP DRIVE?
NUH... NO...
SHITBIRD.
THEY WANTED THE TAPE.
DETECTIVES. THEY... THEY...
WHAT? THEY WHAT?
THEY WHA... WANTED...
THEY WANTED THE TAPE.

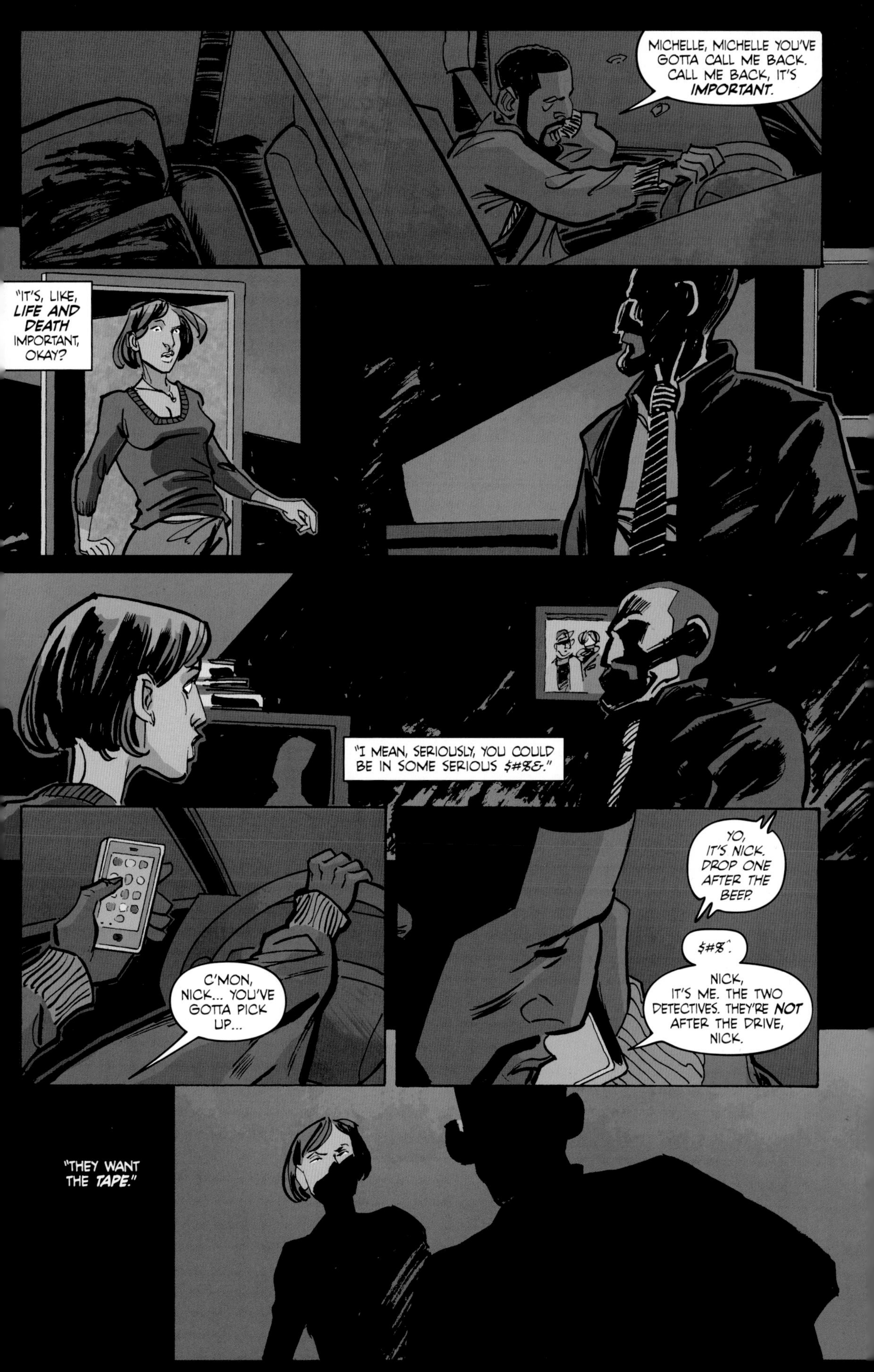
MICHELLE, MICHELLE YOU'VE GOTTA CALL ME BACK. CALL ME BACK, IT'S IMPORTANT.
"IT'S, LIKE, LIFE AND DEATH IMPORTANT, OKAY?
"I MEAN, SERIOUSLY, YOU COULD BE IN SOME SERIOUS $#%&."
C'MON, NICK... YOU'VE GOTTA PICK UP...
YO, IT'S NICK. DROP ONE AFTER THE BEEP.
$#%.
NICK, IT'S ME. THE TWO DETECTIVES. THEY'RE NOT AFTER THE DRIVE, NICK.
"THEY WANT THE TAPE."

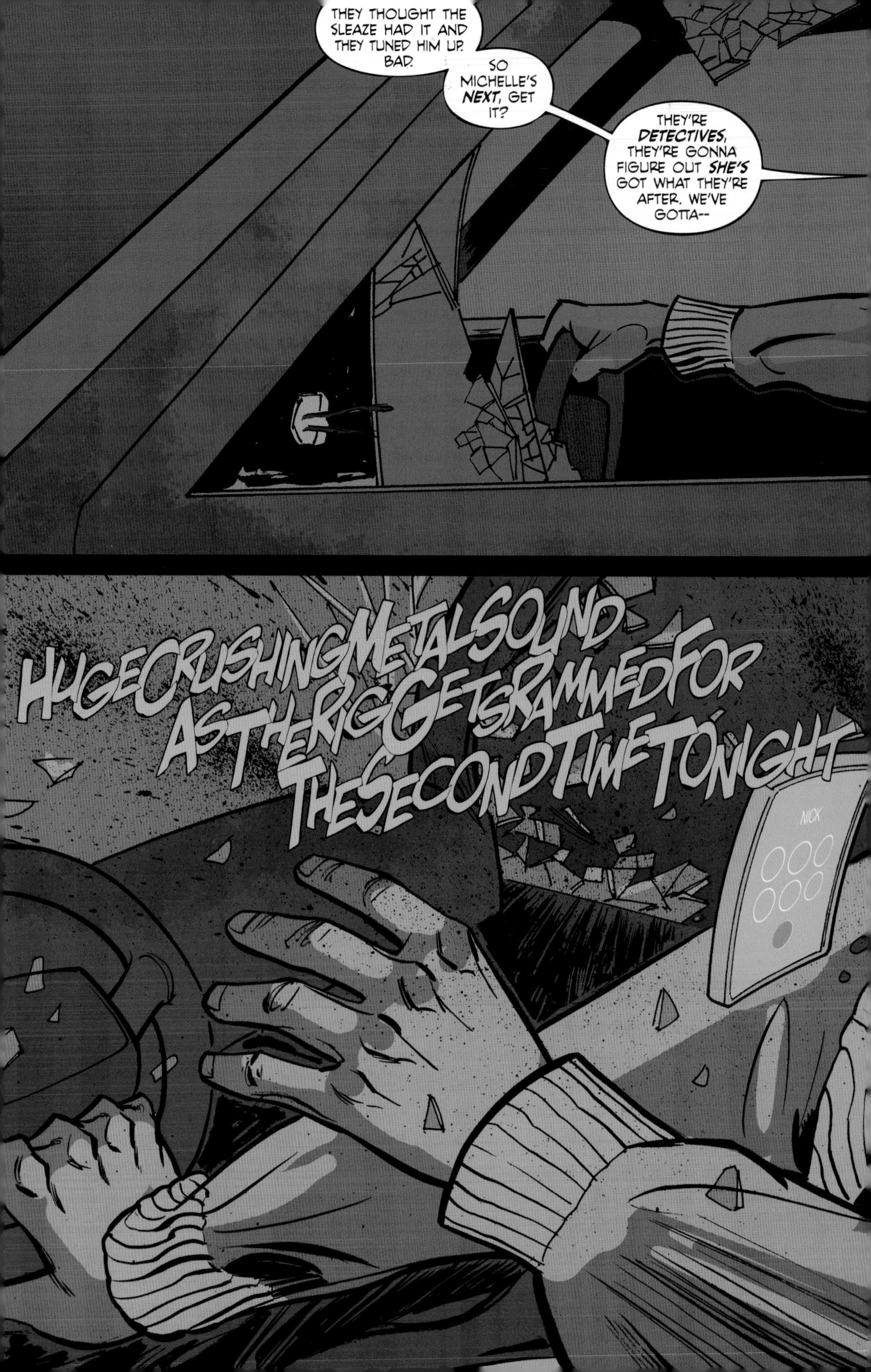
THEY THOUGHT THE SLEAZE HAD IT AND THEY TUNED HIM UP. BAD.
SO MICHELLE'S NEXT, GET IT?
THEY'RE DETECTIVES, THEY'RE GONNA FIGURE OUT SHE'S GOT WHAT THEY'RE AFTER. WE'VE GOTTA--
HUGE CRUSHING METAL SOUND AS THE RIG GETS RAMMED FOR THE SECOND TIME TONIGHT
NICK

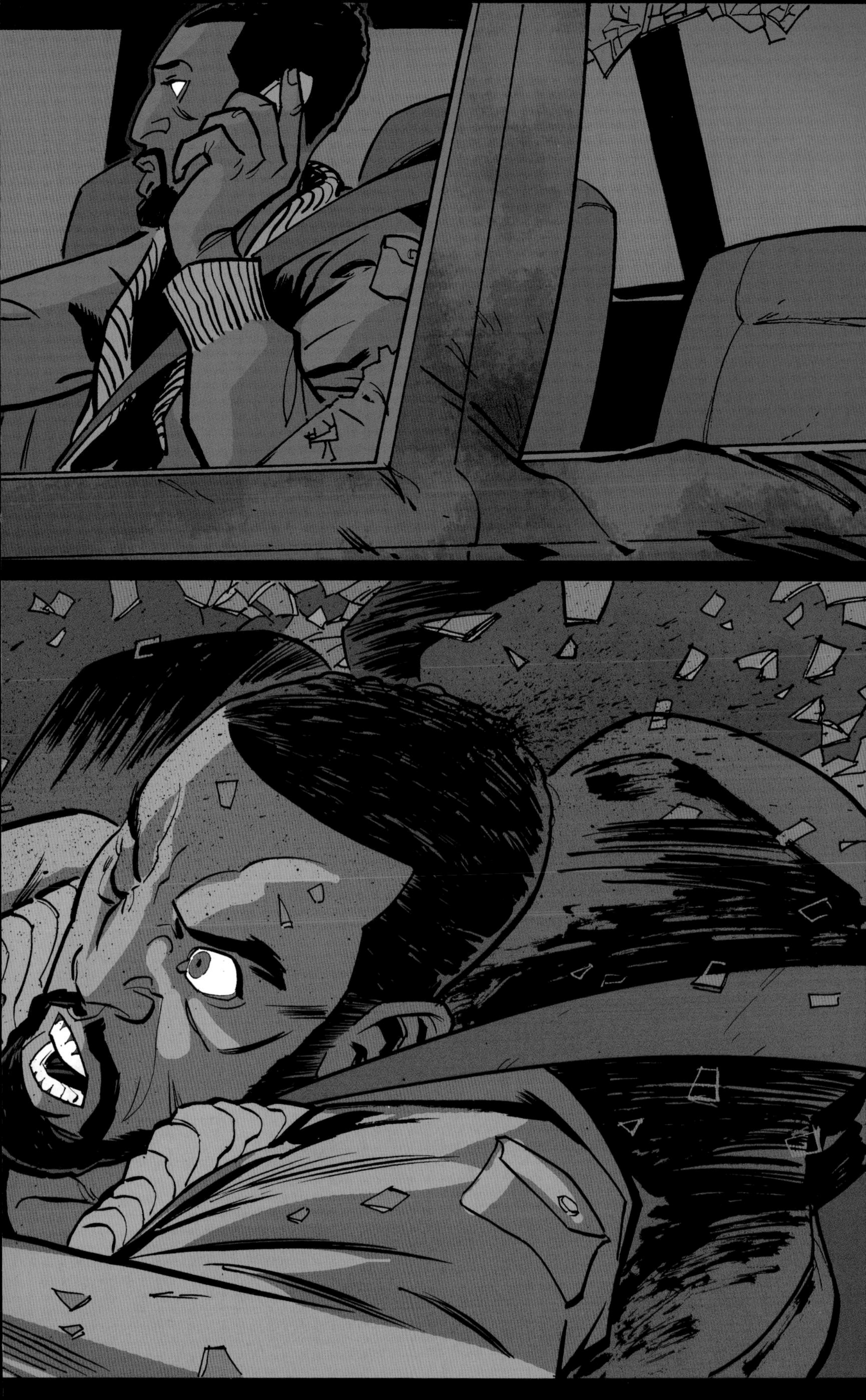

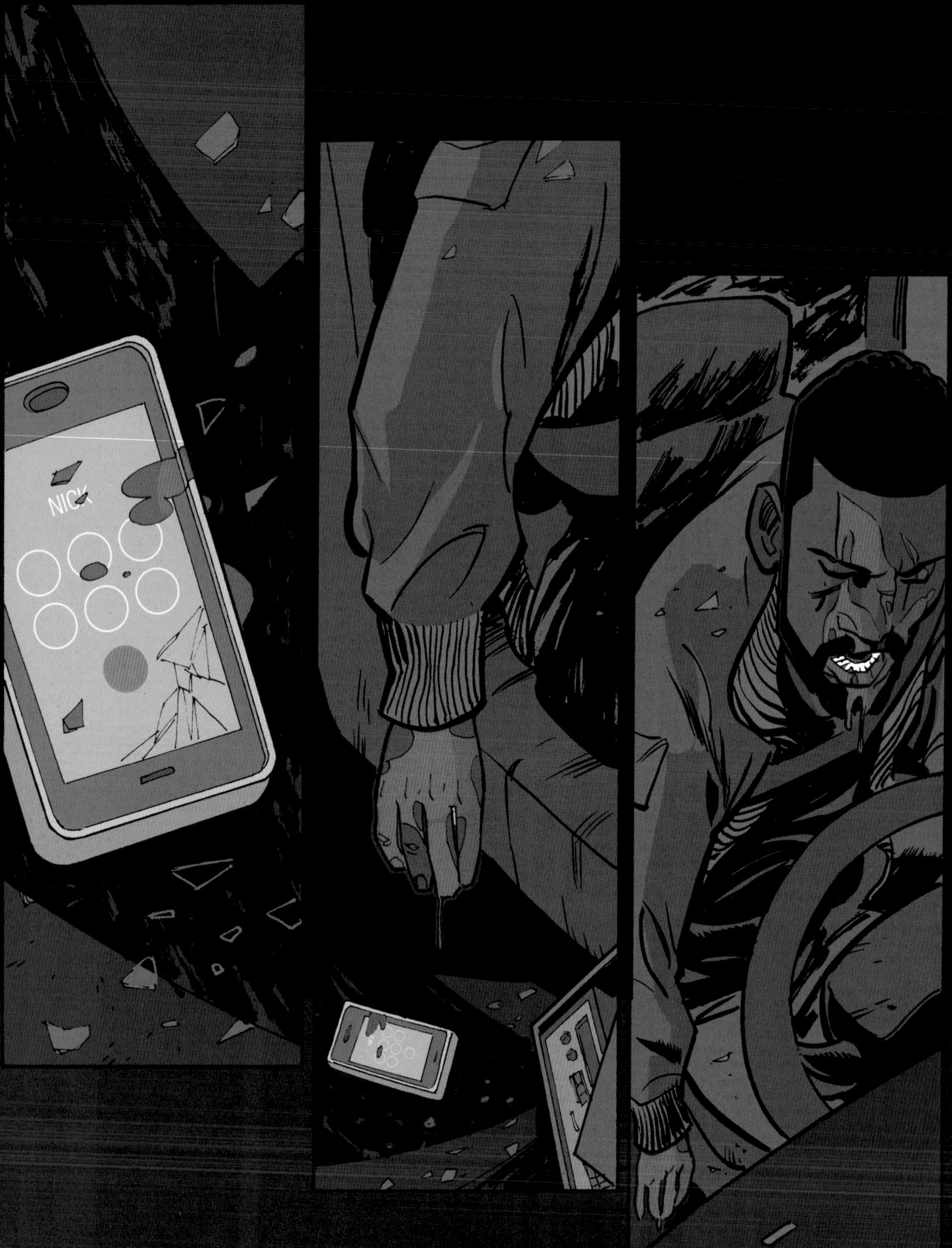
NICK

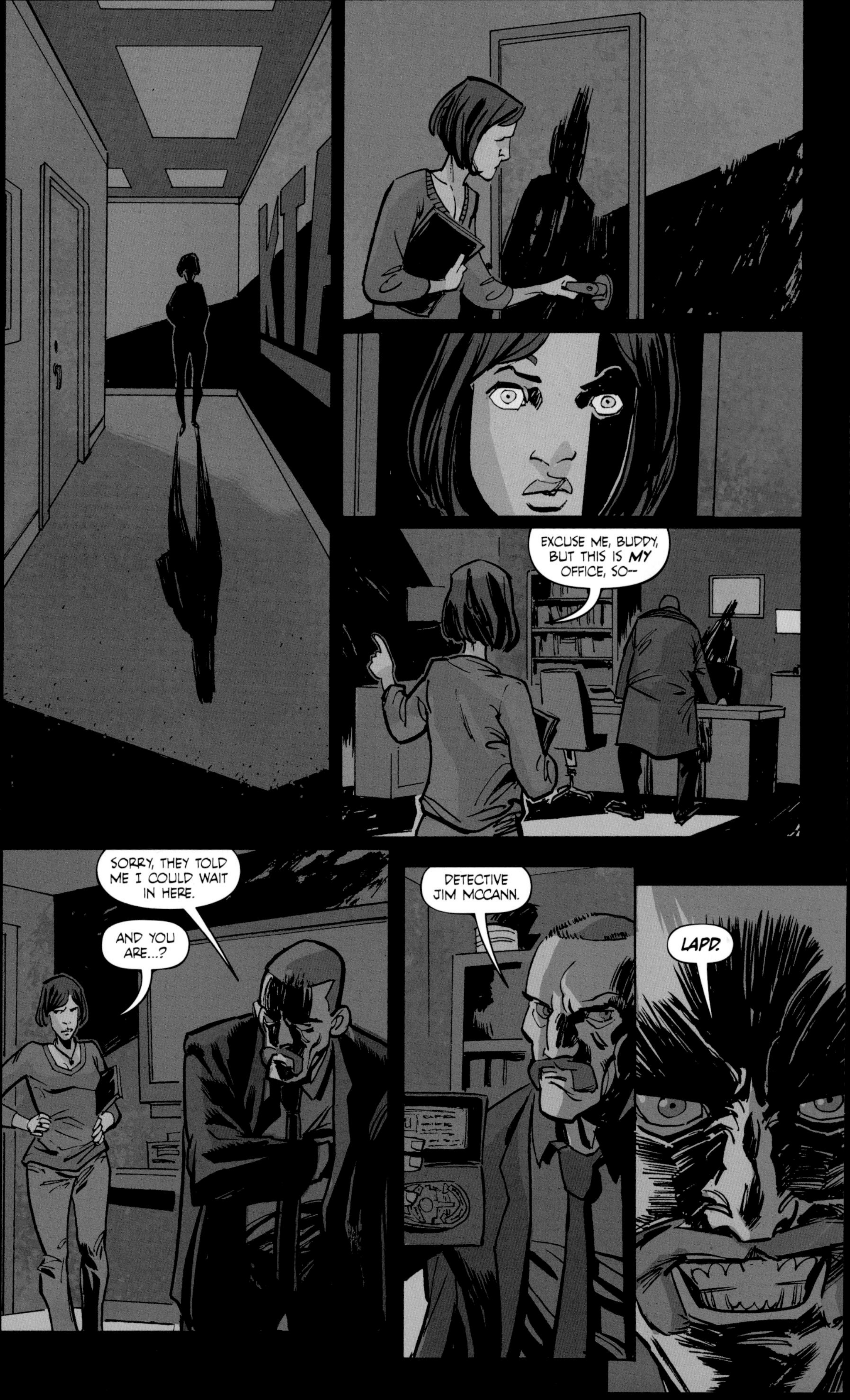

KTA
EXCUSE ME, BUDDY, BUT THIS IS *MY* OFFICE, SO--
SORRY, THEY TOLD ME I COULD WAIT IN HERE.
AND YOU ARE...?
DETECTIVE JIM MCCANN.
LAPD.

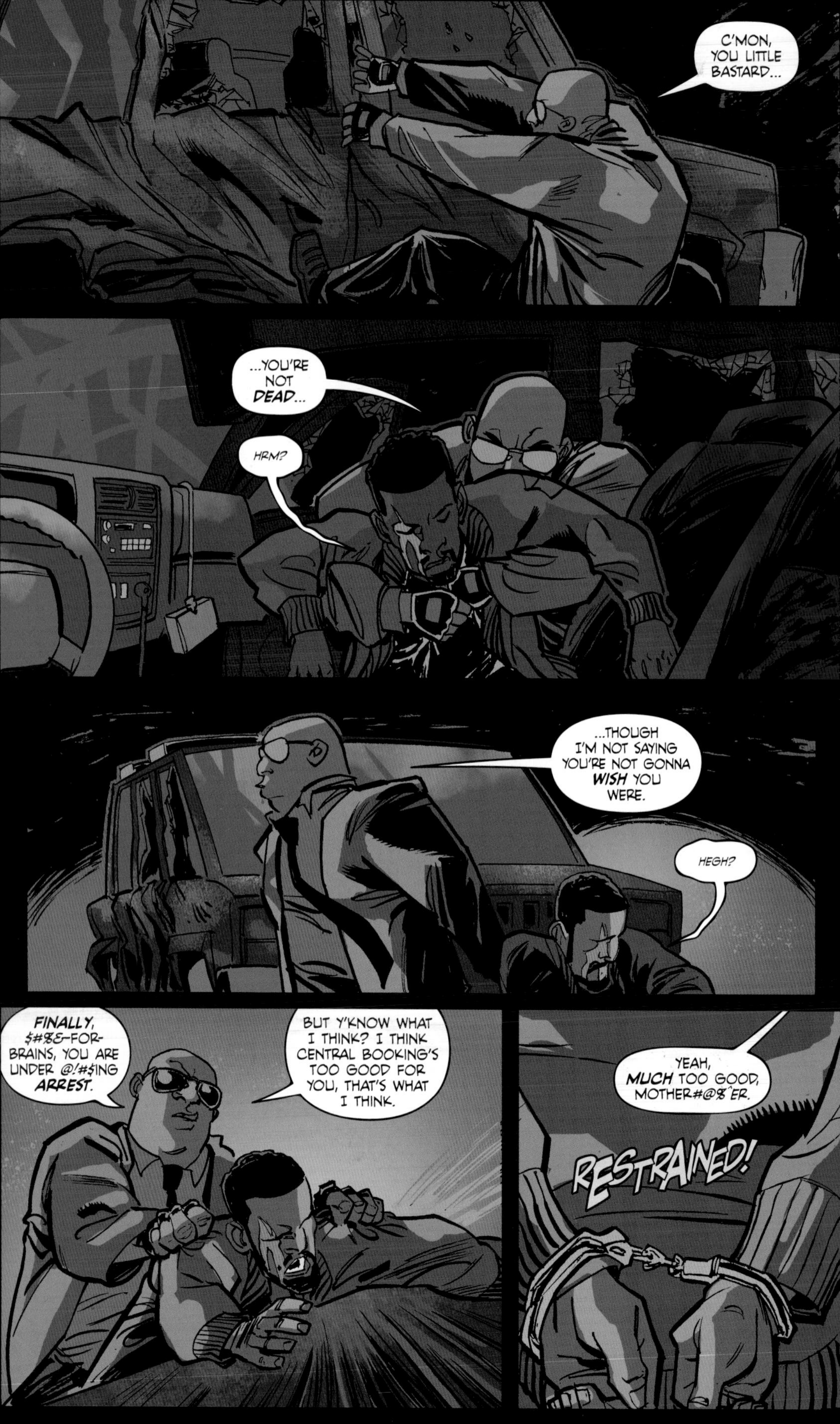
C'MON, YOU LITTLE BASTARD...
...YOU'RE NOT DEAD...
HRM?
...THOUGH I'M NOT SAYING YOU'RE NOT GONNA WISH YOU WERE.
HEGH?
FINALLY, $#%&-FOR-BRAINS, YOU ARE UNDER @!#$ING ARREST.
BUT Y'KNOW WHAT I THINK? I THINK CENTRAL BOOKING'S TOO GOOD FOR YOU, THAT'S WHAT I THINK.
YEAH, MUCH TOO GOOD, MOTHER#@%^ER.
RESTRAINED!

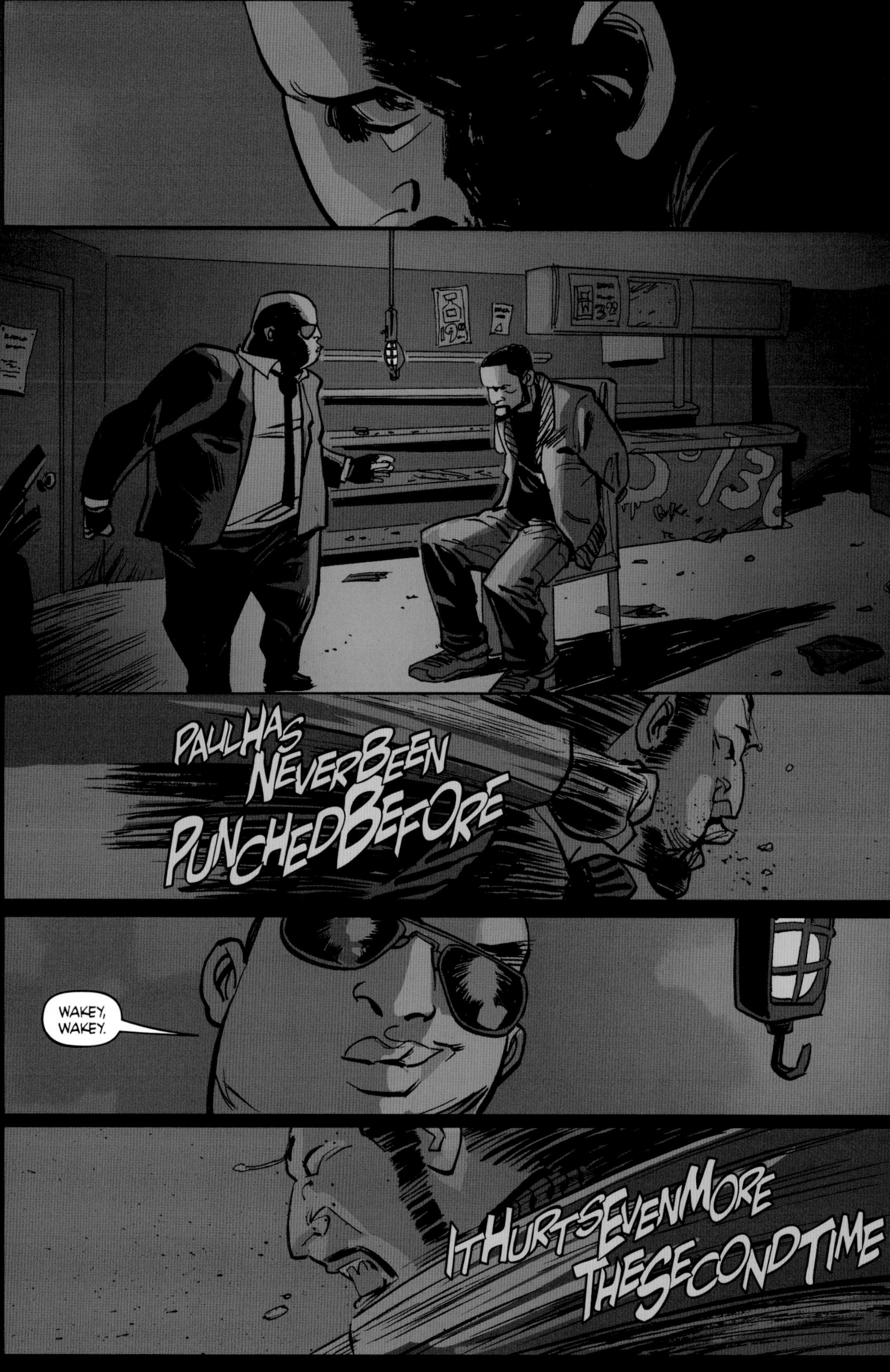
PAUL HAS NEVER BEEN PUNCHED BEFORE
WAKEY, WAKEY.
IT HURTS EVEN MORE THE SECOND TIME

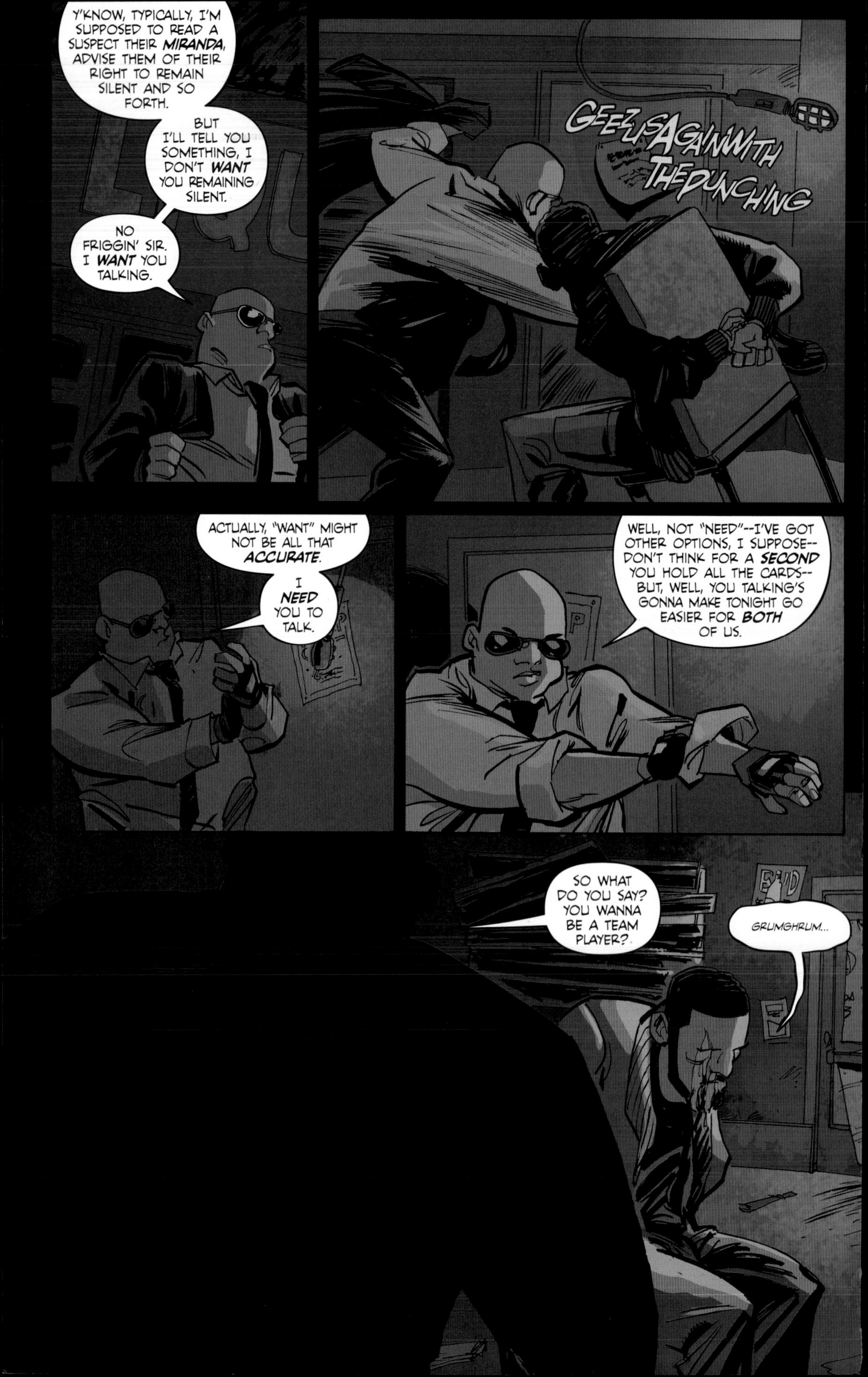
Y'KNOW, TYPICALLY, I'M SUPPOSED TO READ A SUSPECT THEIR MIRANDA, ADVISE THEM OF THEIR RIGHT TO REMAIN SILENT AND SO FORTH.
BUT I'LL TELL YOU SOMETHING, I DON'T WANT YOU REMAINING SILENT.
NO FRIGGIN' SIR. I WANT YOU TALKING.
GEEZ US AGAIN WITH THE PUNCHING
ACTUALLY, "WANT" MIGHT NOT BE ALL THAT ACCURATE.
I NEED YOU TO TALK.
WELL, NOT "NEED"--I'VE GOT OTHER OPTIONS, I SUPPOSE-- DON'T THINK FOR A SECOND YOU HOLD ALL THE CARDS-- BUT, WELL, YOU TALKING'S GONNA MAKE TONIGHT GO EASIER FOR BOTH OF US.
SO WHAT DO YOU SAY? YOU WANNA BE A TEAM PLAYER?
GRUMGHRUM...

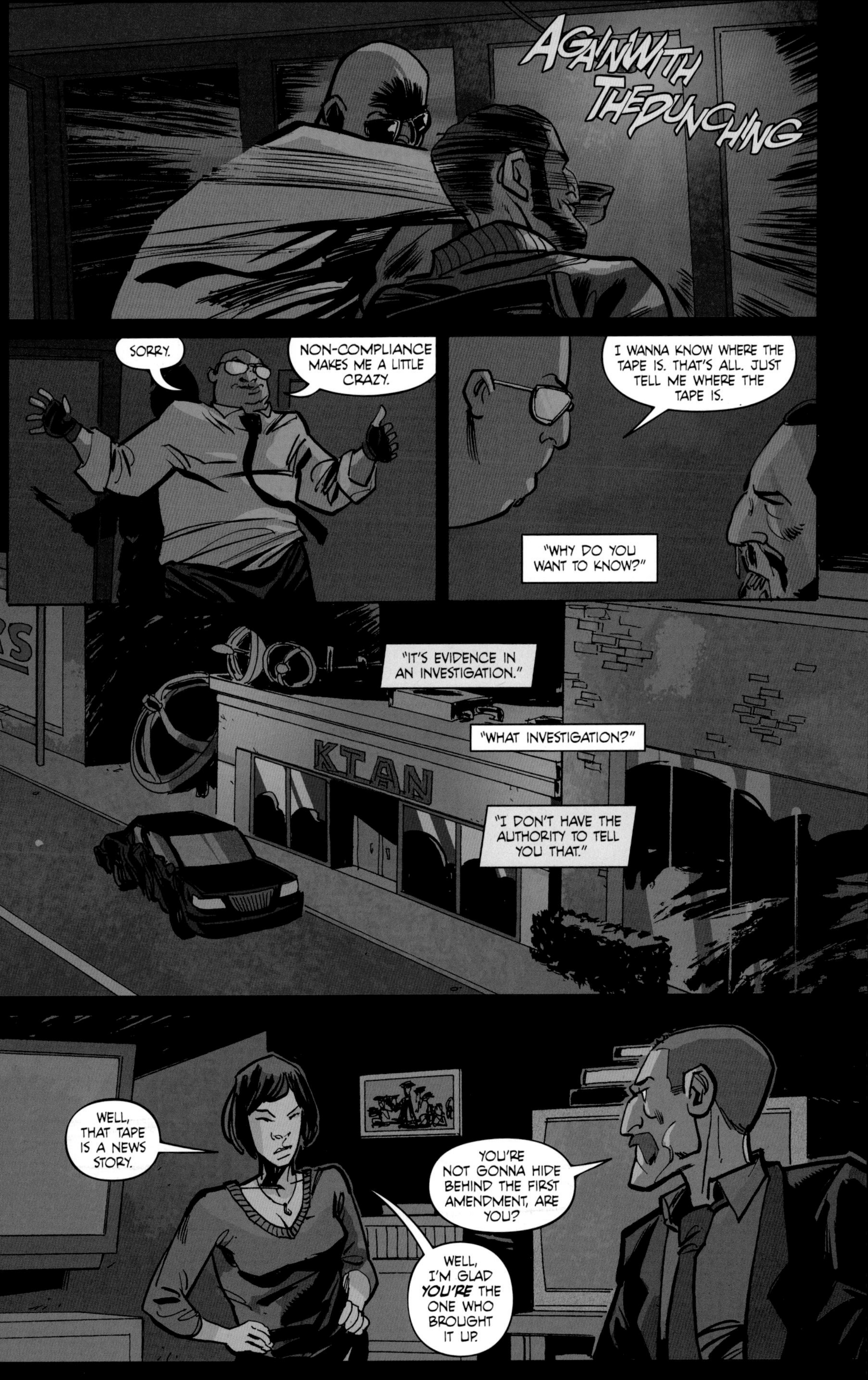
AGAINWITH THEPUNCHING
SORRY.
NON-COMPLIANCE MAKES ME A LITTLE CRAZY.
I WANNA KNOW WHERE THE TAPE IS. THAT'S ALL. JUST TELL ME WHERE THE TAPE IS.
"WHY DO YOU WANT TO KNOW?"
"IT'S EVIDENCE IN AN INVESTIGATION."
KTAN
"WHAT INVESTIGATION?"
"I DON'T HAVE THE AUTHORITY TO TELL YOU THAT."
WELL, THAT TAPE IS A NEWS STORY.
YOU'RE NOT GONNA HIDE BEHIND THE FIRST AMENDMENT, ARE YOU?
WELL, I'M GLAD *YOU'RE* THE ONE WHO BROUGHT IT UP.

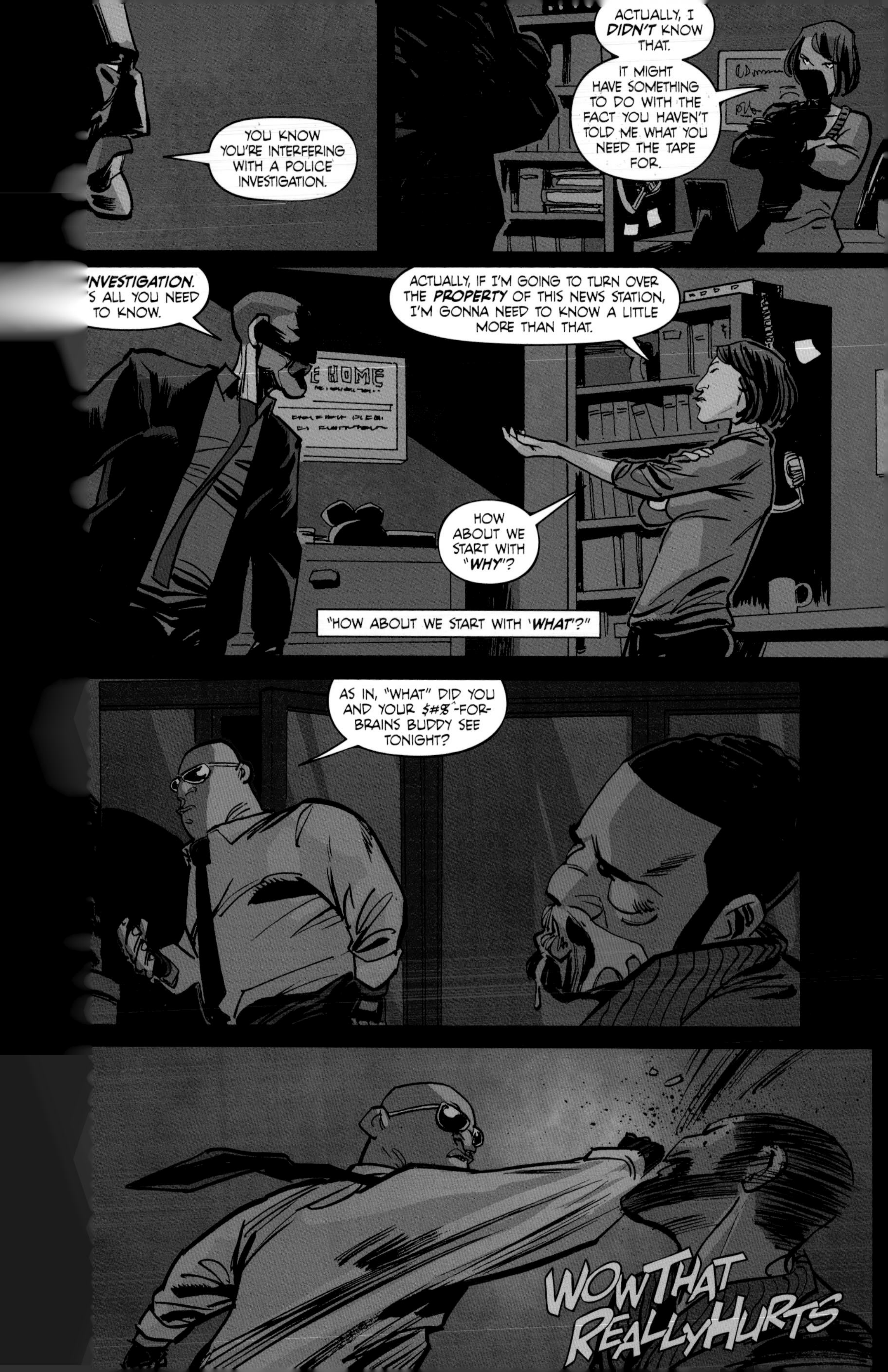
YOU KNOW YOU'RE INTERFERING WITH A POLICE INVESTIGATION.
ACTUALLY, I DIDN'T KNOW THAT.
IT MIGHT HAVE SOMETHING TO DO WITH THE FACT YOU HAVEN'T TOLD ME WHAT YOU NEED THE TAPE FOR.
INVESTIGATION. 'S ALL YOU NEED TO KNOW.
ACTUALLY, IF I'M GOING TO TURN OVER THE PROPERTY OF THIS NEWS STATION, I'M GONNA NEED TO KNOW A LITTLE MORE THAN THAT.
HOW ABOUT WE START WITH "WHY"?
"HOW ABOUT WE START WITH 'WHAT'?"
AS IN, "WHAT" DID YOU AND YOUR $#%-FOR-BRAINS BUDDY SEE TONIGHT?
WOW THAT REALLY HURTS

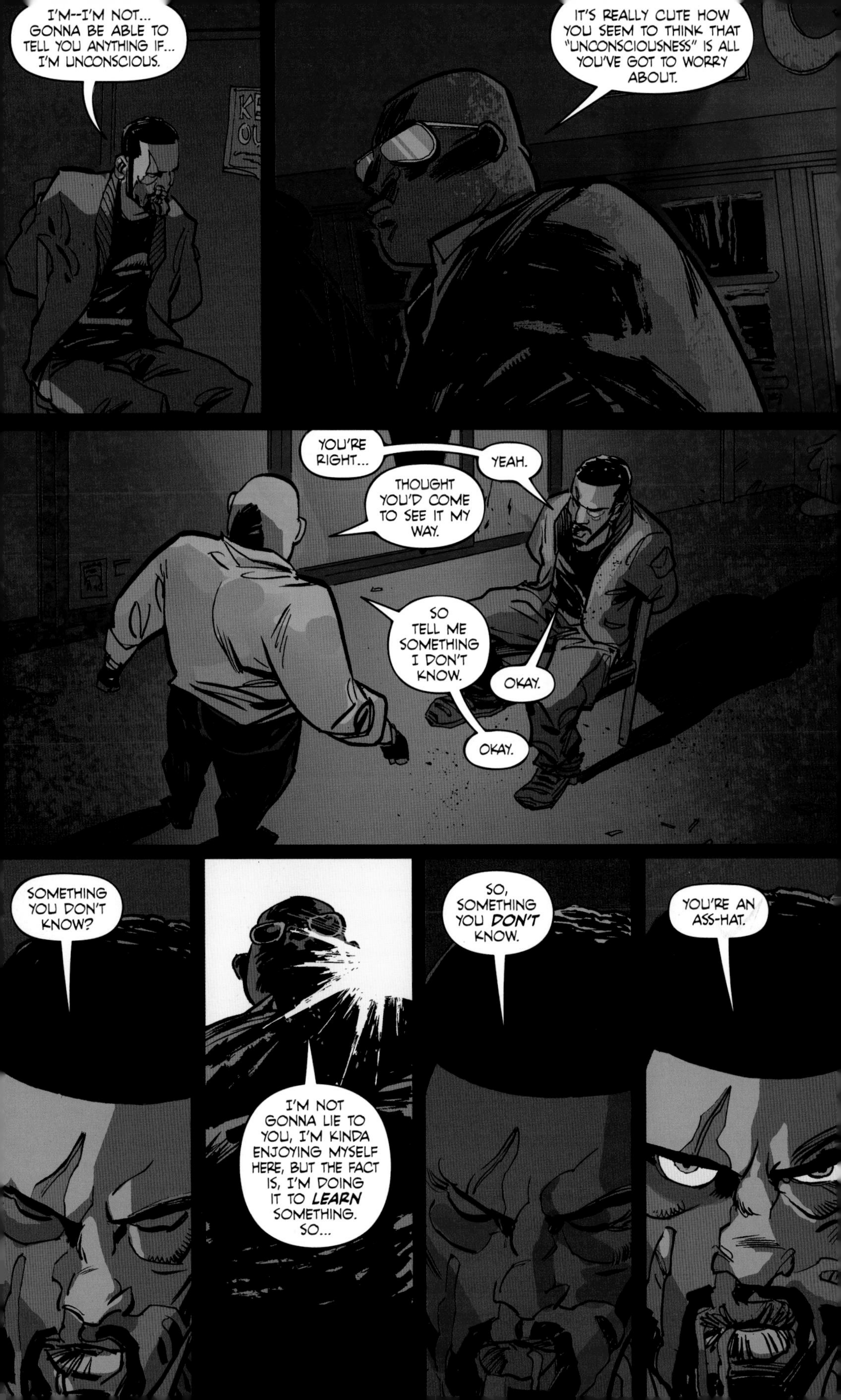
I'M--I'M NOT... GONNA BE ABLE TO TELL YOU ANYTHING IF... I'M UNCONSCIOUS.
IT'S REALLY CUTE HOW YOU SEEM TO THINK THAT "UNCONSCIOUSNESS" IS ALL YOU'VE GOT TO WORRY ABOUT.
YOU'RE RIGHT...
YEAH.
THOUGHT YOU'D COME TO SEE IT MY WAY.
SO TELL ME SOMETHING I DON'T KNOW.
OKAY.
OKAY.
SOMETHING YOU DON'T KNOW?
I'M NOT GONNA LIE TO YOU, I'M KINDA ENJOYING MYSELF HERE, BUT THE FACT IS, I'M DOING IT TO *LEARN* SOMETHING. SO...
SO, SOMETHING YOU *DON'T* KNOW.
YOU'RE AN ASS-HAT.

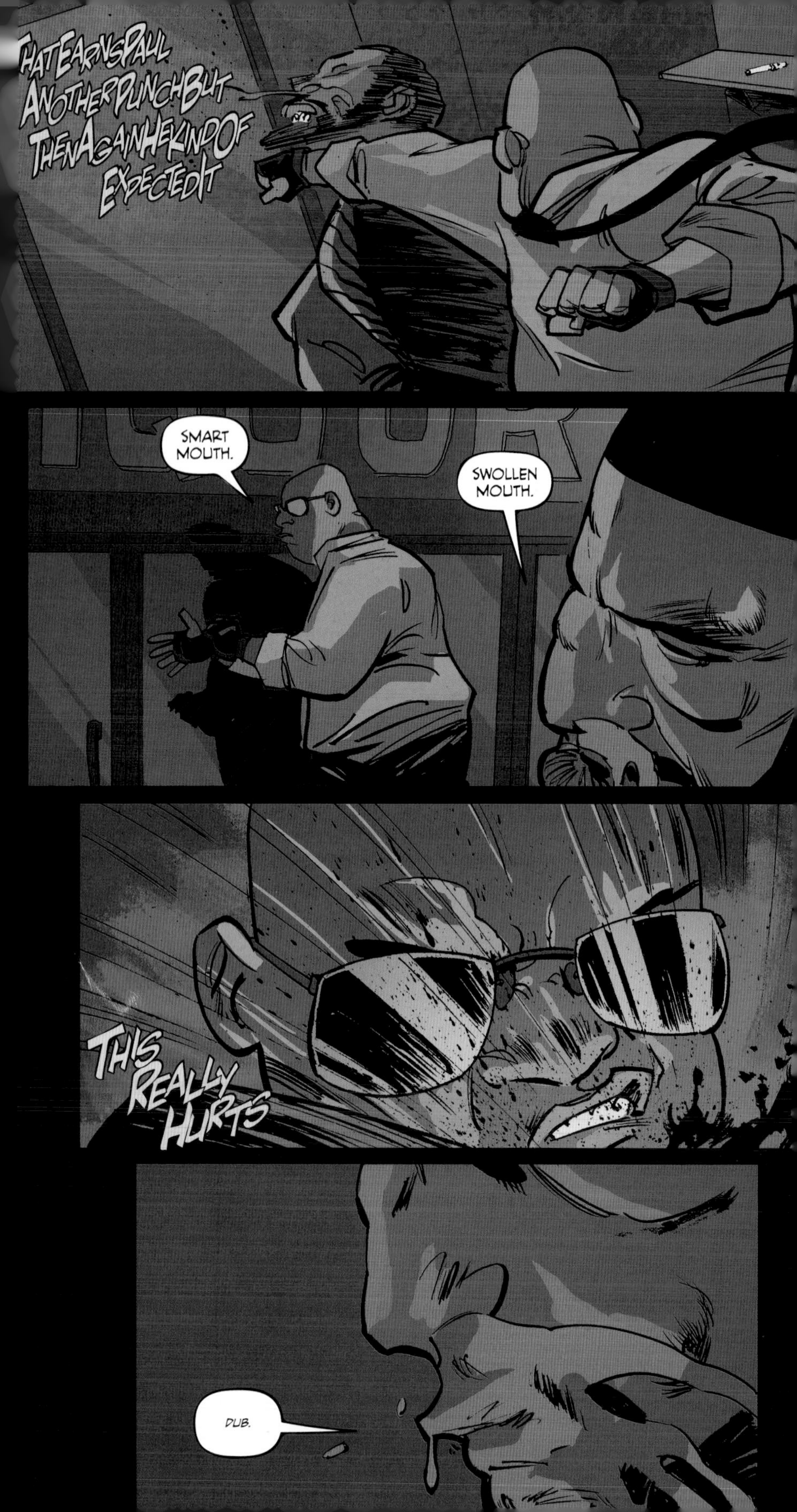
THAT EARNS PAUL ANOTHER PUNCH BUT THEN AGAIN HE KIND OF EXPECTED IT
SMART MOUTH.
SWOLLEN MOUTH.
THIS REALLY HURTS
DUB.

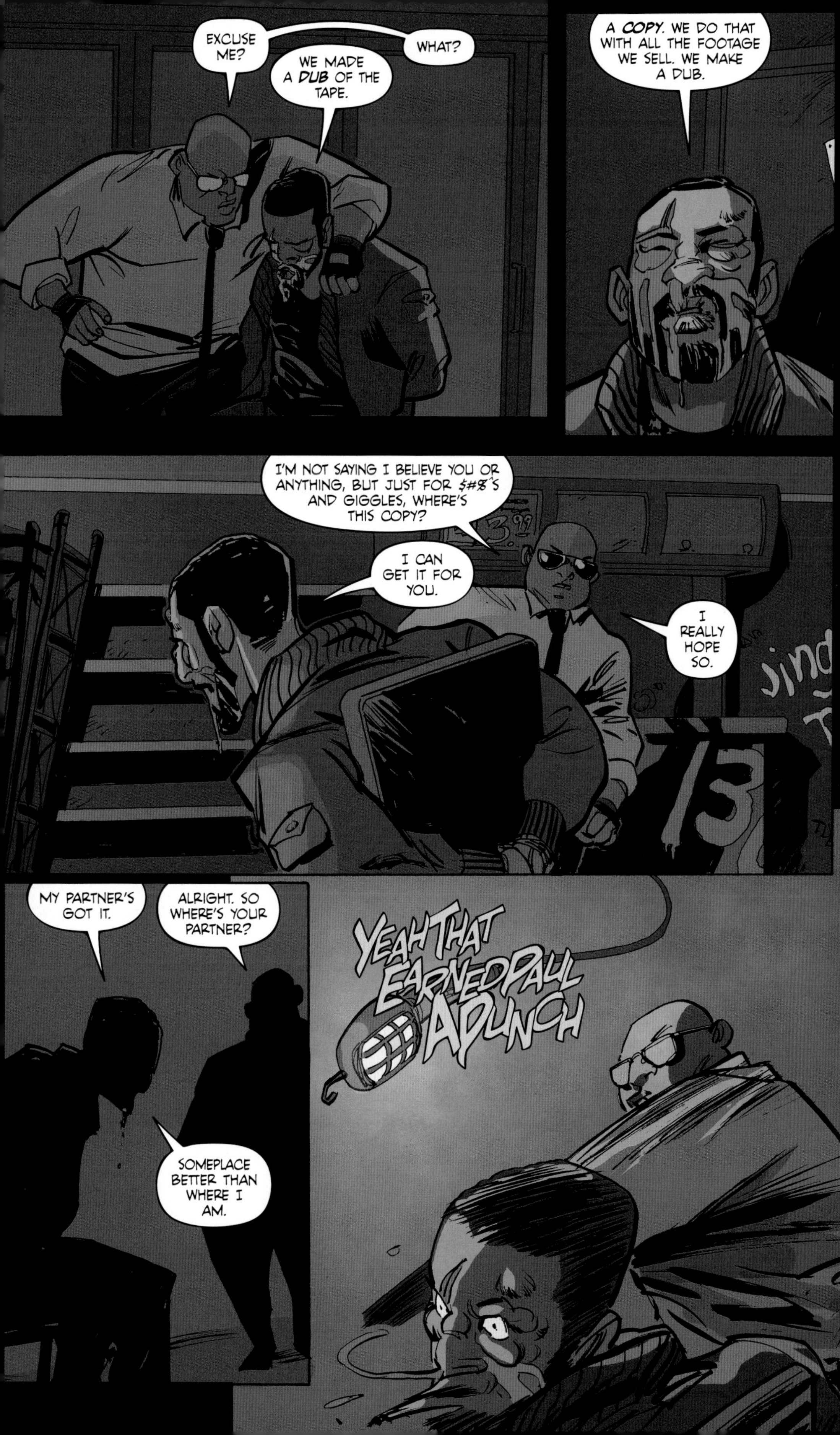
EXCUSE ME?
WHAT?
WE MADE A DUB OF THE TAPE.
A COPY. WE DO THAT WITH ALL THE FOOTAGE WE SELL. WE MAKE A DUB.
I'M NOT SAYING I BELIEVE YOU OR ANYTHING, BUT JUST FOR $#%^'S AND GIGGLES, WHERE'S THIS COPY?
I CAN GET IT FOR YOU.
I REALLY HOPE SO.
MY PARTNER'S GOT IT.
ALRIGHT. SO WHERE'S YOUR PARTNER?
SOMEPLACE BETTER THAN WHERE I AM.
YEAH THAT EARNED PAUL A PUNCH

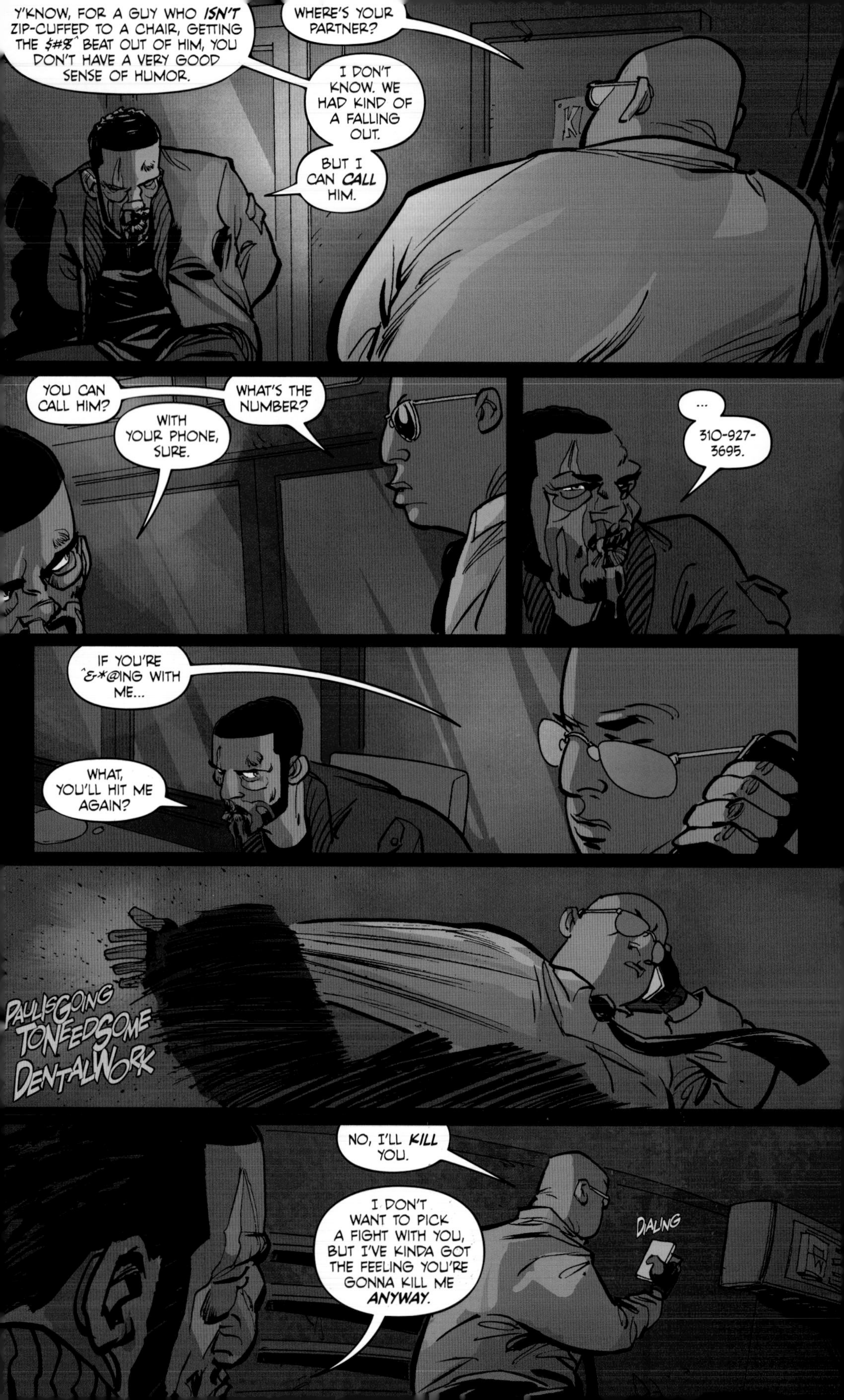
Y'KNOW, FOR A GUY WHO ISN'T ZIP-CUFFED TO A CHAIR, GETTING THE $#%^ BEAT OUT OF HIM, YOU DON'T HAVE A VERY GOOD SENSE OF HUMOR.
WHERE'S YOUR PARTNER?
I DON'T KNOW. WE HAD KIND OF A FALLING OUT.
BUT I CAN CALL HIM.
YOU CAN CALL HIM?
WITH YOUR PHONE, SURE.
WHAT'S THE NUMBER?
...
310-927-3695.
IF YOU'RE ^&*@ING WITH ME...
WHAT, YOU'LL HIT ME AGAIN?
PAULISGOING TONEEDSOME DENTALWORK
NO, I'LL KILL YOU.
I DON'T WANT TO PICK A FIGHT WITH YOU, BUT I'VE KINDA GOT THE FEELING YOU'RE GONNA KILL ME ANYWAY.
DIALING

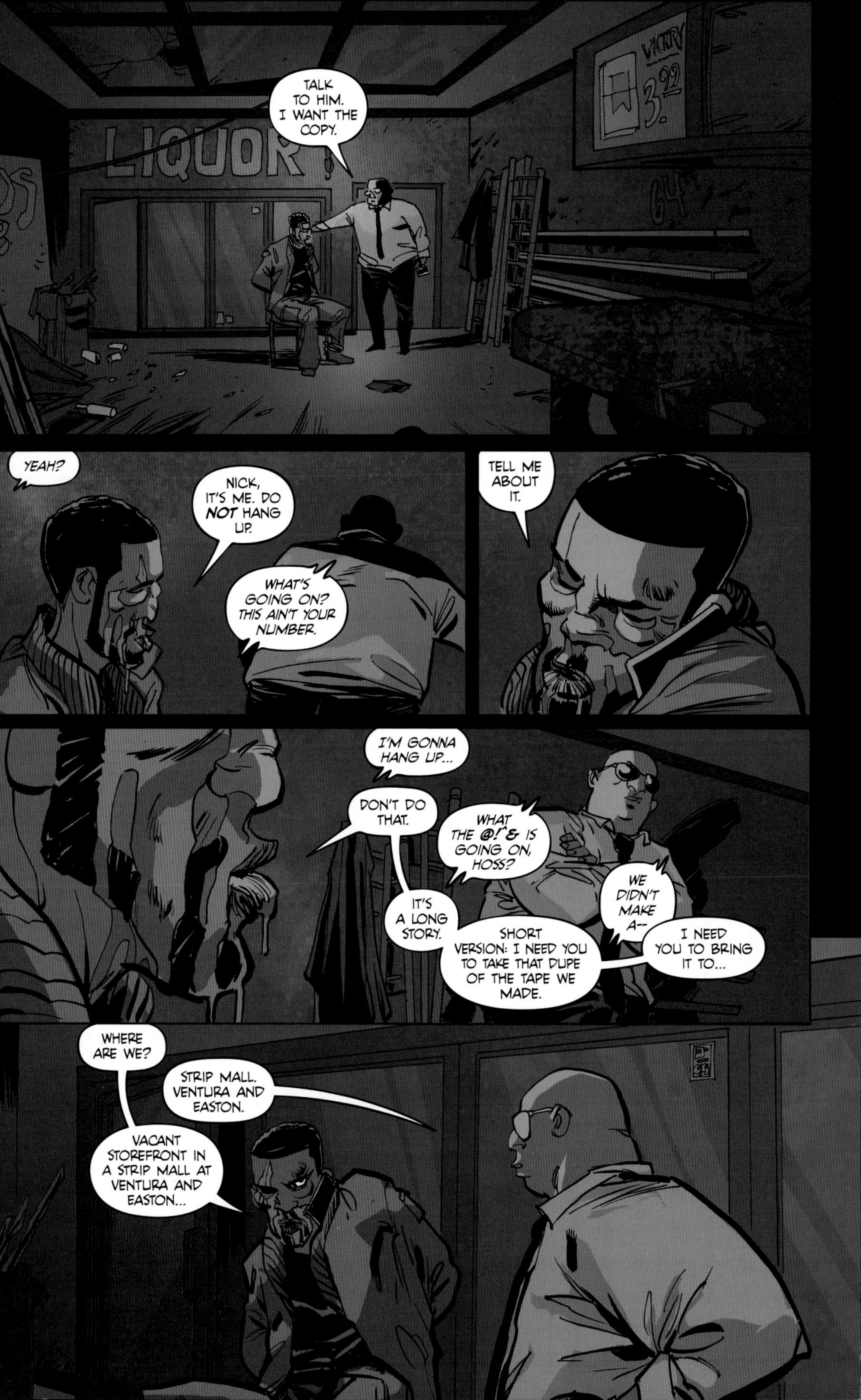
LIQUOR
VICTORY
3.99
64¢
TALK TO HIM. I WANT THE COPY.
YEAH?
NICK, IT'S ME. DO **NOT** HANG UP.
WHAT'S GOING ON? THIS AIN'T YOUR NUMBER.
TELL ME ABOUT IT.
I'M GONNA HANG UP...
DON'T DO THAT.
WHAT THE @!^& IS GOING ON, HOSS?
IT'S A LONG STORY.
WE DIDN'T MAKE A--
SHORT VERSION: I NEED YOU TO TAKE THAT DUPE OF THE TAPE WE MADE.
I NEED YOU TO BRING IT TO...
WHERE ARE WE?
STRIP MALL. VENTURA AND EASTON.
VACANT STOREFRONT IN A STRIP MALL AT VENTURA AND EASTON...

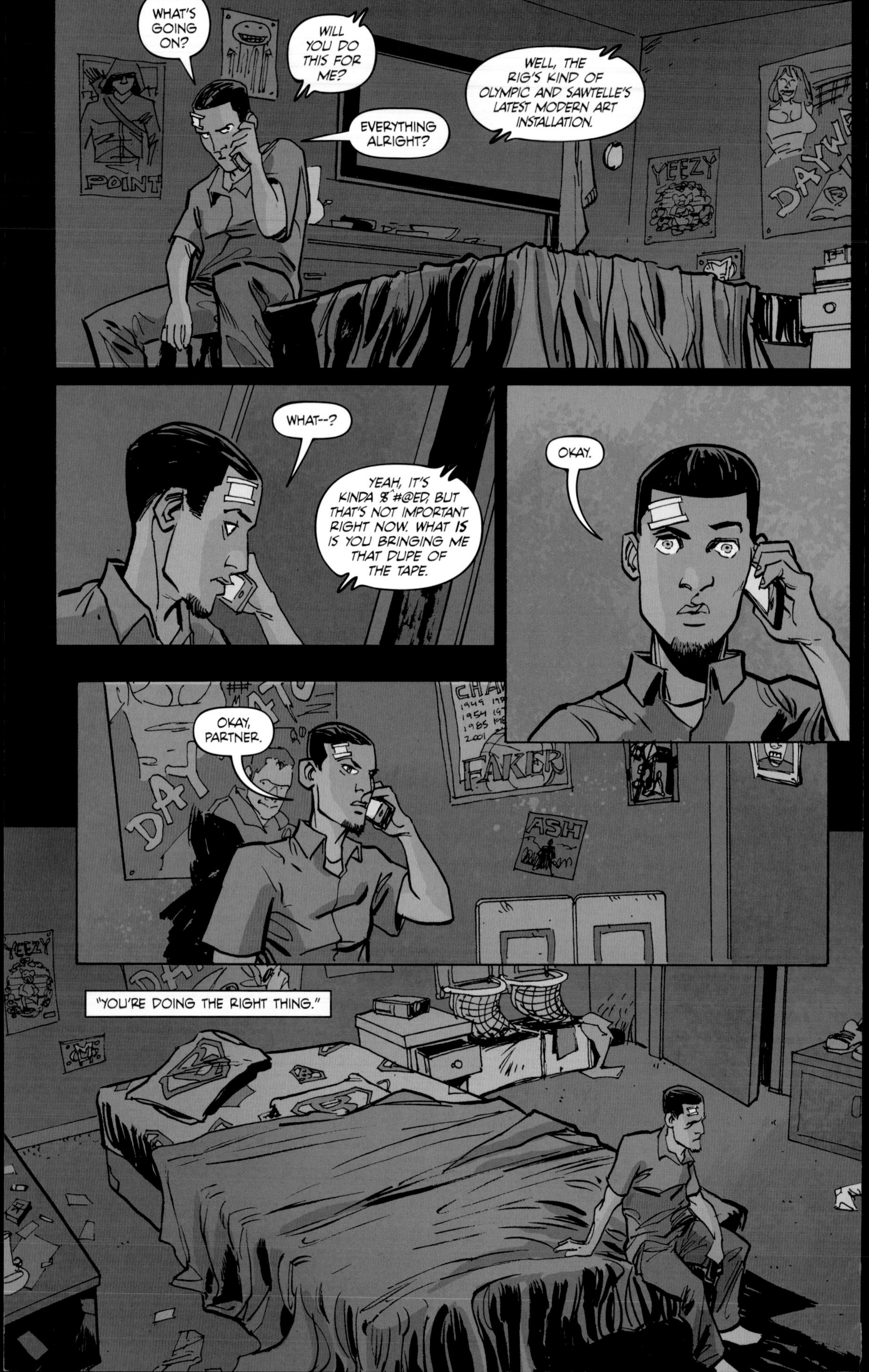
WHAT'S GOING ON?
WILL YOU DO THIS FOR ME?
EVERYTHING ALRIGHT?
WELL, THE RIG'S KIND OF OLYMPIC AND SAWTELLE'S LATEST MODERN ART INSTALLATION.
POINT
YEEZY
WHAT--?
YEAH, IT'S KINDA $^#@ED, BUT THAT'S NOT IMPORTANT RIGHT NOW. WHAT IS IS YOU BRINGING ME THAT DUPE OF THE TAPE.
OKAY.
OKAY, PARTNER.
FAKER
ASH
"YOU'RE DOING THE RIGHT THING."

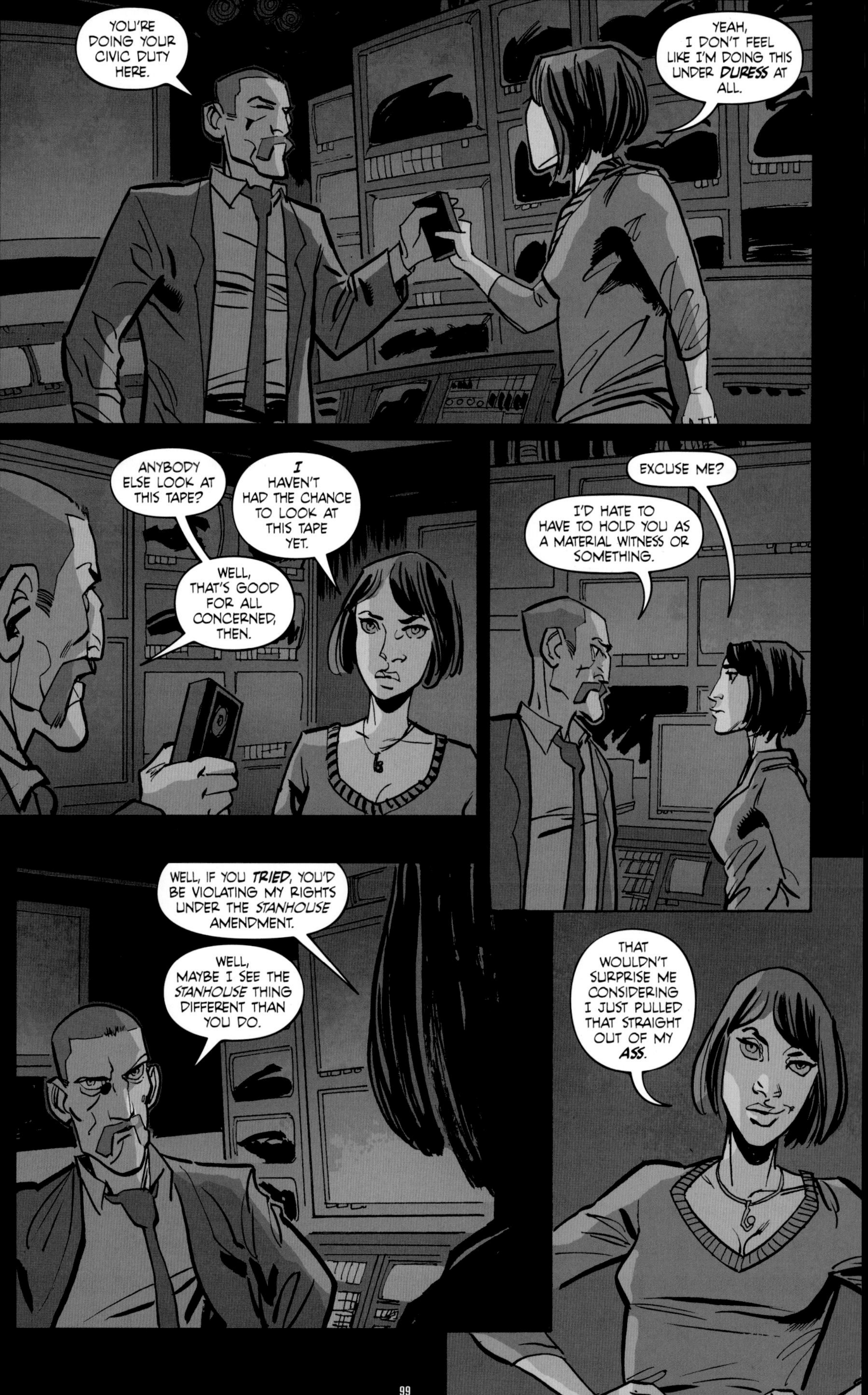
YOU'RE DOING YOUR CIVIC DUTY HERE.
YEAH, I DON'T FEEL LIKE I'M DOING THIS UNDER DURESS AT ALL.
ANYBODY ELSE LOOK AT THIS TAPE?
I HAVEN'T HAD THE CHANCE TO LOOK AT THIS TAPE YET.
WELL, THAT'S GOOD FOR ALL CONCERNED, THEN.
I'D HATE TO HAVE TO HOLD YOU AS A MATERIAL WITNESS OR SOMETHING.
EXCUSE ME?
WELL, IF YOU TRIED, YOU'D BE VIOLATING MY RIGHTS UNDER THE STANHOUSE AMENDMENT.
WELL, MAYBE I SEE THE STANHOUSE THING DIFFERENT THAN YOU DO.
THAT WOULDN'T SURPRISE ME CONSIDERING I JUST PULLED THAT STRAIGHT OUT OF MY ASS.

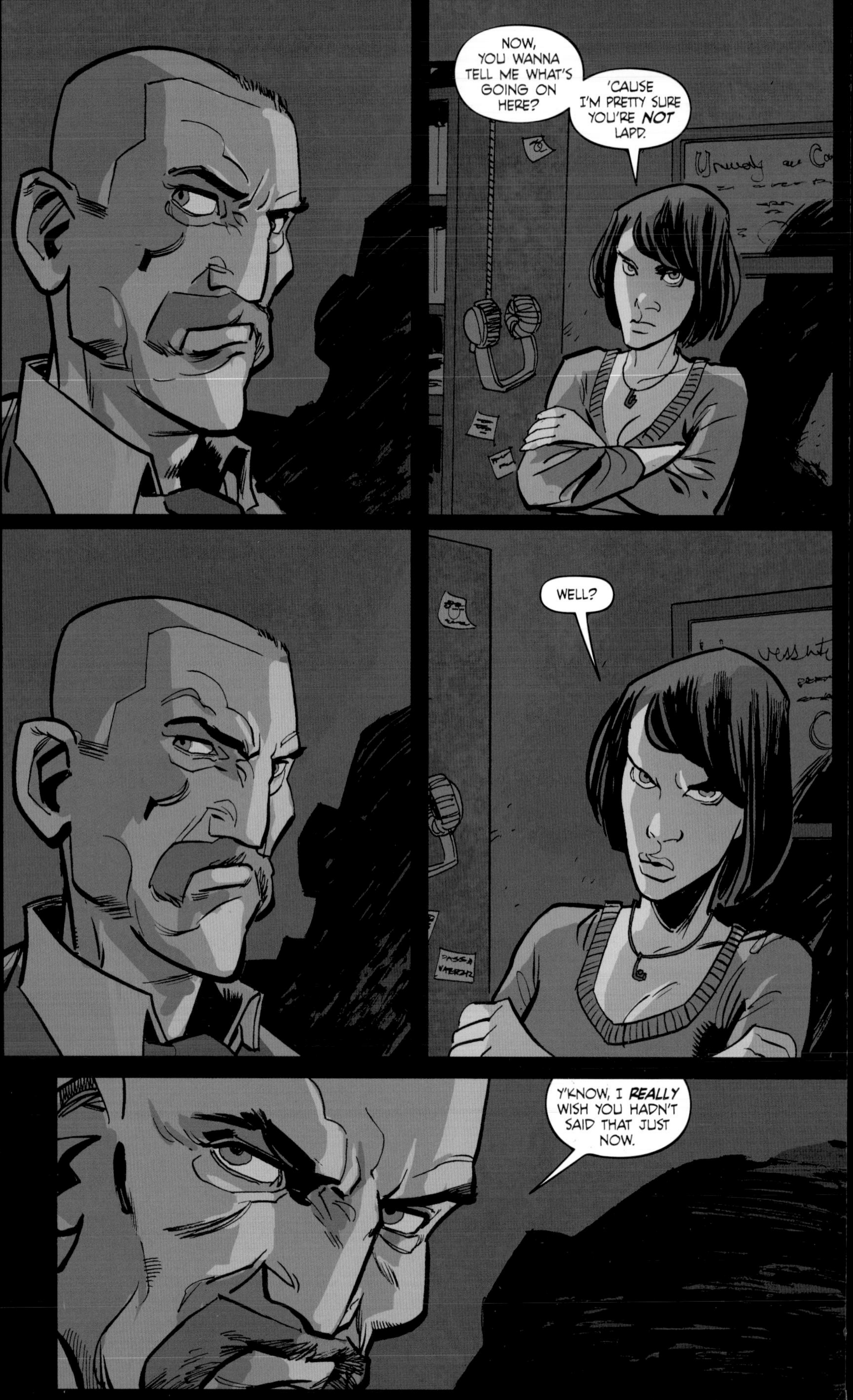
NOW, YOU WANNA TELL ME WHAT'S GOING ON HERE?
'CAUSE I'M PRETTY SURE YOU'RE NOT LAPD.
WELL?
Y'KNOW, I REALLY WISH YOU HADN'T SAID THAT JUST NOW.

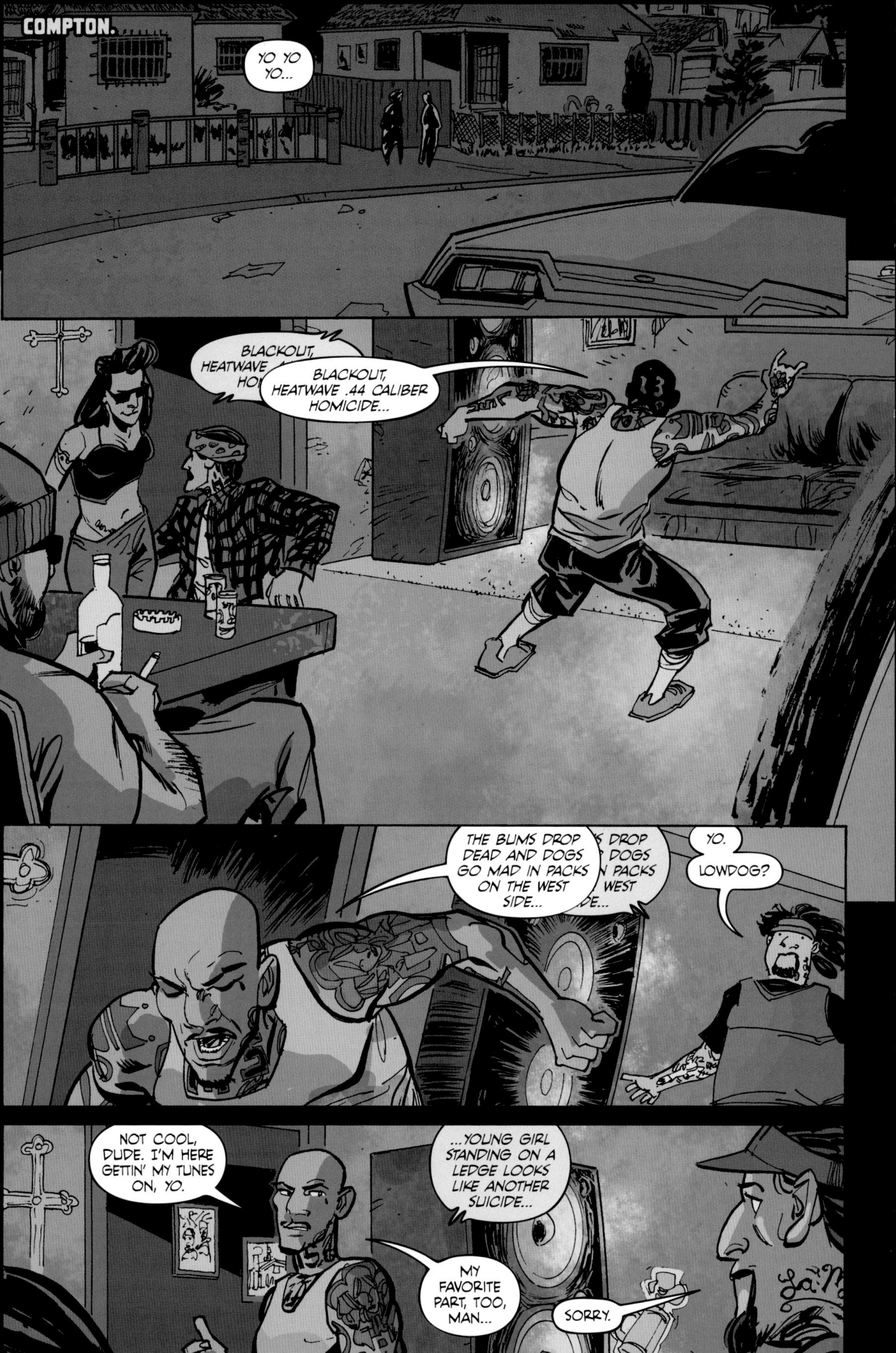
COMPTON.
YO YO YO...
BLACKOUT, HEATWAVE .44 CALIBER HOMICIDE...
THE BUMS DROP DEAD AND DOGS GO MAD IN PACKS ON THE WEST SIDE...
YO.
LOWDOG?
NOT COOL, DUDE. I'M HERE GETTIN' MY TUNES ON, YO.
...YOUNG GIRL STANDING ON A LEDGE LOOKS LIKE ANOTHER SUICIDE...
MY FAVORITE PART, TOO, MAN...
SORRY.

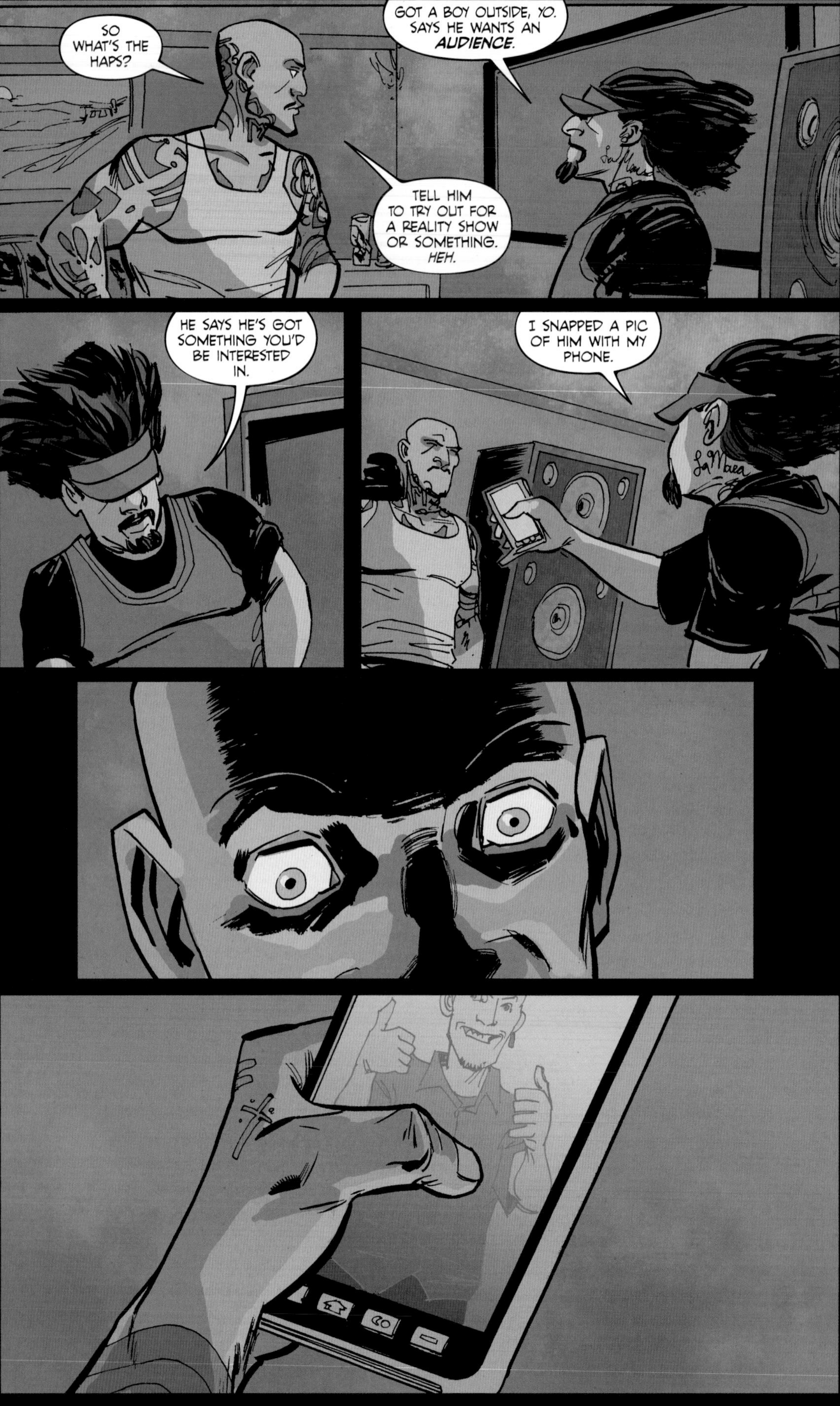
SO WHAT'S THE HAPS?
GOT A BOY OUTSIDE, YO. SAYS HE WANTS AN AUDIENCE.
TELL HIM TO TRY OUT FOR A REALITY SHOW OR SOMETHING. HEH.
HE SAYS HE'S GOT SOMETHING YOU'D BE INTERESTED IN.
I SNAPPED A PIC OF HIM WITH MY PHONE.

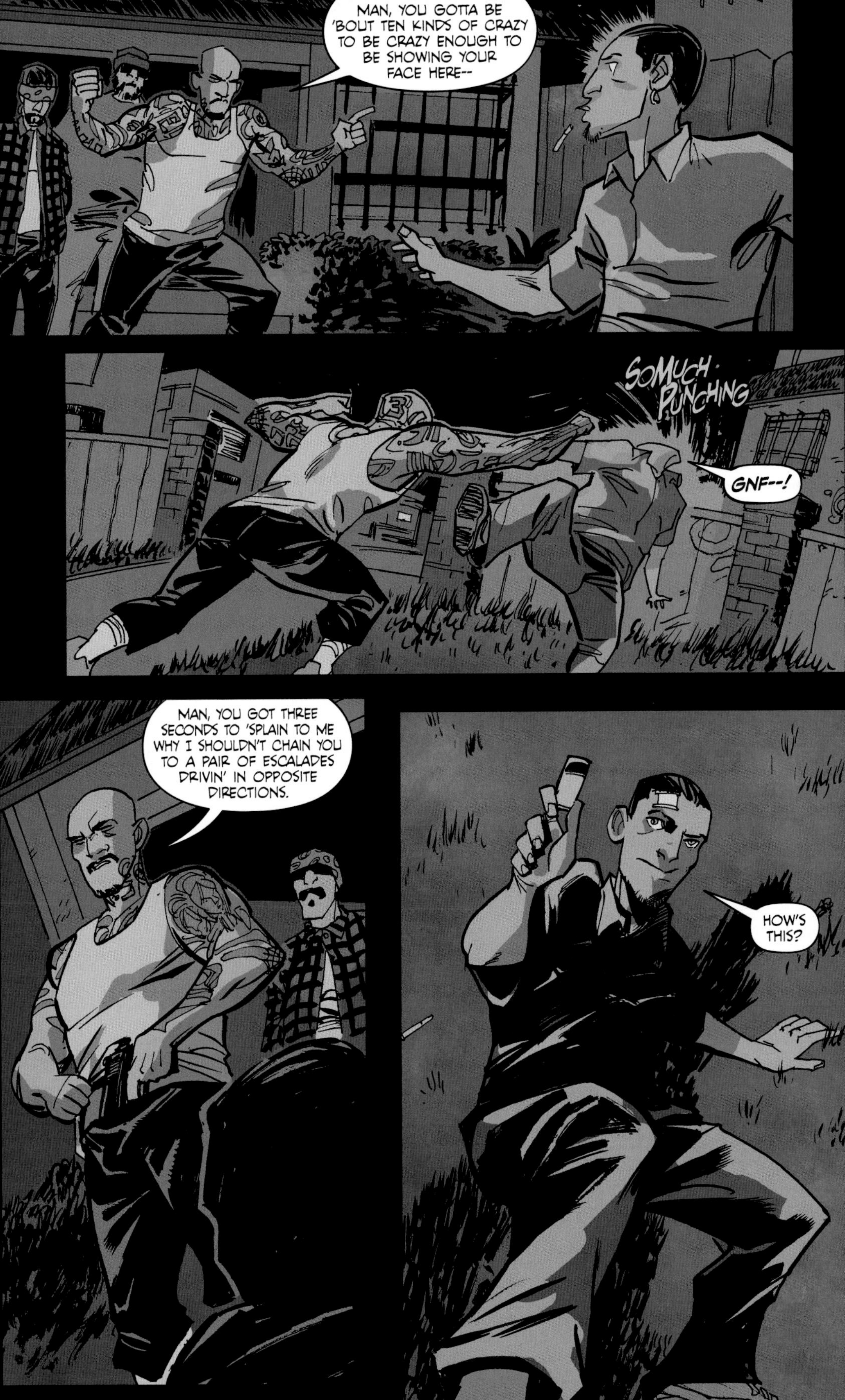
MAN, YOU GOTTA BE 'BOUT TEN KINDS OF CRAZY TO BE CRAZY ENOUGH TO BE SHOWING YOUR FACE HERE--
SOMUCH PUNCHING
GNF--!
MAN, YOU GOT THREE SECONDS TO 'SPLAIN TO ME WHY I SHOULDN'T CHAIN YOU TO A PAIR OF ESCALADES DRIVIN' IN OPPOSITE DIRECTIONS.
HOW'S THIS?

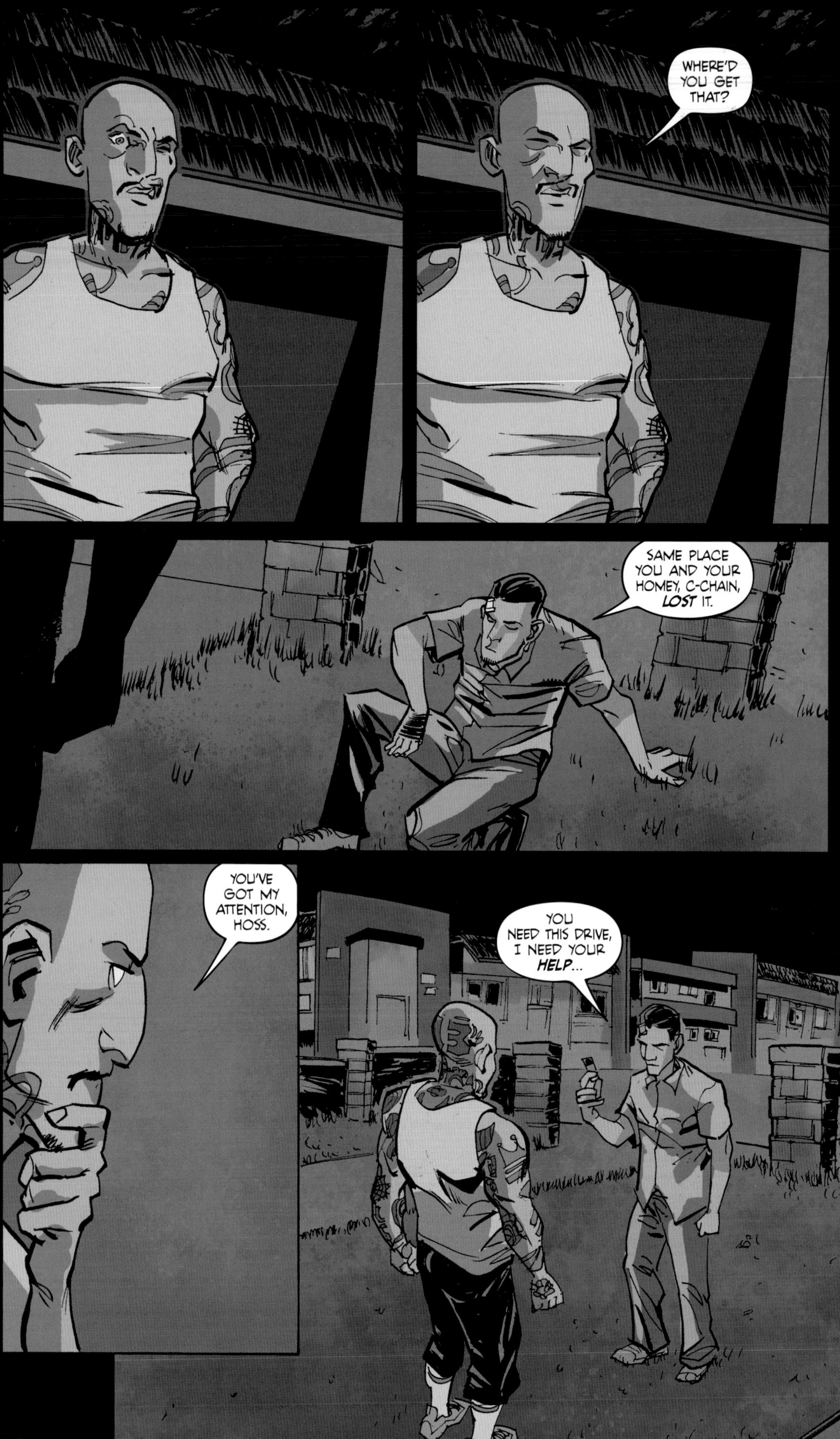
WHERE'D YOU GET THAT?
SAME PLACE YOU AND YOUR HOMEY, C-CHAIN, LOST IT.
YOU'VE GOT MY ATTENTION, HOSS.
YOU NEED THIS DRIVE, I NEED YOUR HELP...

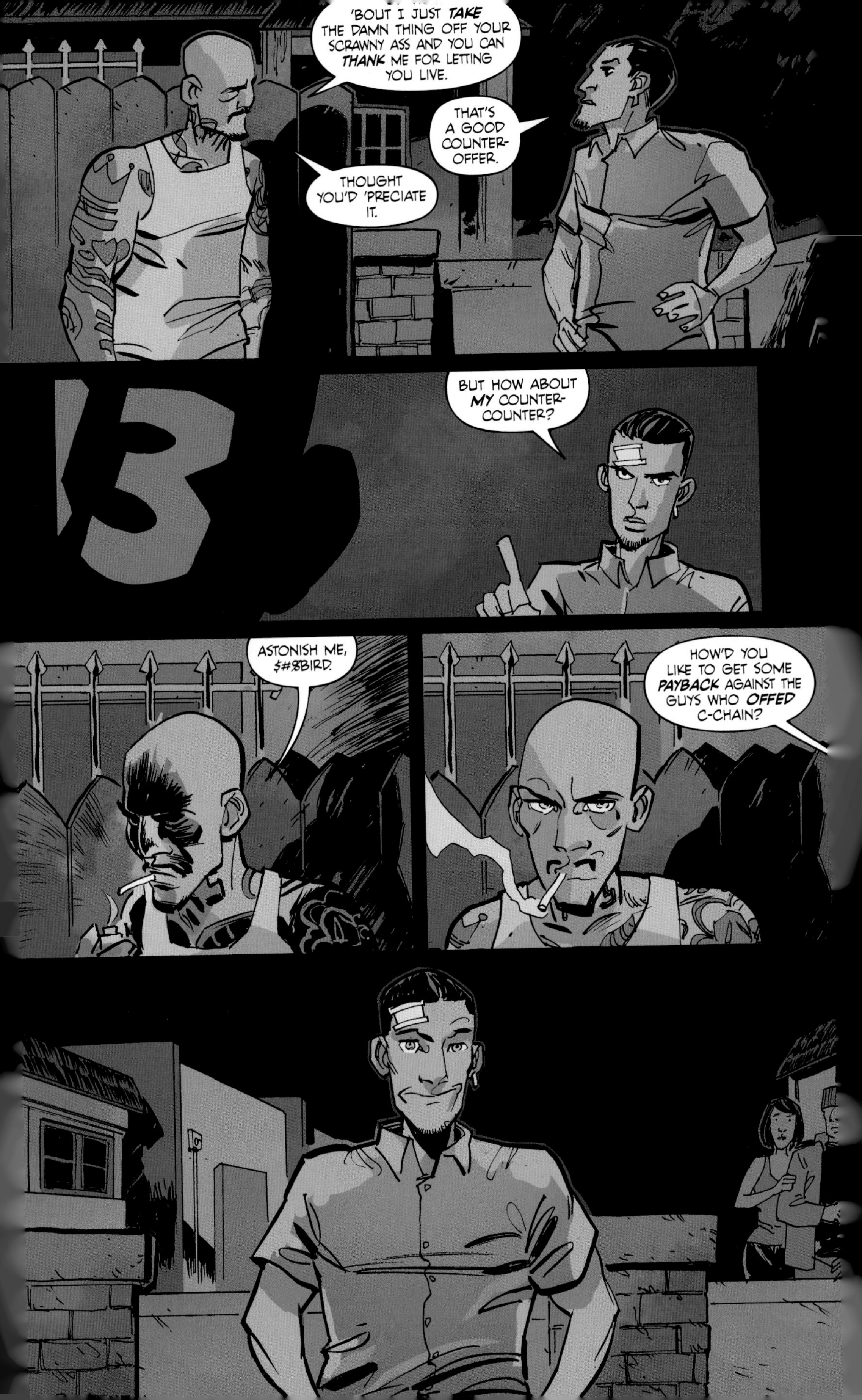
'BOUT I JUST TAKE THE DAMN THING OFF YOUR SCRAWNY ASS AND YOU CAN THANK ME FOR LETTING YOU LIVE.
THAT'S A GOOD COUNTER-OFFER.
THOUGHT YOU'D 'PRECIATE IT.
BUT HOW ABOUT MY COUNTER-COUNTER?
ASTONISH ME, $#%BIRD.
HOW'D YOU LIKE TO GET SOME PAYBACK AGAINST THE GUYS WHO OFFED C-CHAIN?

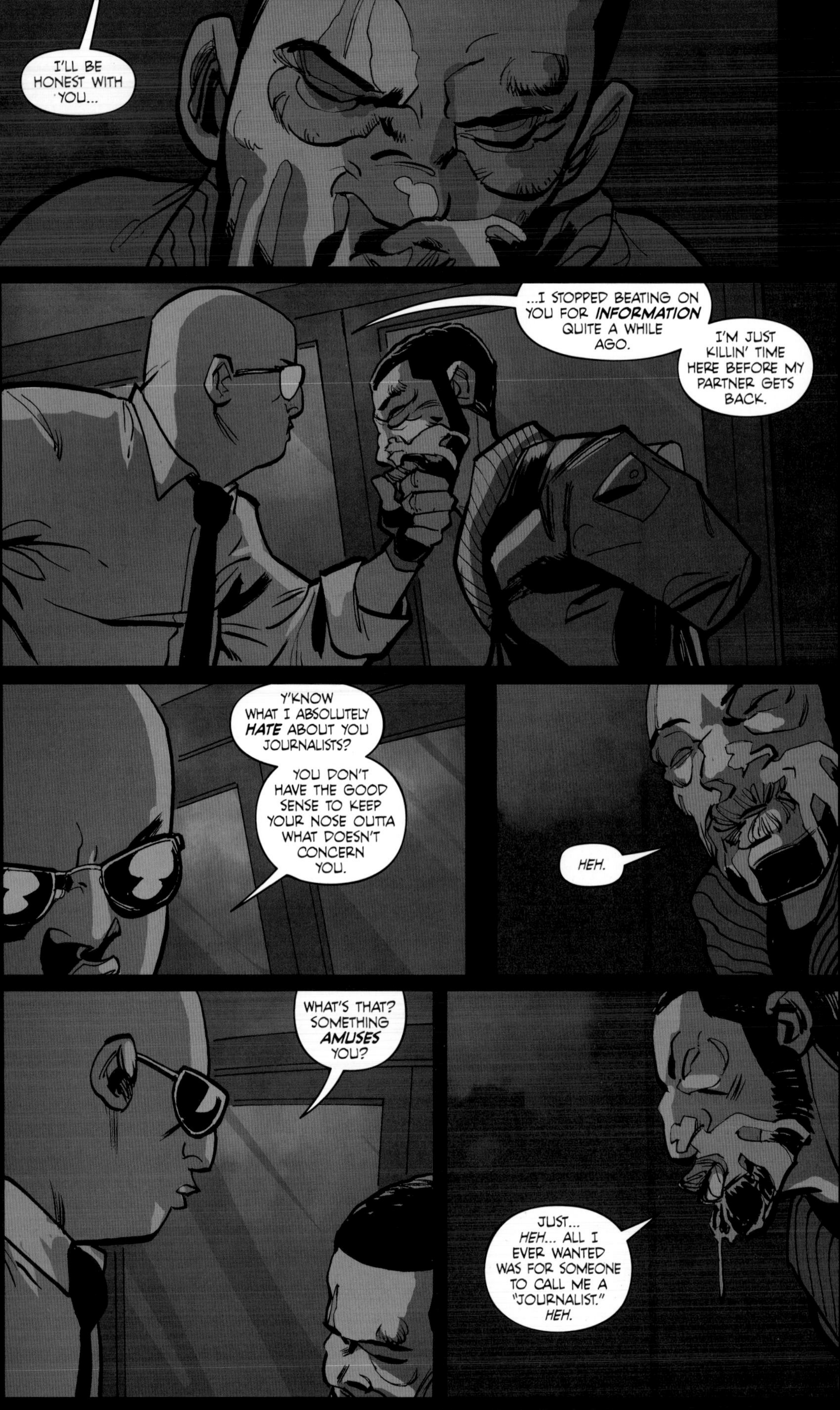
I'LL BE HONEST WITH YOU...
...I STOPPED BEATING ON YOU FOR *INFORMATION* QUITE A WHILE AGO.
I'M JUST KILLIN' TIME HERE BEFORE MY PARTNER GETS BACK.
Y'KNOW WHAT I ABSOLUTELY *HATE* ABOUT YOU JOURNALISTS?
YOU DON'T HAVE THE GOOD SENSE TO KEEP YOUR NOSE OUTTA WHAT DOESN'T CONCERN YOU.
HEH.
WHAT'S THAT? SOMETHING *AMUSES* YOU?
JUST... *HEH*... ALL I EVER WANTED WAS FOR SOMEONE TO CALL ME A "JOURNALIST." *HEH.*

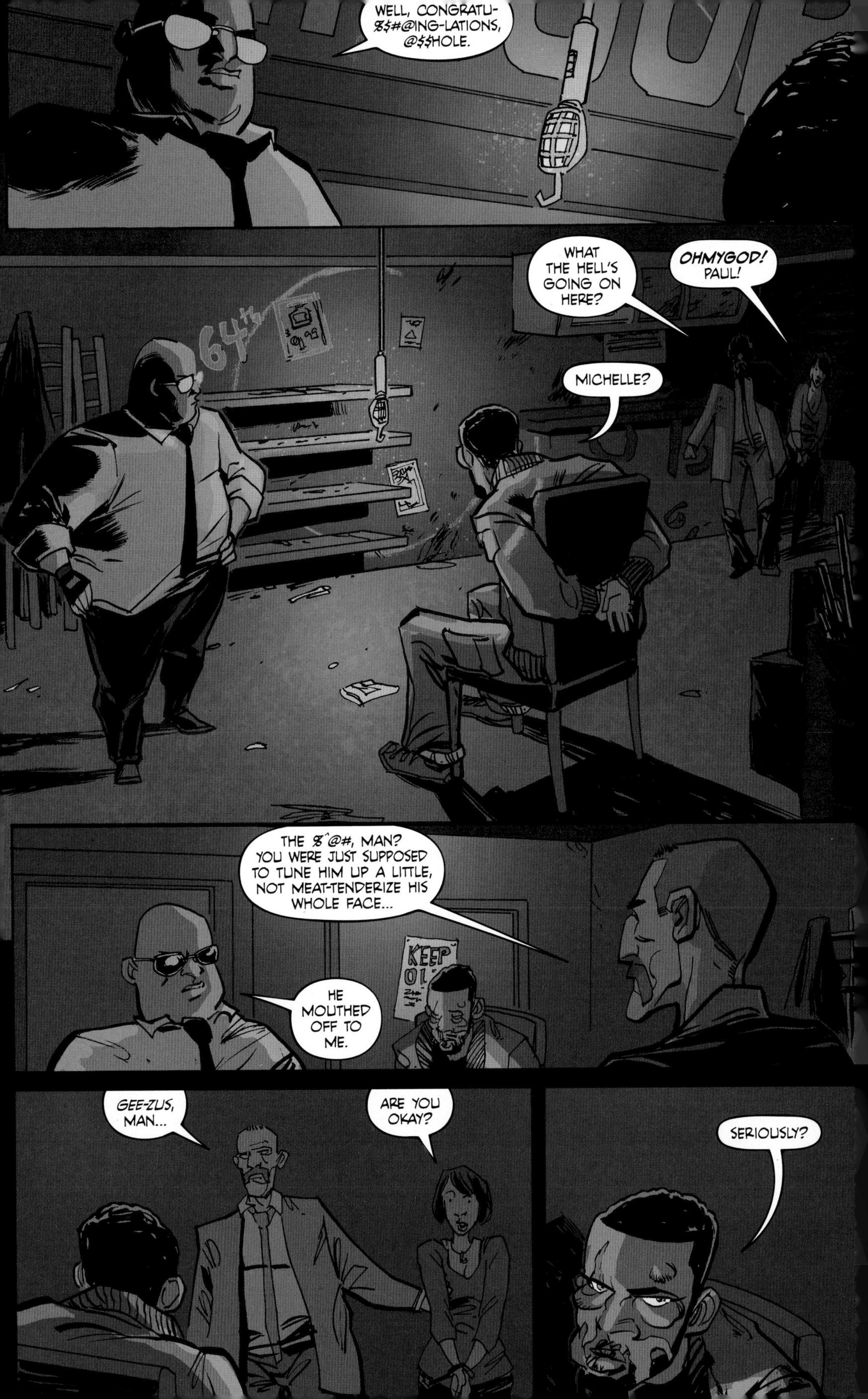
WELL, CONGRATU-%$#@ING-LATIONS, @$$HOLE.
WHAT THE HELL'S GOING ON HERE?
OHMYGOD! PAUL!
MICHELLE?
THE %^@#, MAN? YOU WERE JUST SUPPOSED TO TUNE HIM UP A LITTLE, NOT MEAT-TENDERIZE HIS WHOLE FACE...
HE MOUTHED OFF TO ME.
GEE-ZUS, MAN...
ARE YOU OKAY?
SERIOUSLY?

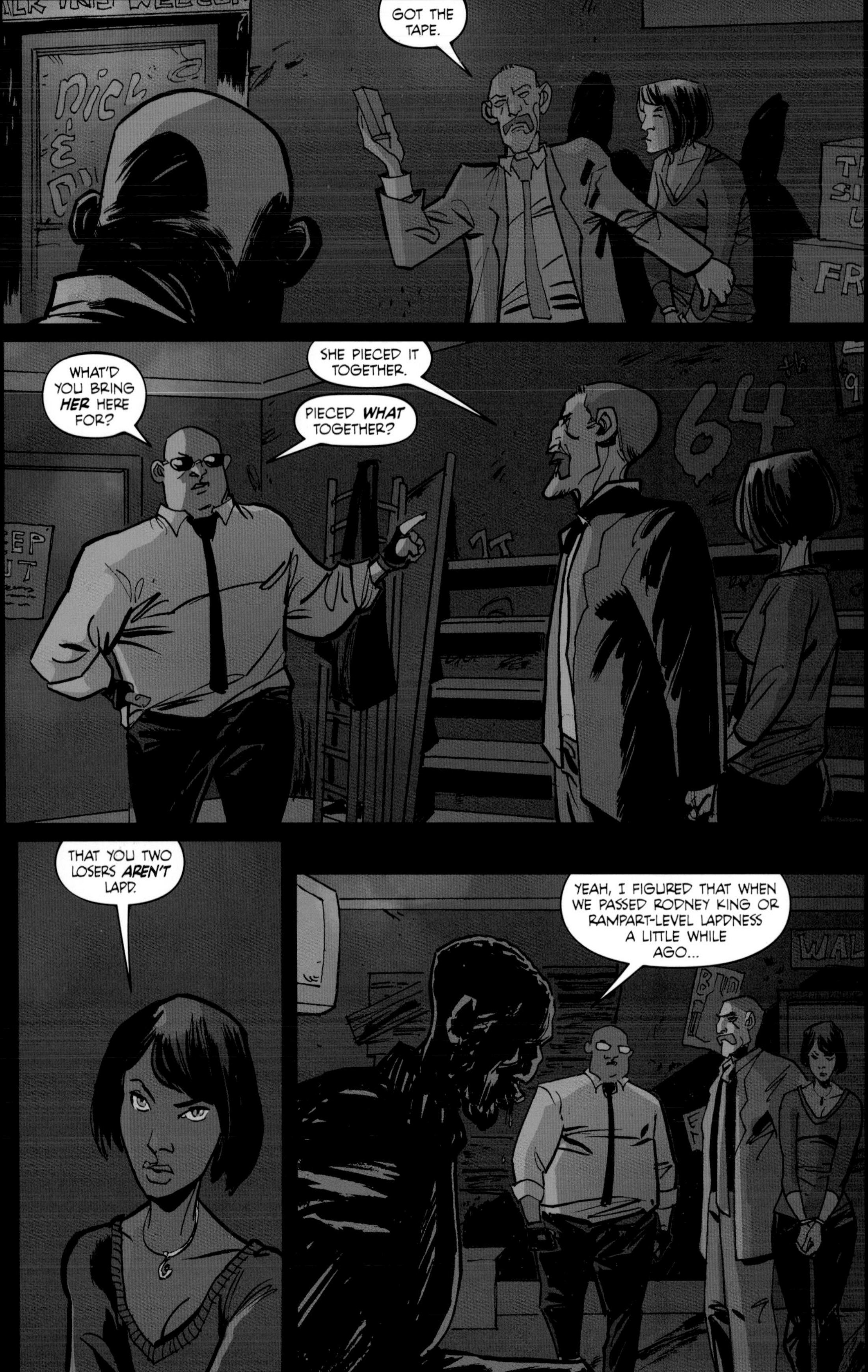
GOT THE TAPE.
WHAT'D YOU BRING HER HERE FOR?
SHE PIECED IT TOGETHER.
PIECED WHAT TOGETHER?
THAT YOU TWO LOSERS AREN'T LAPD.
YEAH, I FIGURED THAT WHEN WE PASSED RODNEY KING OR RAMPART-LEVEL LAPDNESS A LITTLE WHILE AGO...

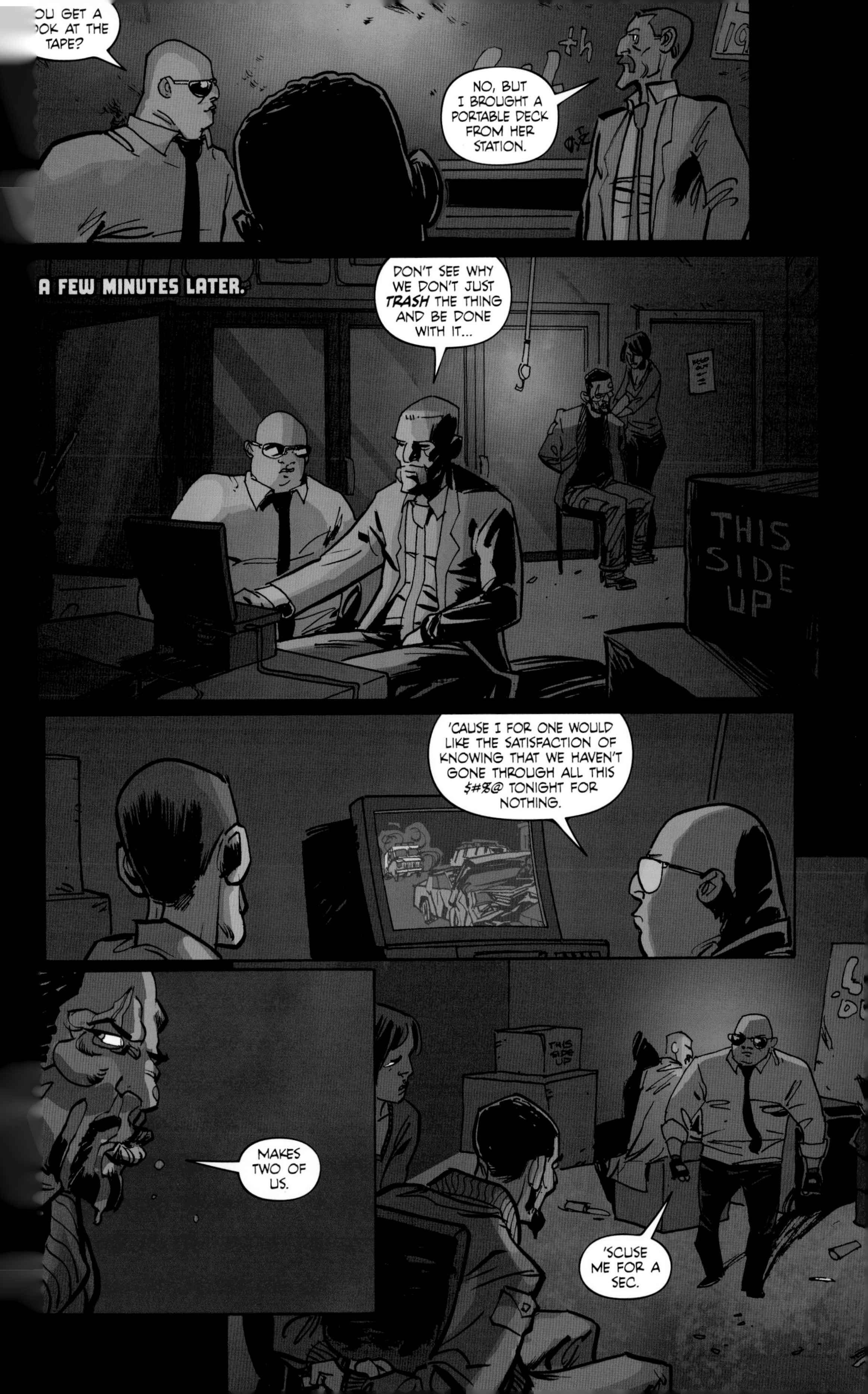
OU GET A
OOK AT THE
TAPE?
NO, BUT I BROUGHT A PORTABLE DECK FROM HER STATION.
A FEW MINUTES LATER.
DON'T SEE WHY WE DON'T JUST TRASH THE THING AND BE DONE WITH IT...
THIS SIDE UP
'CAUSE I FOR ONE WOULD LIKE THE SATISFACTION OF KNOWING THAT WE HAVEN'T GONE THROUGH ALL THIS $#%@ TONIGHT FOR NOTHING.
MAKES TWO OF US.
'SCUSE ME FOR A SEC.

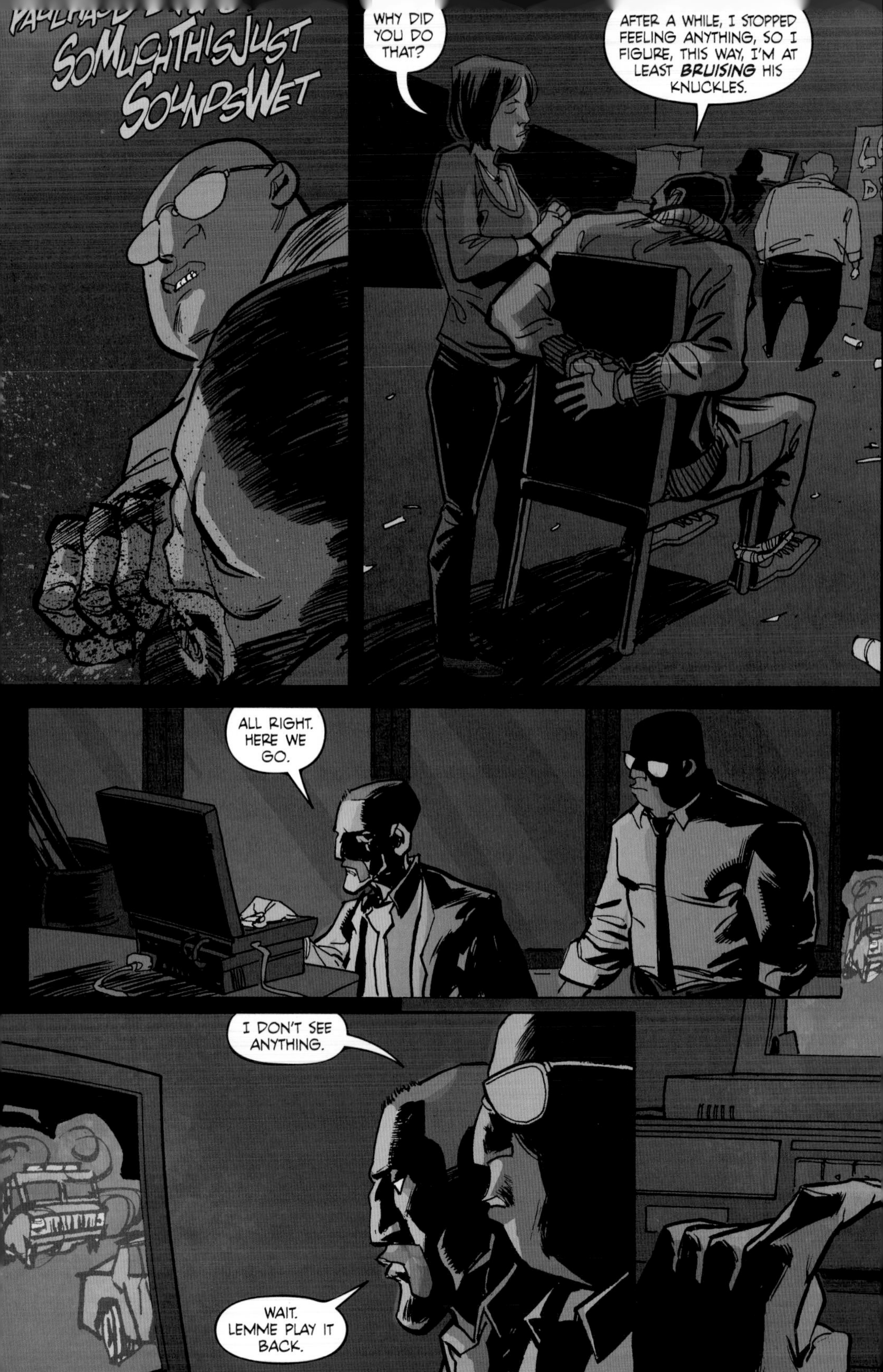
SoMuchThisJust
SoundsWet
WHY DID YOU DO THAT?
AFTER A WHILE, I STOPPED FEELING ANYTHING, SO I FIGURE, THIS WAY, I'M AT LEAST **BRUISING** HIS KNUCKLES.
ALL RIGHT. HERE WE GO.
I DON'T SEE ANYTHING.
WAIT. LEMME PLAY IT BACK.

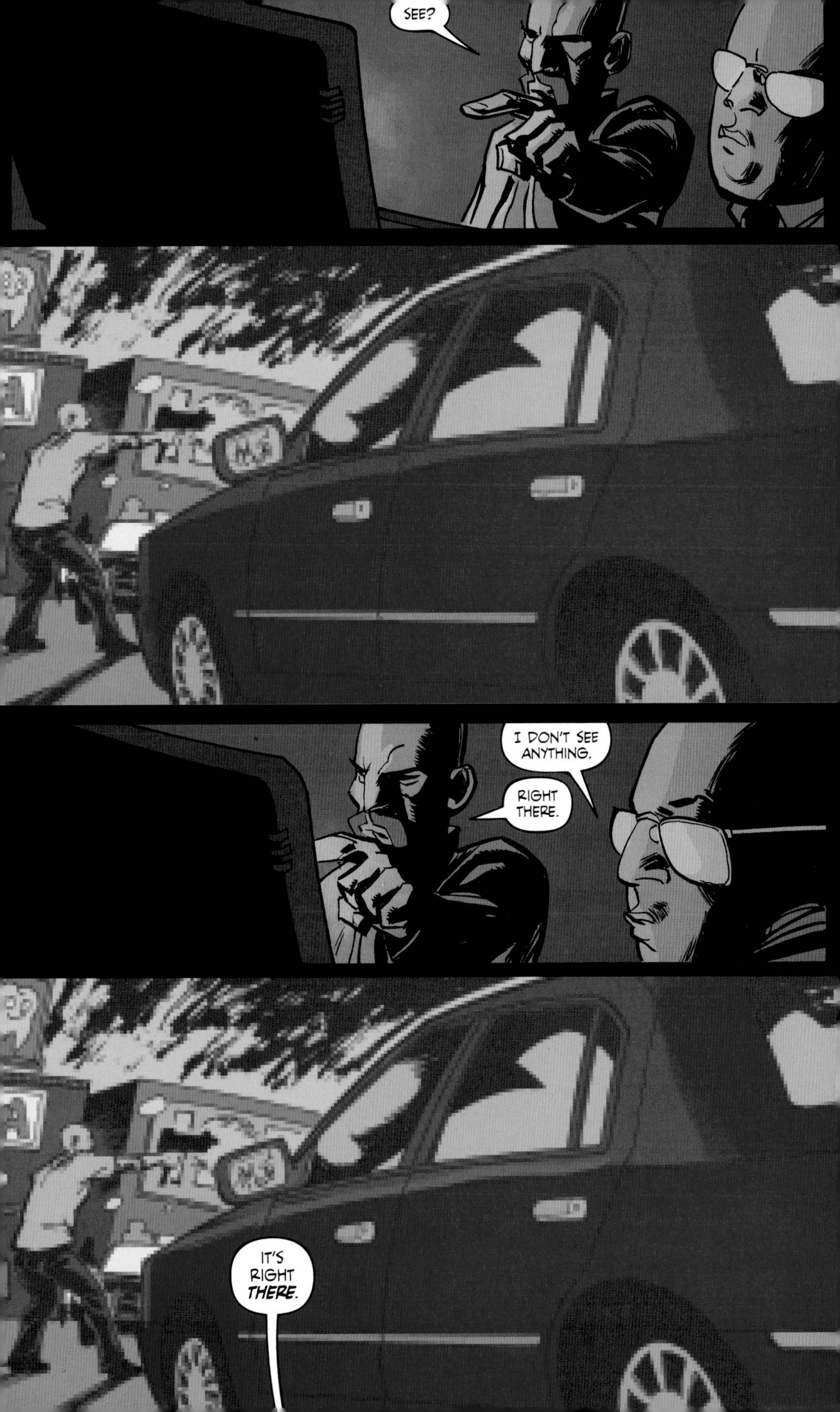
SEE?
I DON'T SEE ANYTHING.
RIGHT THERE.
IT'S RIGHT THERE.

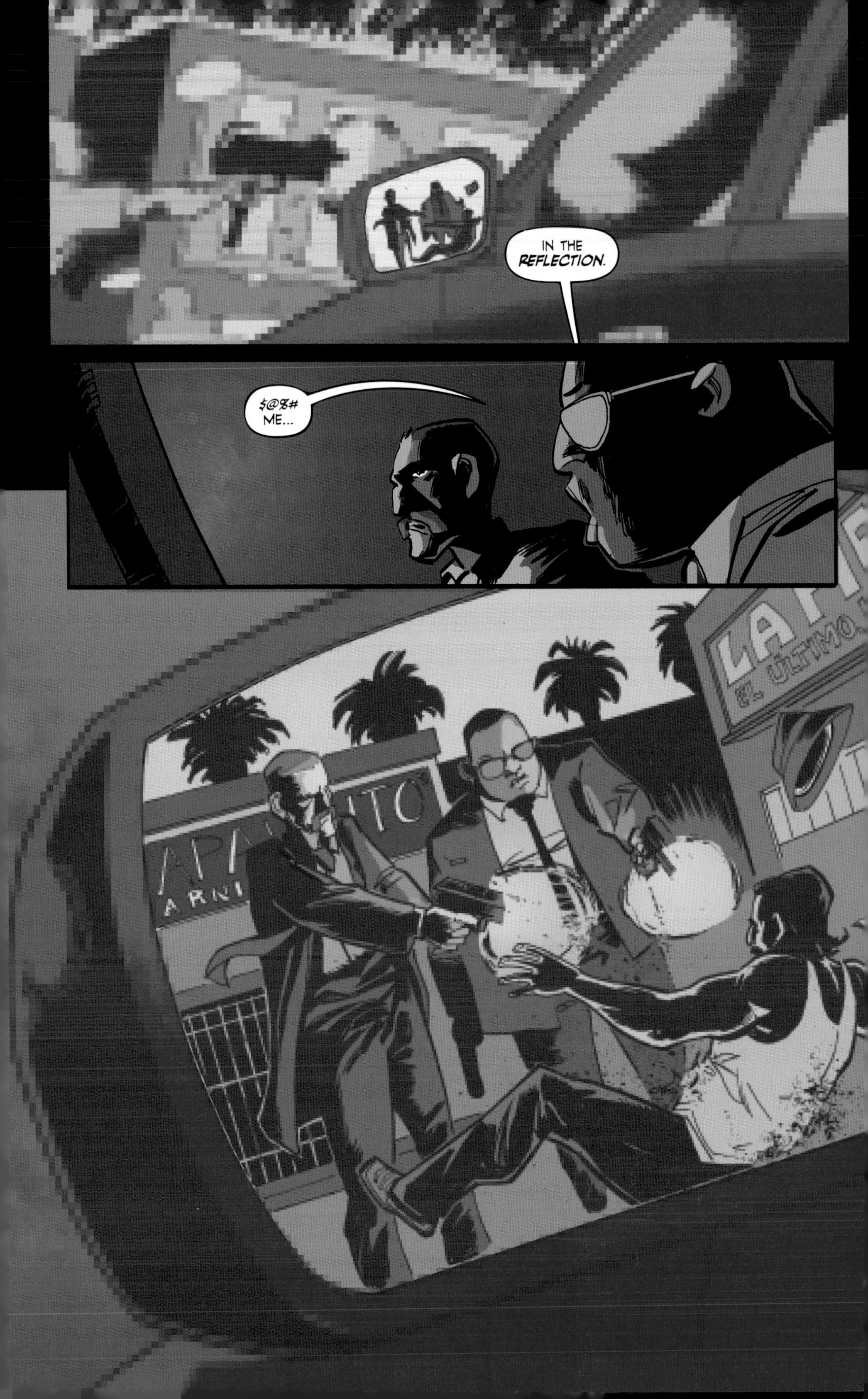
IN THE REFLECTION.
$@%# ME...
LA
EL ÚLTIMO

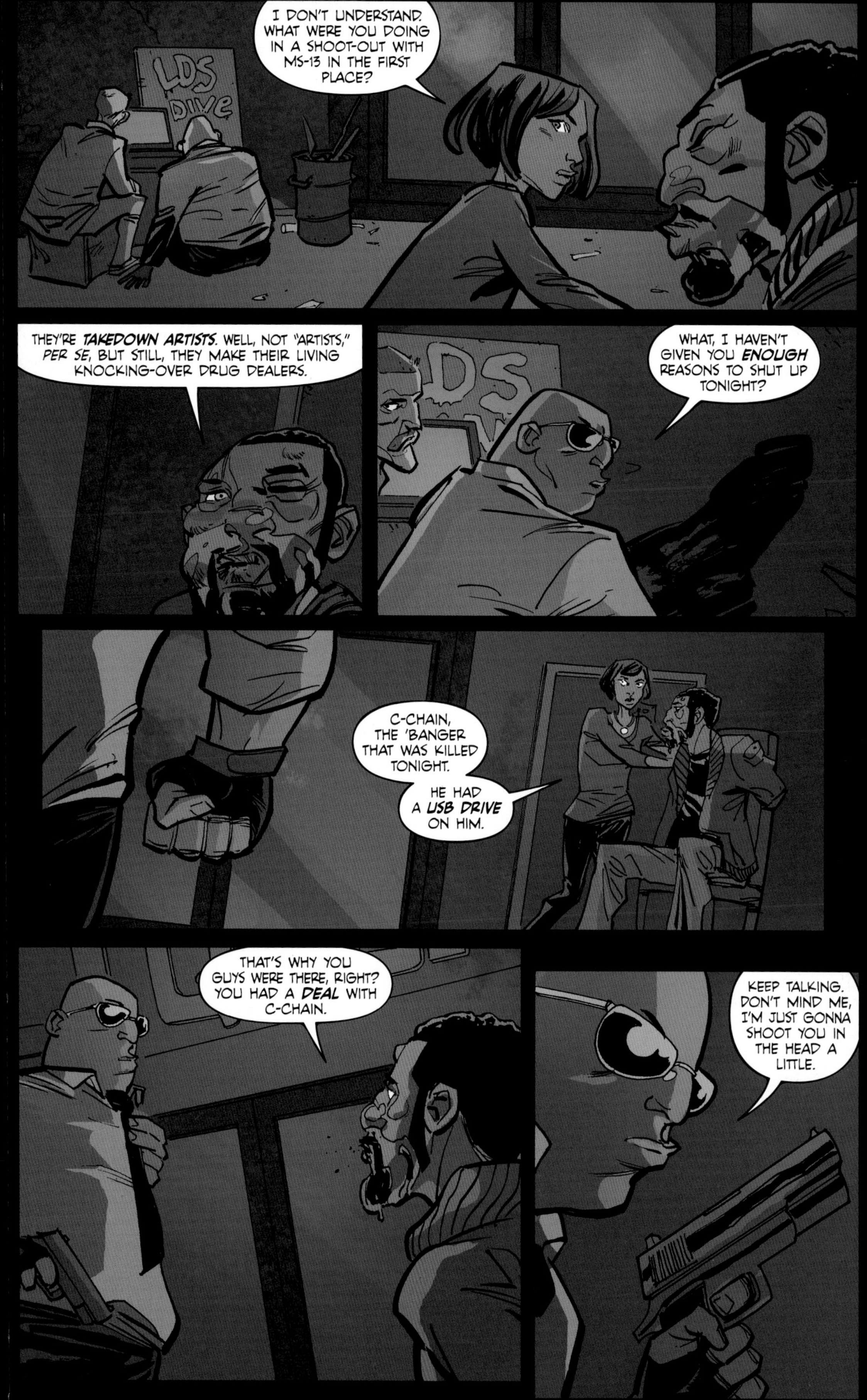
I DON'T UNDERSTAND. WHAT WERE YOU DOING IN A SHOOT-OUT WITH MS-13 IN THE FIRST PLACE?
LDS DIVE
THEY'RE *TAKEDOWN ARTISTS*. WELL, NOT "ARTISTS," *PER SE*, BUT STILL, THEY MAKE THEIR LIVING KNOCKING-OVER DRUG DEALERS.
WHAT, I HAVEN'T GIVEN YOU *ENOUGH* REASONS TO SHUT UP TONIGHT?
C-CHAIN, THE 'BANGER THAT WAS KILLED TONIGHT.
HE HAD A *USB DRIVE* ON HIM.
THAT'S WHY YOU GUYS WERE THERE, RIGHT? YOU HAD A *DEAL* WITH C-CHAIN.
KEEP TALKING. DON'T MIND ME, I'M JUST GONNA SHOOT YOU IN THE HEAD A LITTLE.

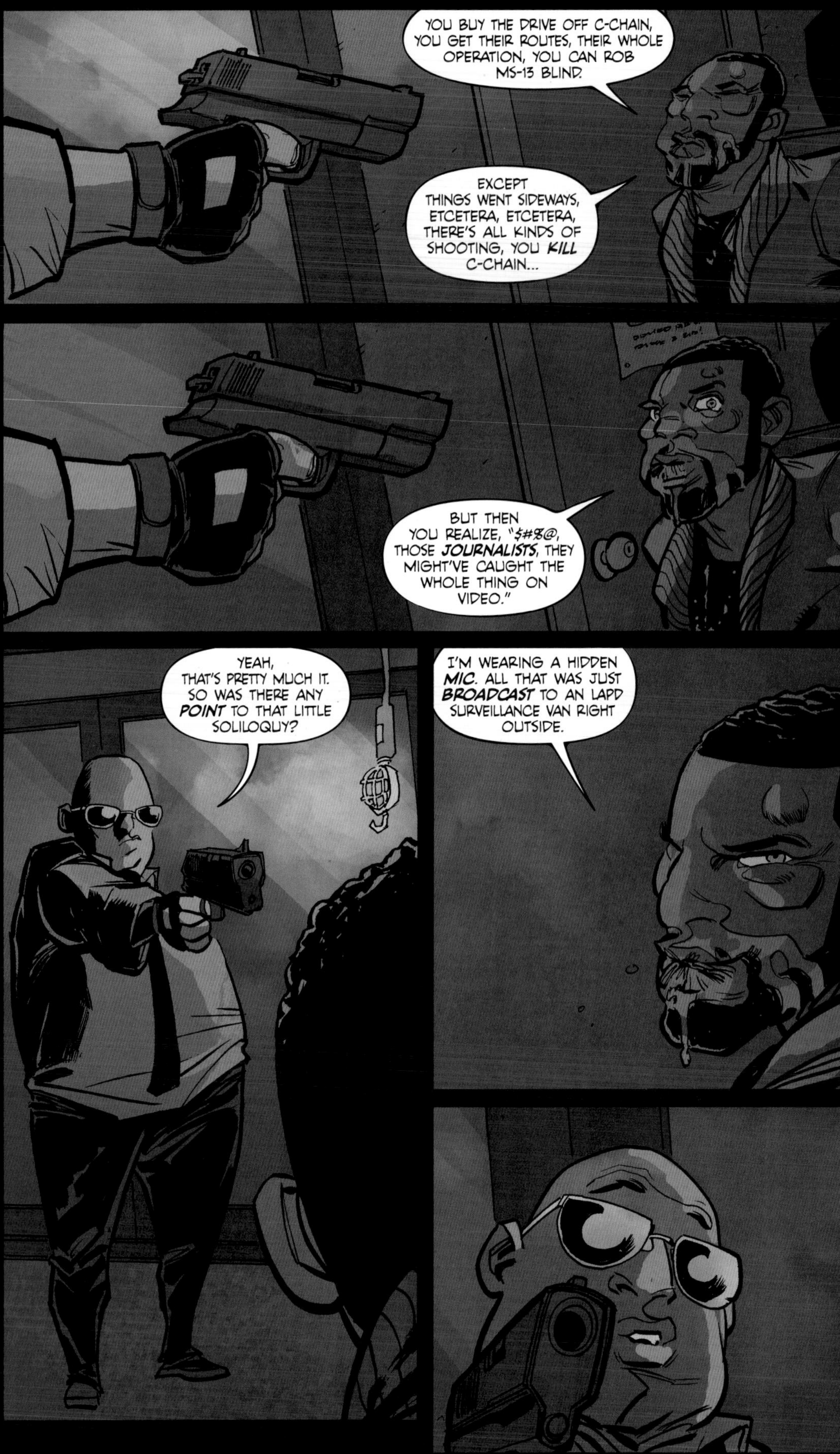

YOU BUY THE DRIVE OFF C-CHAIN, YOU GET THEIR ROUTES, THEIR WHOLE OPERATION, YOU CAN ROB MS-13 BLIND.
EXCEPT THINGS WENT SIDEWAYS, ETCETERA, ETCETERA, THERE'S ALL KINDS OF SHOOTING, YOU KILL C-CHAIN...
BUT THEN YOU REALIZE, "$#%@, THOSE JOURNALISTS, THEY MIGHT'VE CAUGHT THE WHOLE THING ON VIDEO."
YEAH, THAT'S PRETTY MUCH IT. SO WAS THERE ANY POINT TO THAT LITTLE SOLILOQUY?
I'M WEARING A HIDDEN MIC. ALL THAT WAS JUST BROADCAST TO AN LAPD SURVEILLANCE VAN RIGHT OUTSIDE.

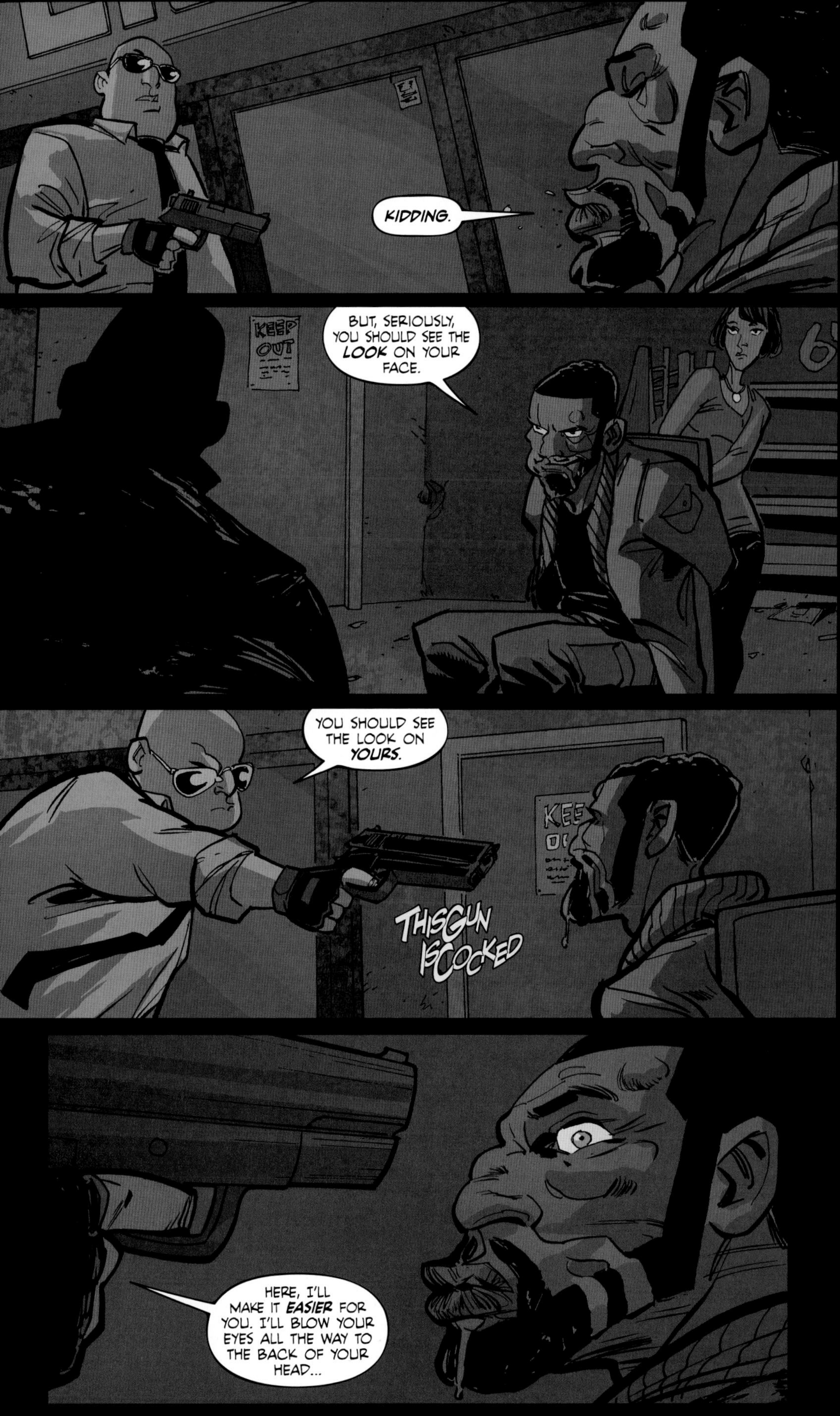
KIDDING.
KEEP OUT
BUT, SERIOUSLY, YOU SHOULD SEE THE LOOK ON YOUR FACE.
YOU SHOULD SEE THE LOOK ON YOURS.
THIS GUN IS COCKED
HERE, I'LL MAKE IT EASIER FOR YOU. I'LL BLOW YOUR EYES ALL THE WAY TO THE BACK OF YOUR HEAD...

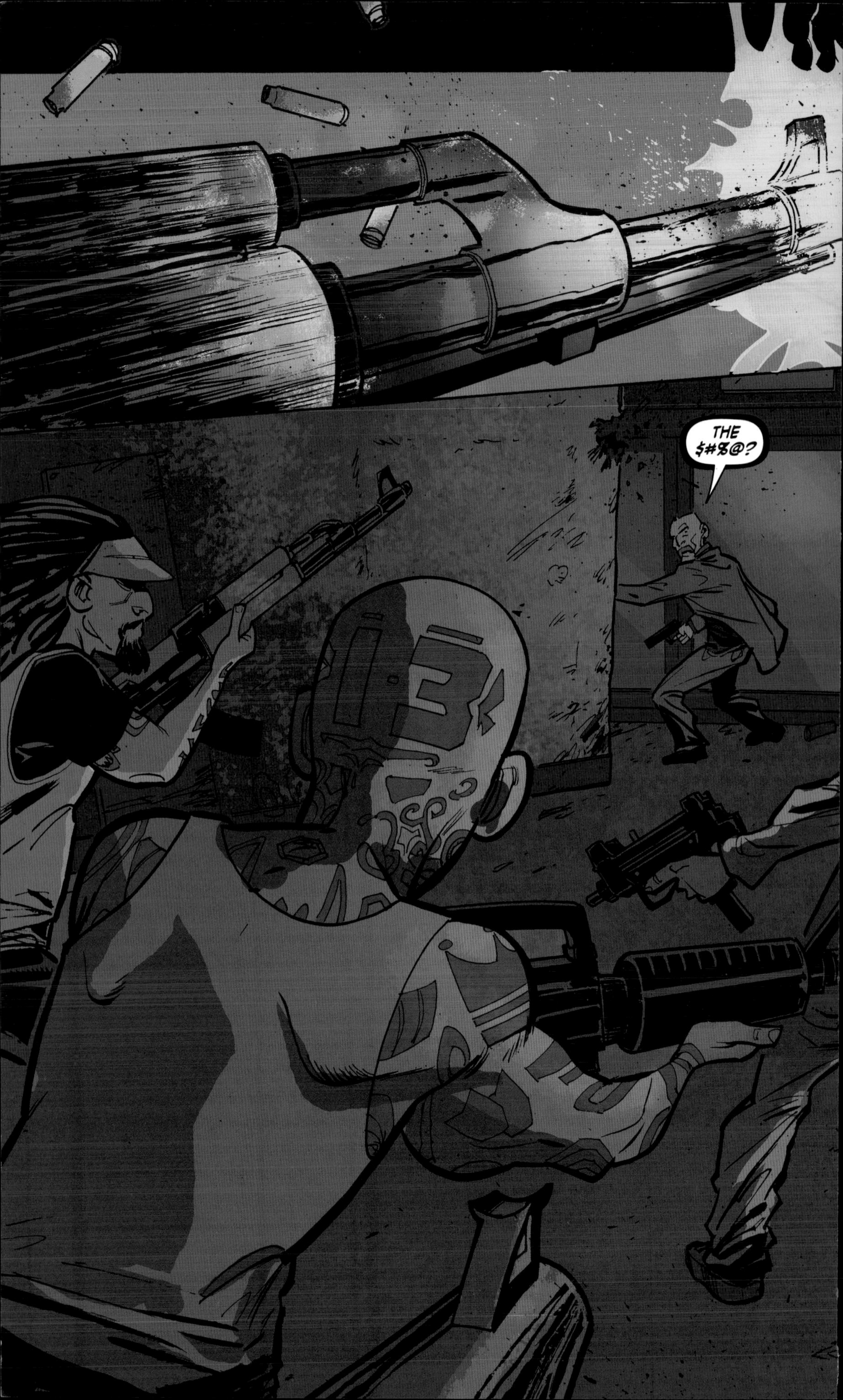
THE $#%@?

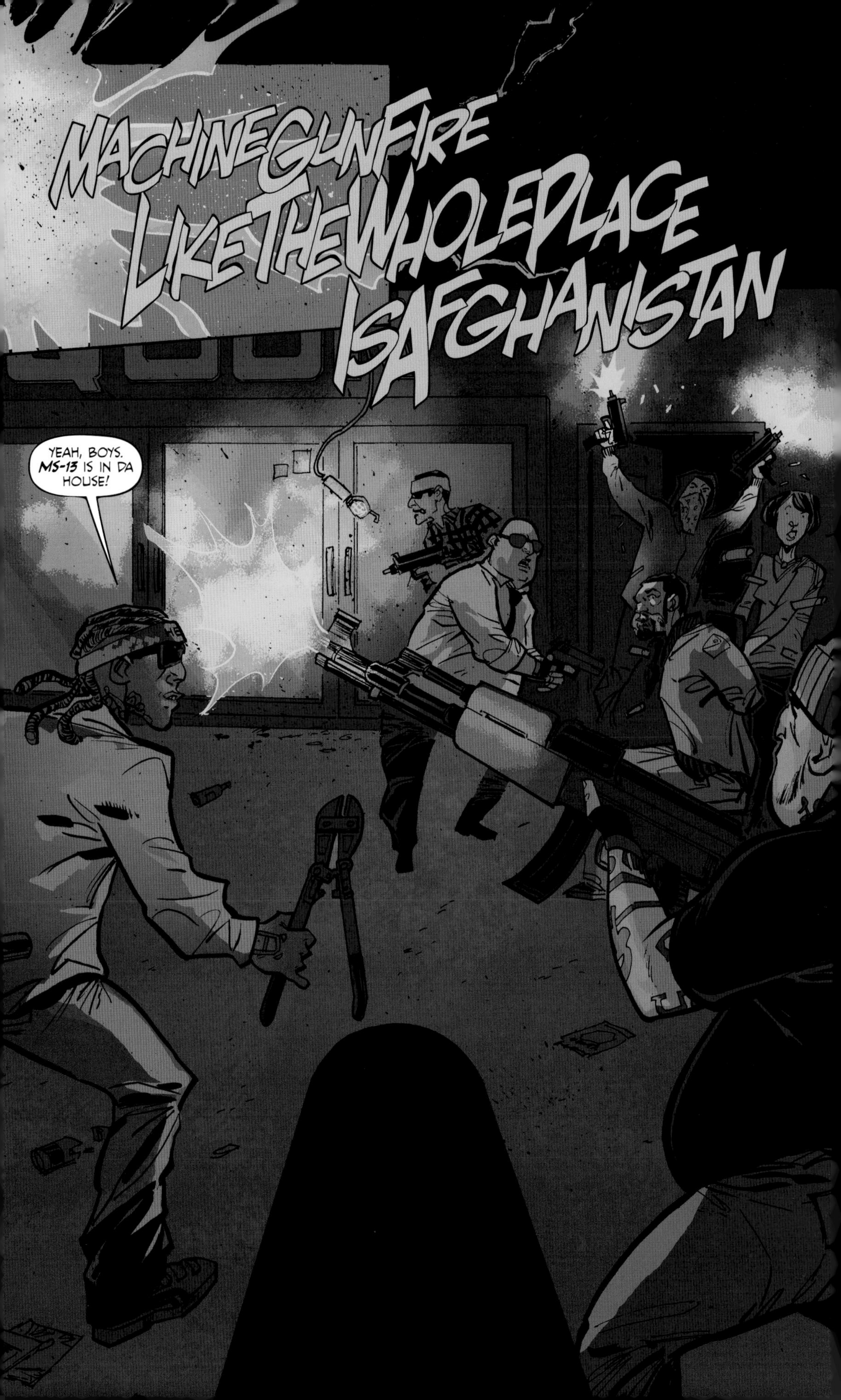
MACHINE GUN FIRE LIKE THE WHOLE PLACE IS AFGHANISTAN
YEAH, BOYS. MS-13 IS IN DA HOUSE!

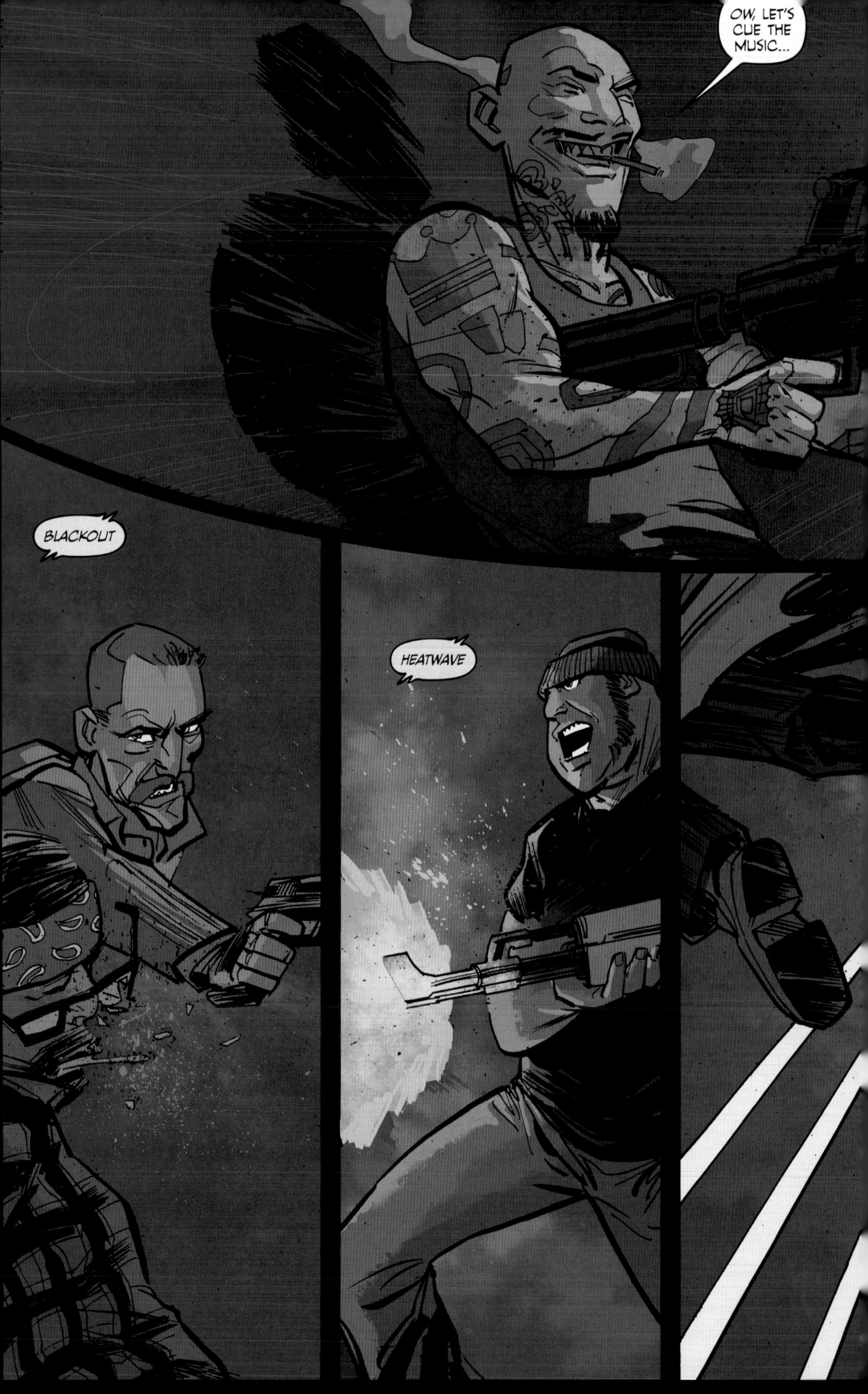
OW, LET'S CUE THE MUSIC...
BLACKOUT
HEATWAVE

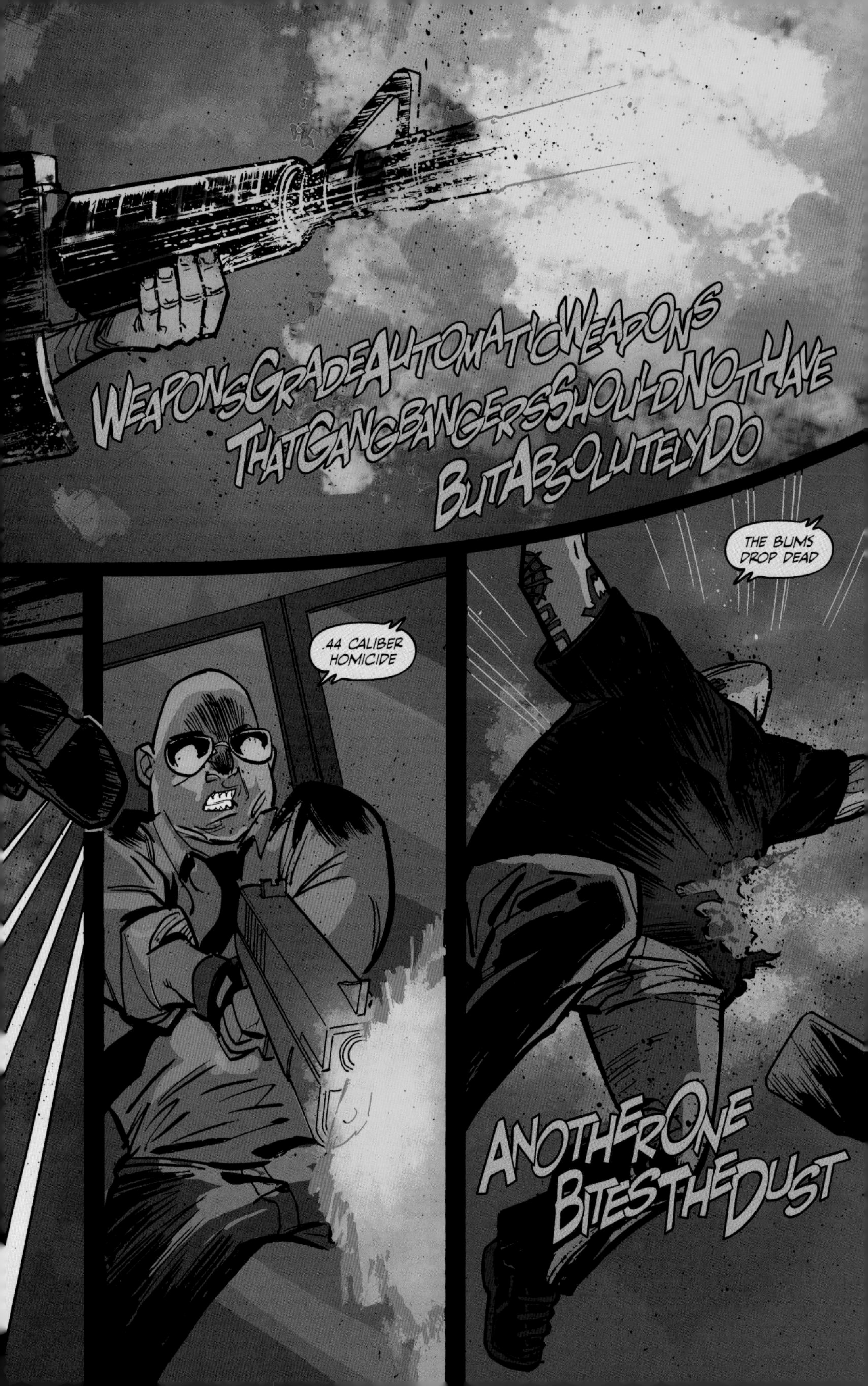
WEAPONS GRADE AUTOMATIC WEAPONS THAT GANGBANGERS SHOULD NOT HAVE BUT ABSOLUTELY DO
THE BUMS DROP DEAD
.44 CALIBER HOMICIDE
ANOTHER ONE BITES THE DUST

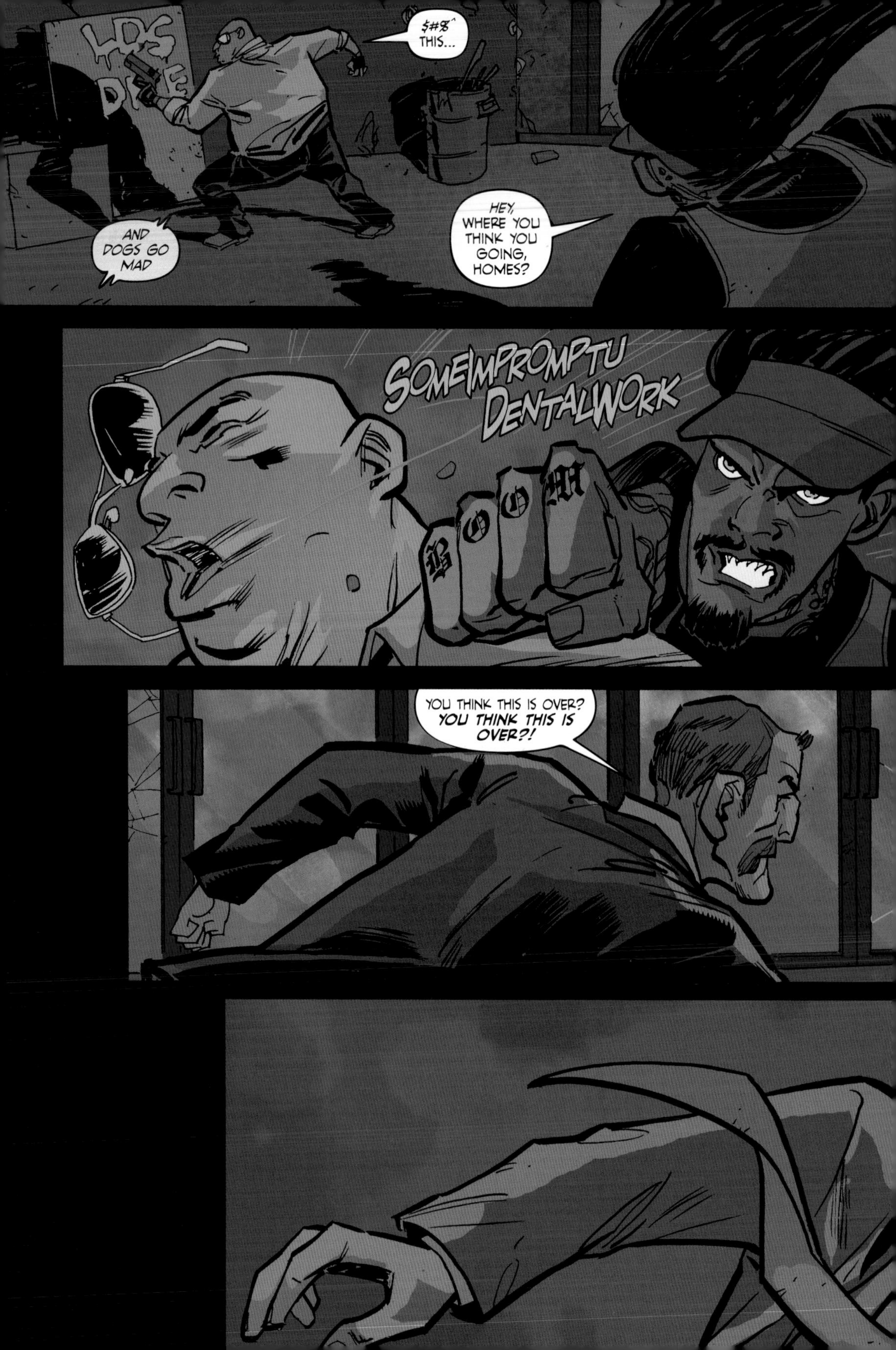

$#&^ THIS...
AND DOGS GO MAD
HEY, WHERE YOU THINK YOU GOING, HOMES?
SOMEIMPROMPTU DENTALWORK
B O O M
YOU THINK THIS IS OVER? YOU THINK THIS IS OVER?!

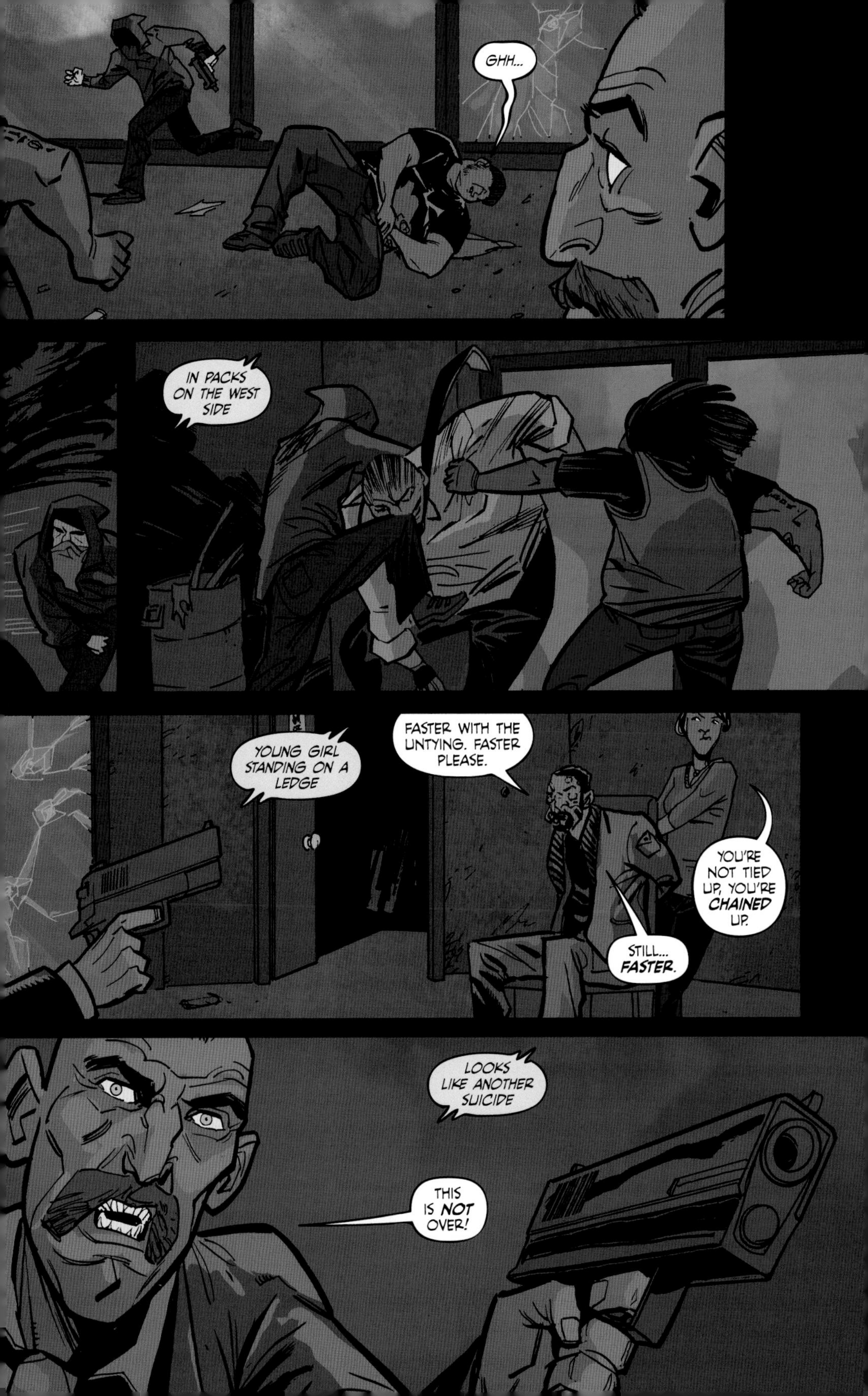
GHH...
IN PACKS ON THE WEST SIDE
YOUNG GIRL STANDING ON A LEDGE
FASTER WITH THE UNTYING. FASTER PLEASE.
YOU'RE NOT TIED UP, YOU'RE **CHAINED** UP.
STILL... **FASTER.**
LOOKS LIKE ANOTHER SUICIDE
THIS IS **NOT** OVER!

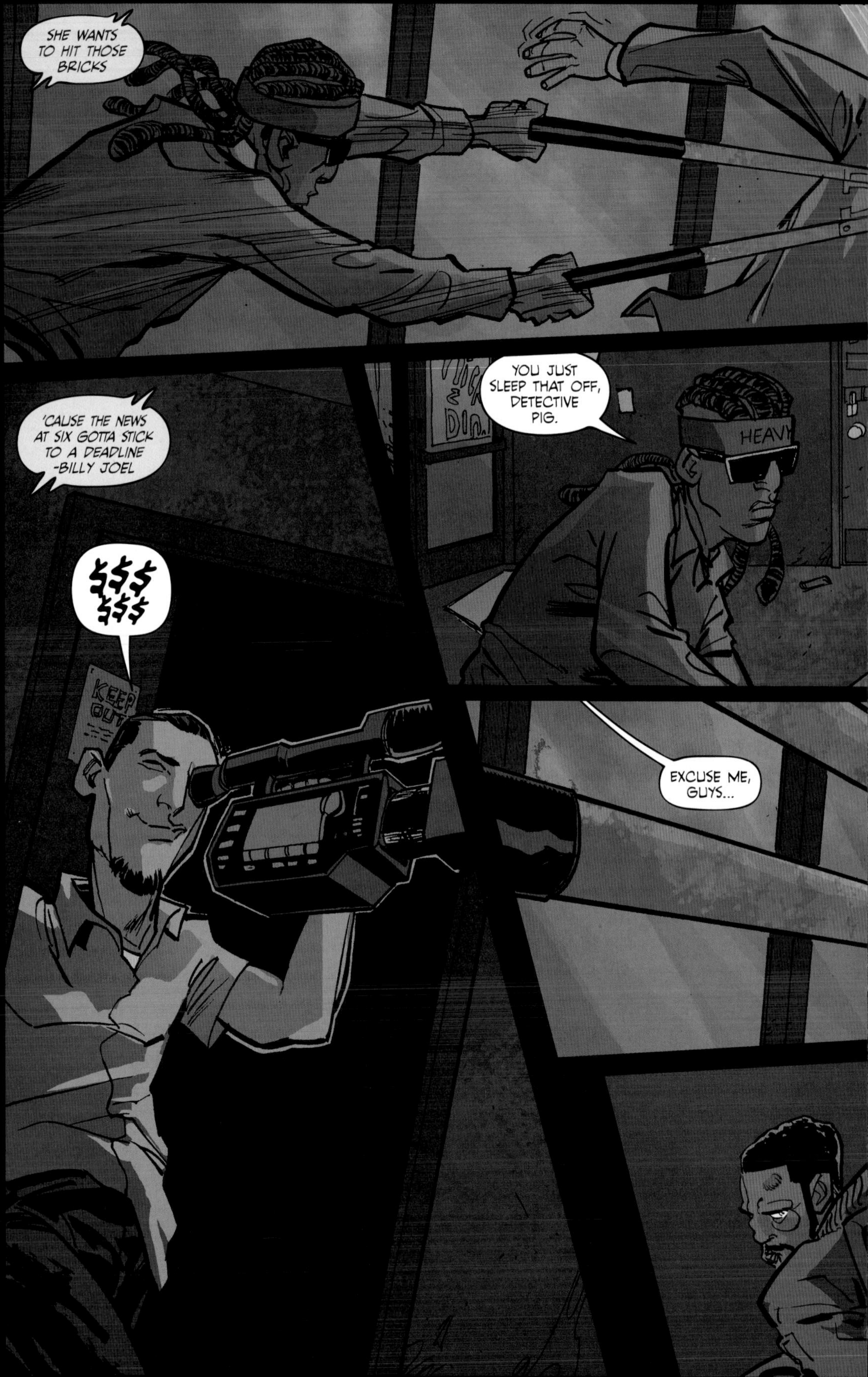
SHE WANTS TO HIT THOSE BRICKS
'CAUSE THE NEWS AT SIX GOTTA STICK TO A DEADLINE -BILLY JOEL
YOU JUST SLEEP THAT OFF, DETECTIVE PIG.
HEAVY
$$$ $$$
KEEP OUT
EXCUSE ME, GUYS...

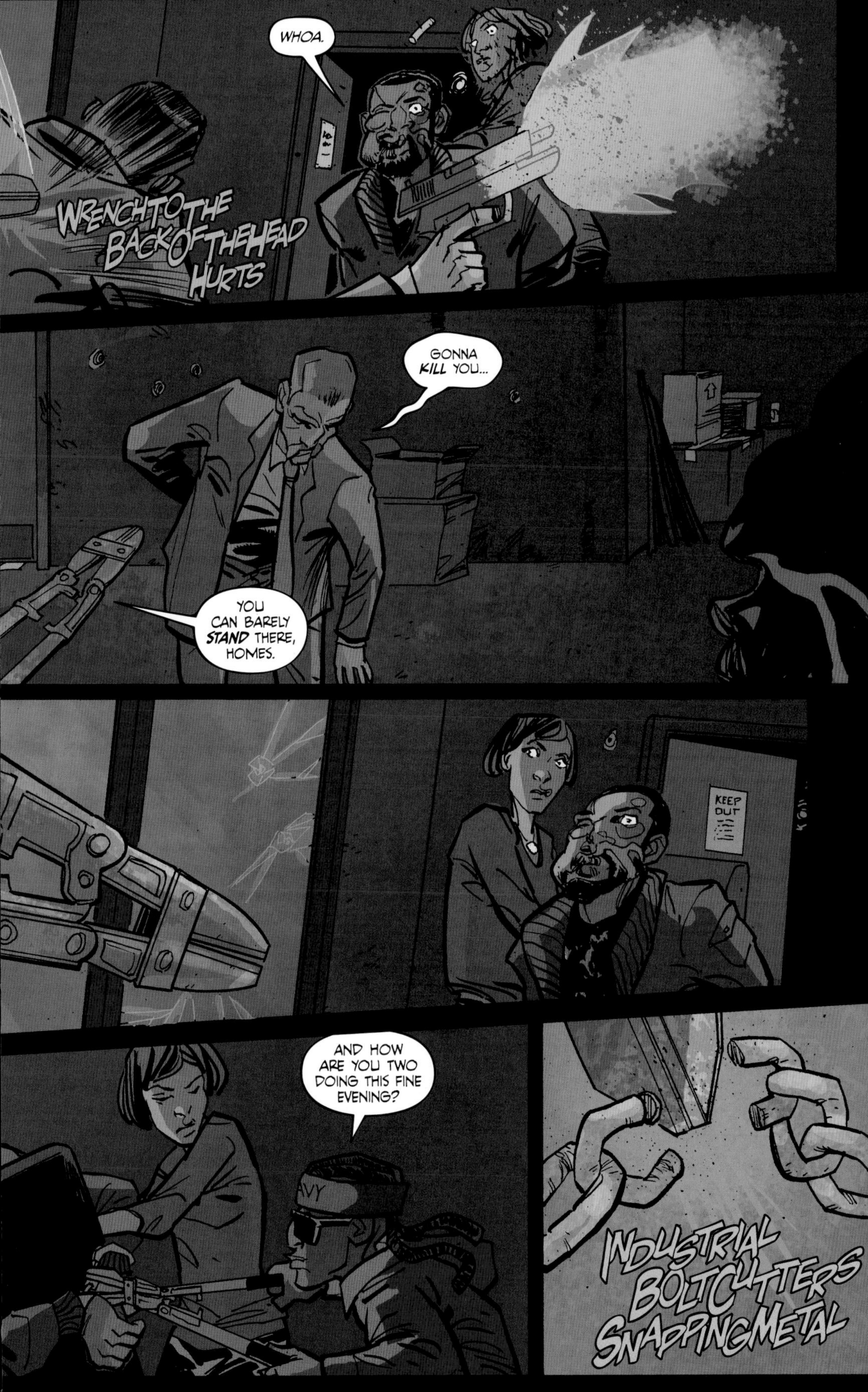

WHOA.
WRENCH TO THE BACK OF THE HEAD HURTS
GONNA KILL YOU...
YOU CAN BARELY STAND THERE, HOMES.
KEEP OUT
AND HOW ARE YOU TWO DOING THIS FINE EVENING?
INDUSTRIAL BOLTCUTTERS SNAPPING METAL

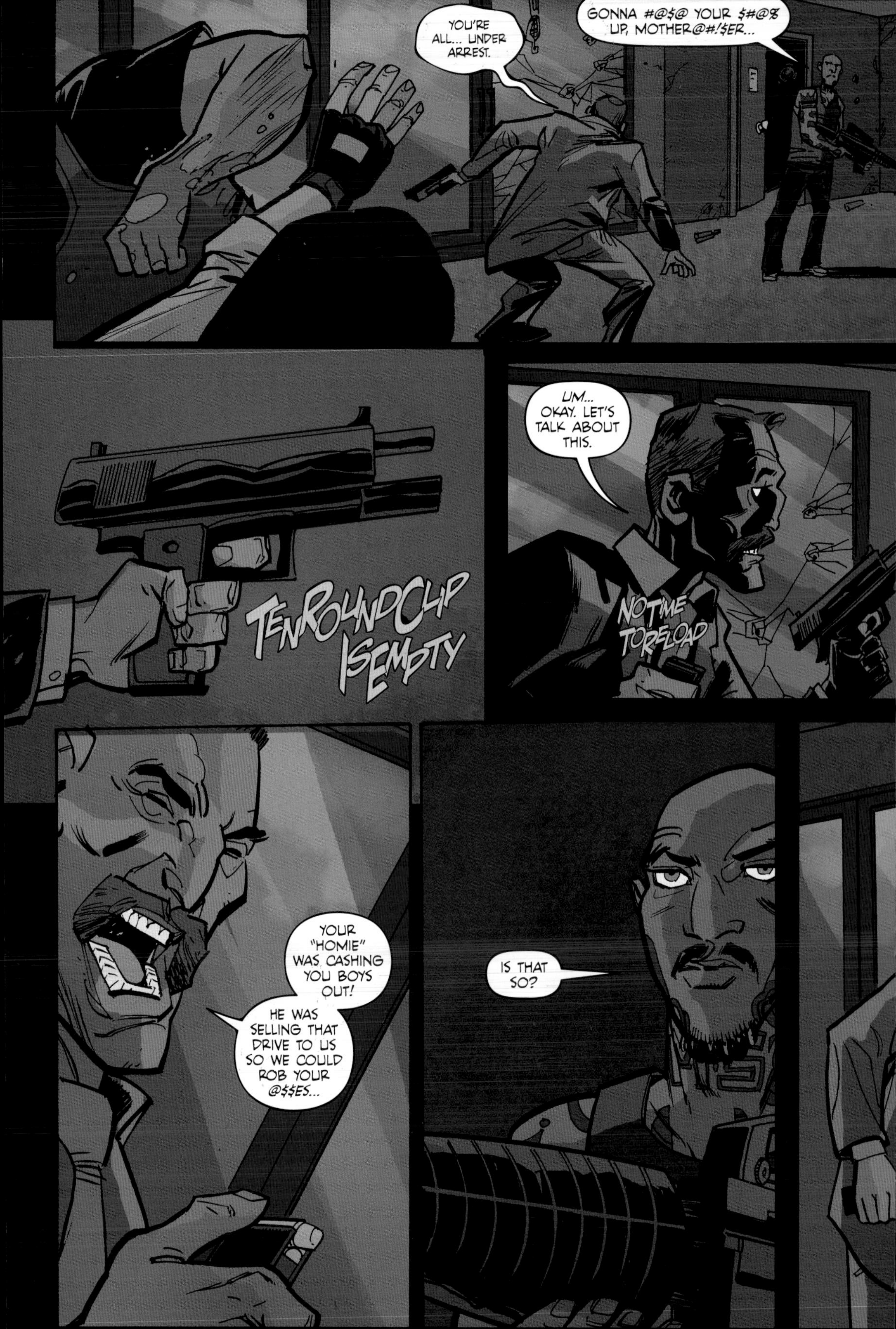

YOU'RE ALL... UNDER ARREST.
GONNA #@$@ YOUR $#@% UP, MOTHER@#!$ER...
TEN ROUND CLIP IS EMPTY
UM... OKAY. LET'S TALK ABOUT THIS.
NO TIME TO RELOAD
YOUR "HOMIE" WAS CASHING YOU BOYS OUT!
HE WAS SELLING THAT DRIVE TO US SO WE COULD ROB YOUR @$$ES...
IS THAT SO?

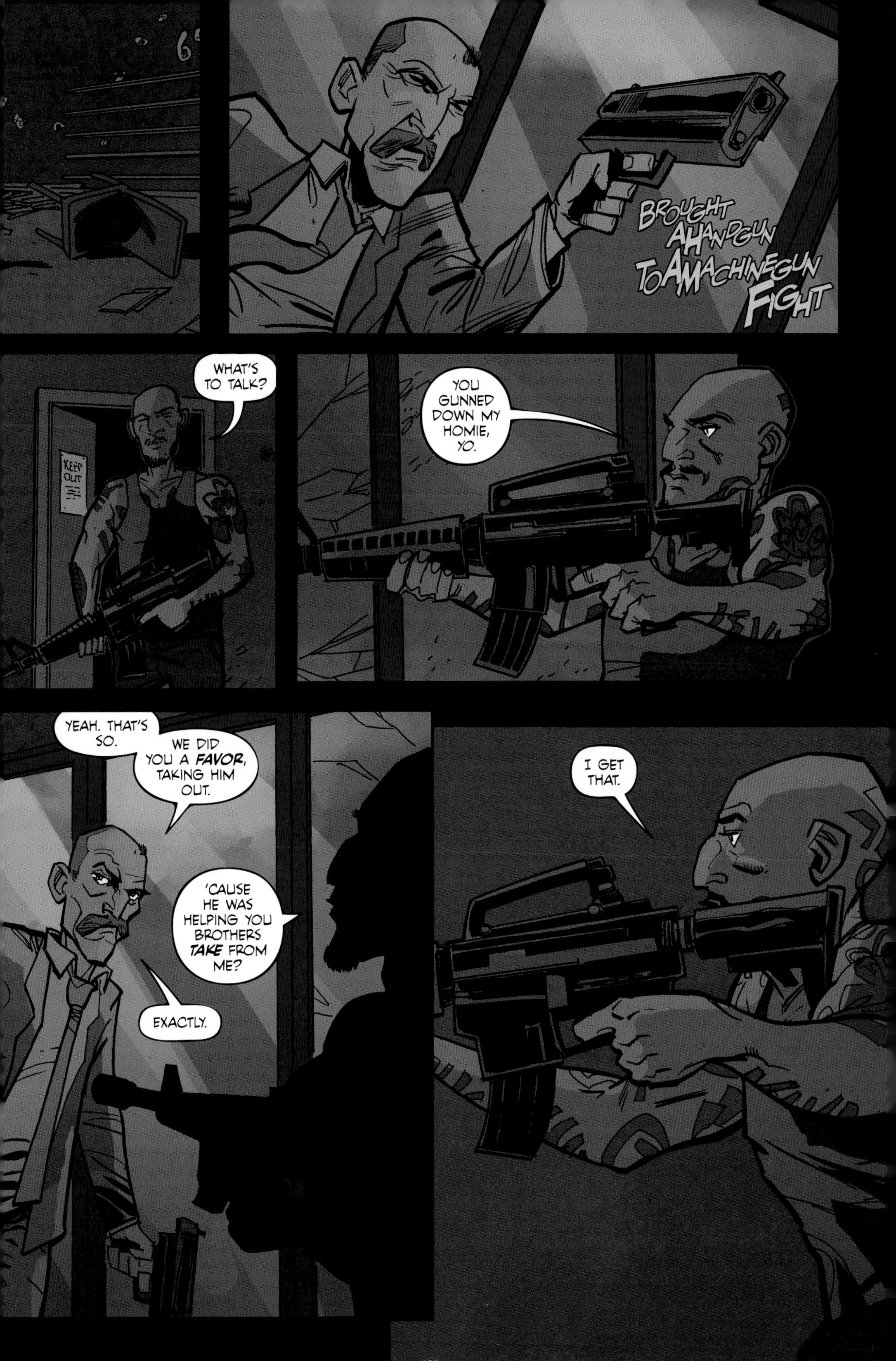
BROUGHT A HANDGUN TO A MACHINEGUN FIGHT
WHAT'S TO TALK?
YOU GUNNED DOWN MY HOMIE, YO.
YEAH. THAT'S SO.
WE DID YOU A FAVOR, TAKING HIM OUT.
'CAUSE HE WAS HELPING YOU BROTHERS TAKE FROM ME?
EXACTLY.
I GET THAT.

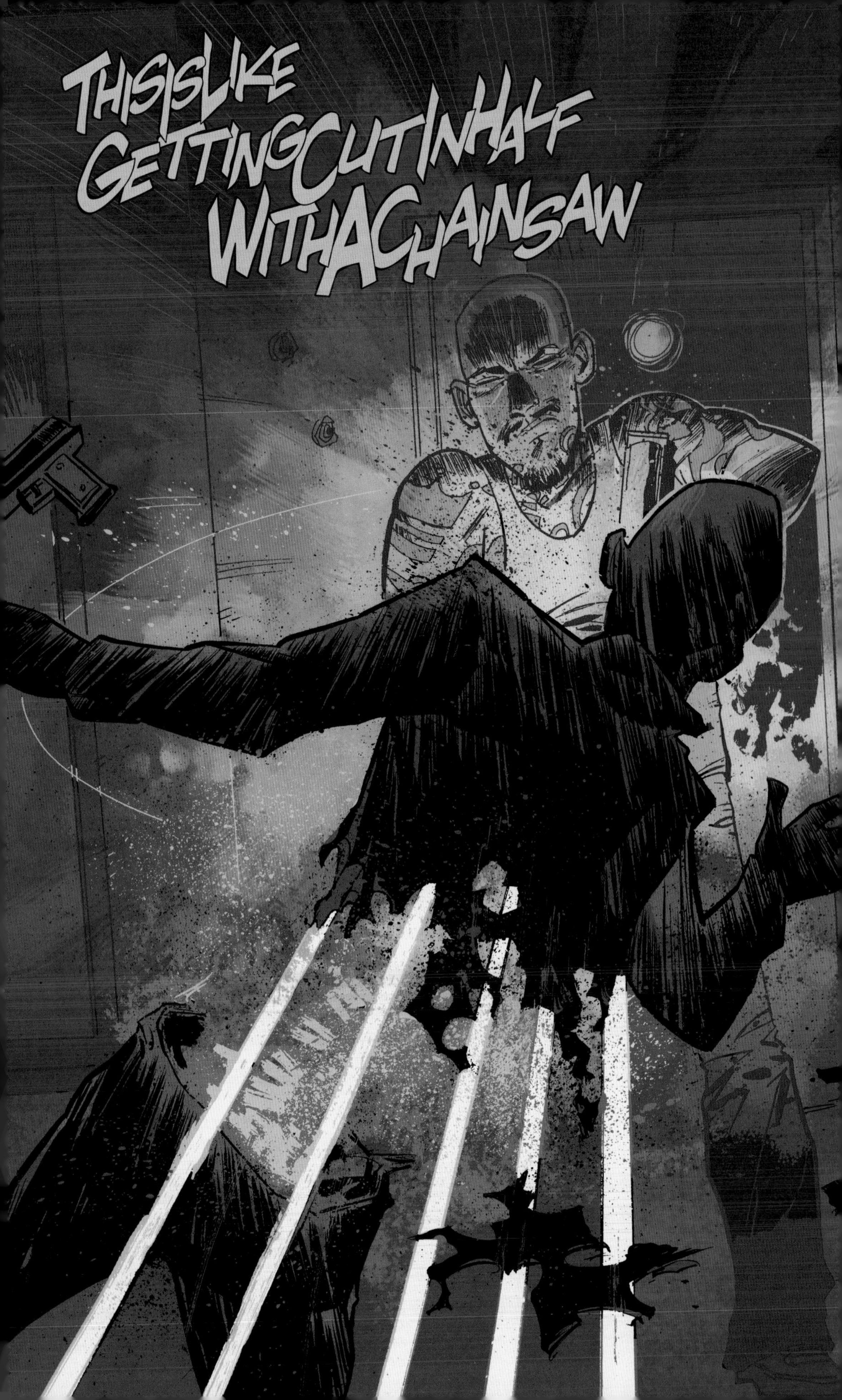
THIS IS LIKE GETTING CUT IN HALF WITH A CHAINSAW

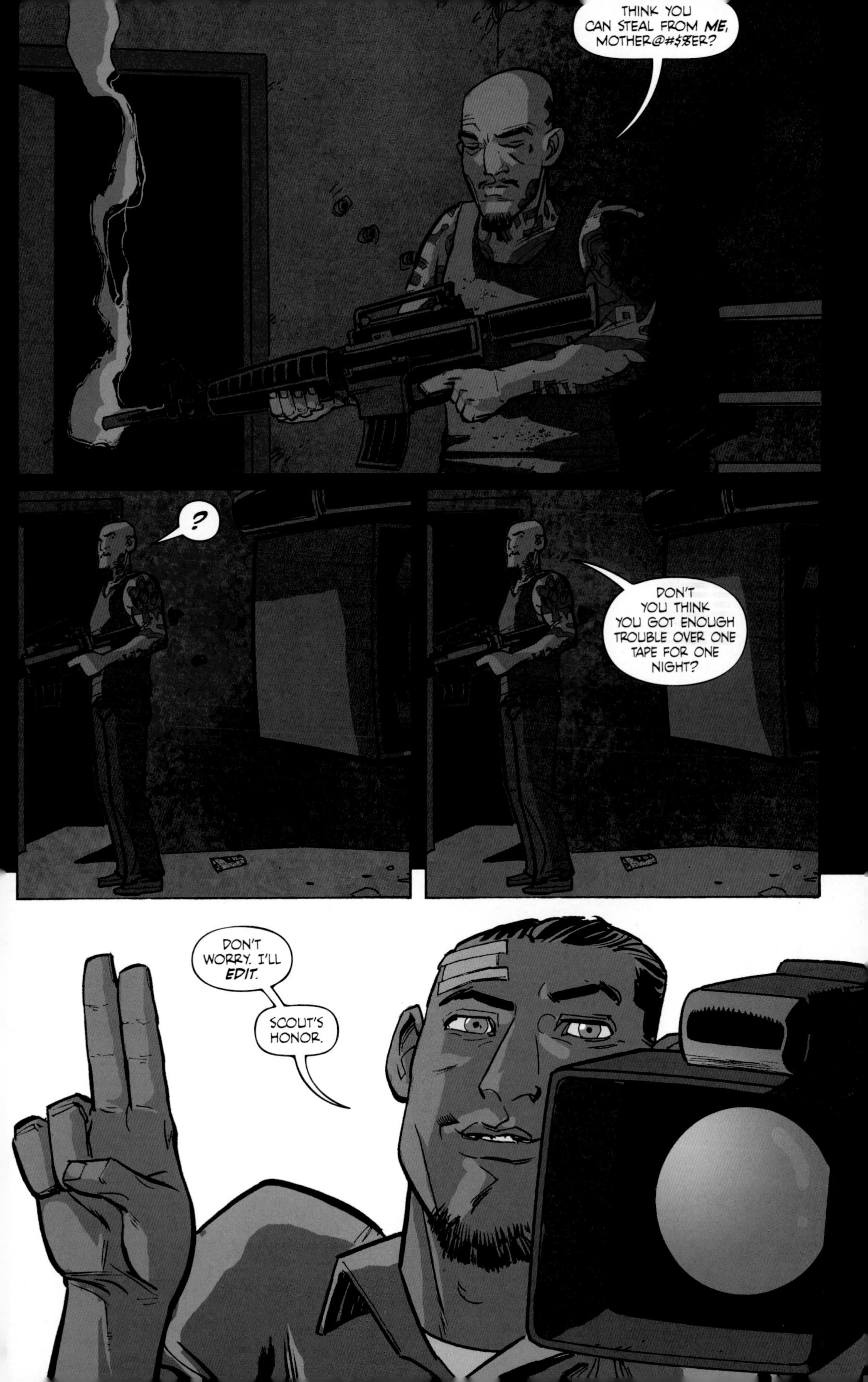
THINK YOU CAN STEAL FROM ME, MOTHER@#$%ER?
?
DON'T YOU THINK YOU GOT ENOUGH TROUBLE OVER ONE TAPE FOR ONE NIGHT?
DON'T WORRY. I'LL EDIT.
SCOUT'S HONOR.

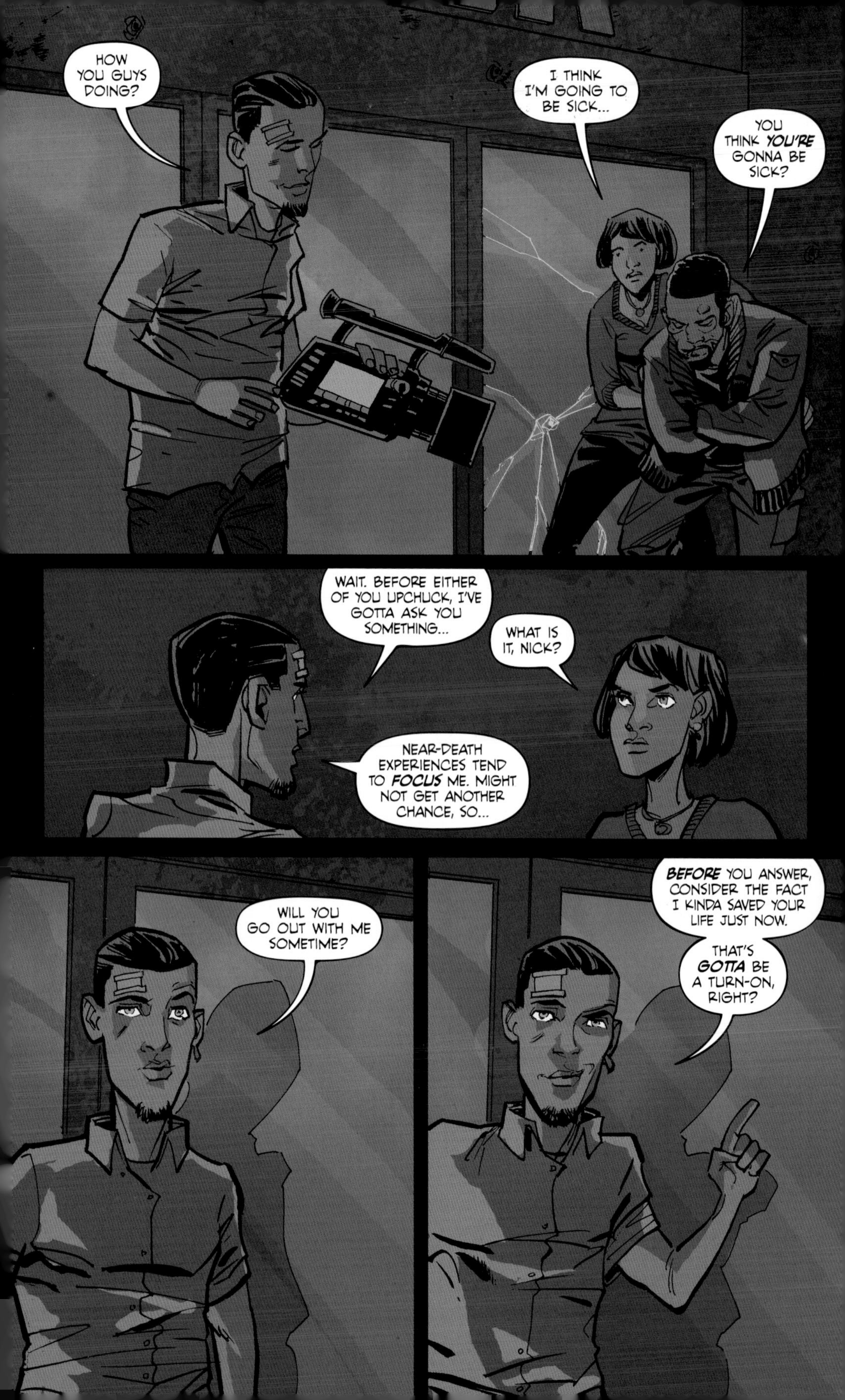
HOW YOU GUYS DOING?
I THINK I'M GOING TO BE SICK...
YOU THINK YOU'RE GONNA BE SICK?
WAIT. BEFORE EITHER OF YOU UPCHUCK, I'VE GOTTA ASK YOU SOMETHING...
WHAT IS IT, NICK?
NEAR-DEATH EXPERIENCES TEND TO FOCUS ME. MIGHT NOT GET ANOTHER CHANCE, SO...
WILL YOU GO OUT WITH ME SOMETIME?
BEFORE YOU ANSWER, CONSIDER THE FACT I KINDA SAVED YOUR LIFE JUST NOW.
THAT'S GOTTA BE A TURN-ON, RIGHT?

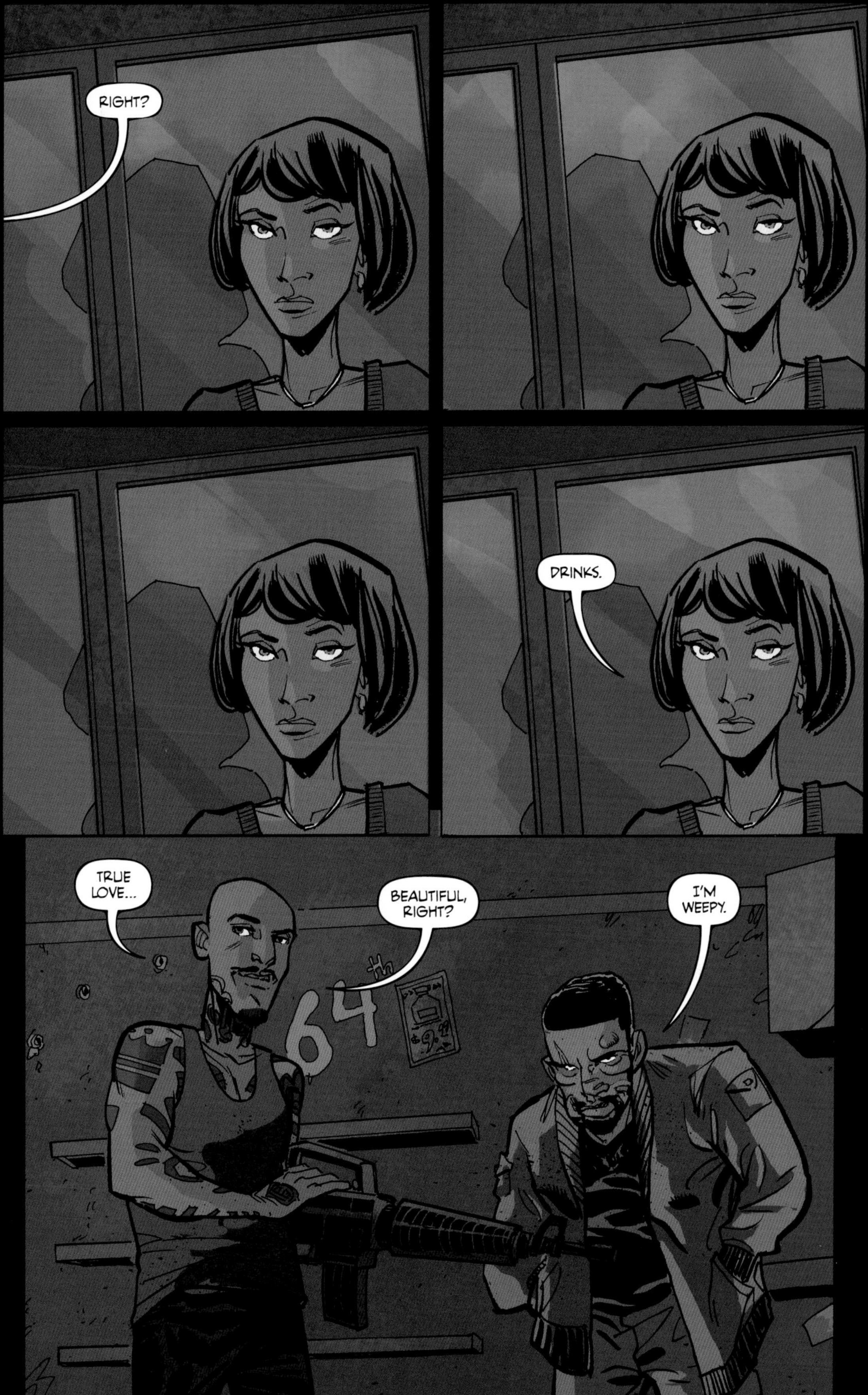
RIGHT?
DRINKS.
TRUE LOVE...
BEAUTIFUL, RIGHT?
I'M WEEPY.

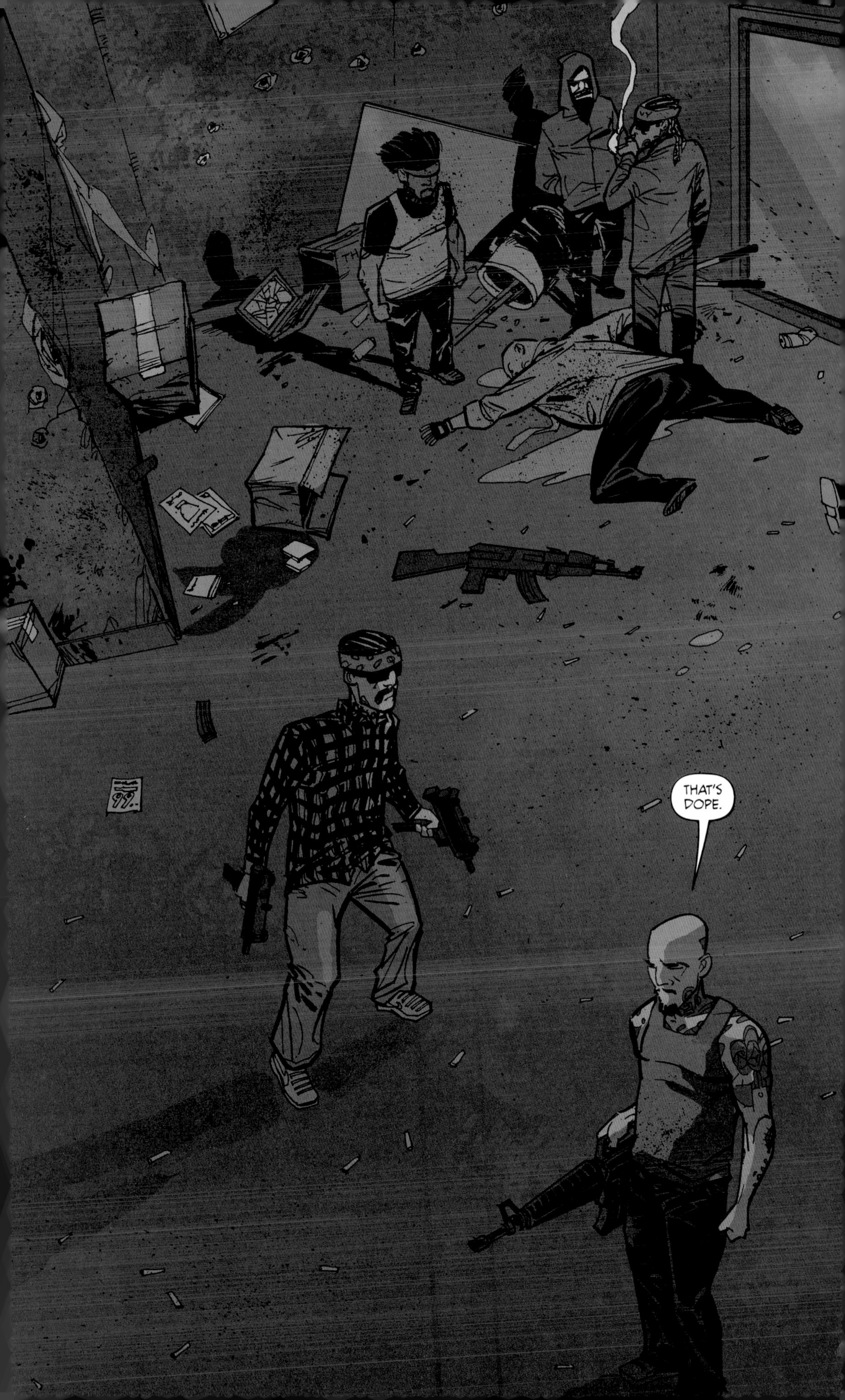
THAT'S DOPE.

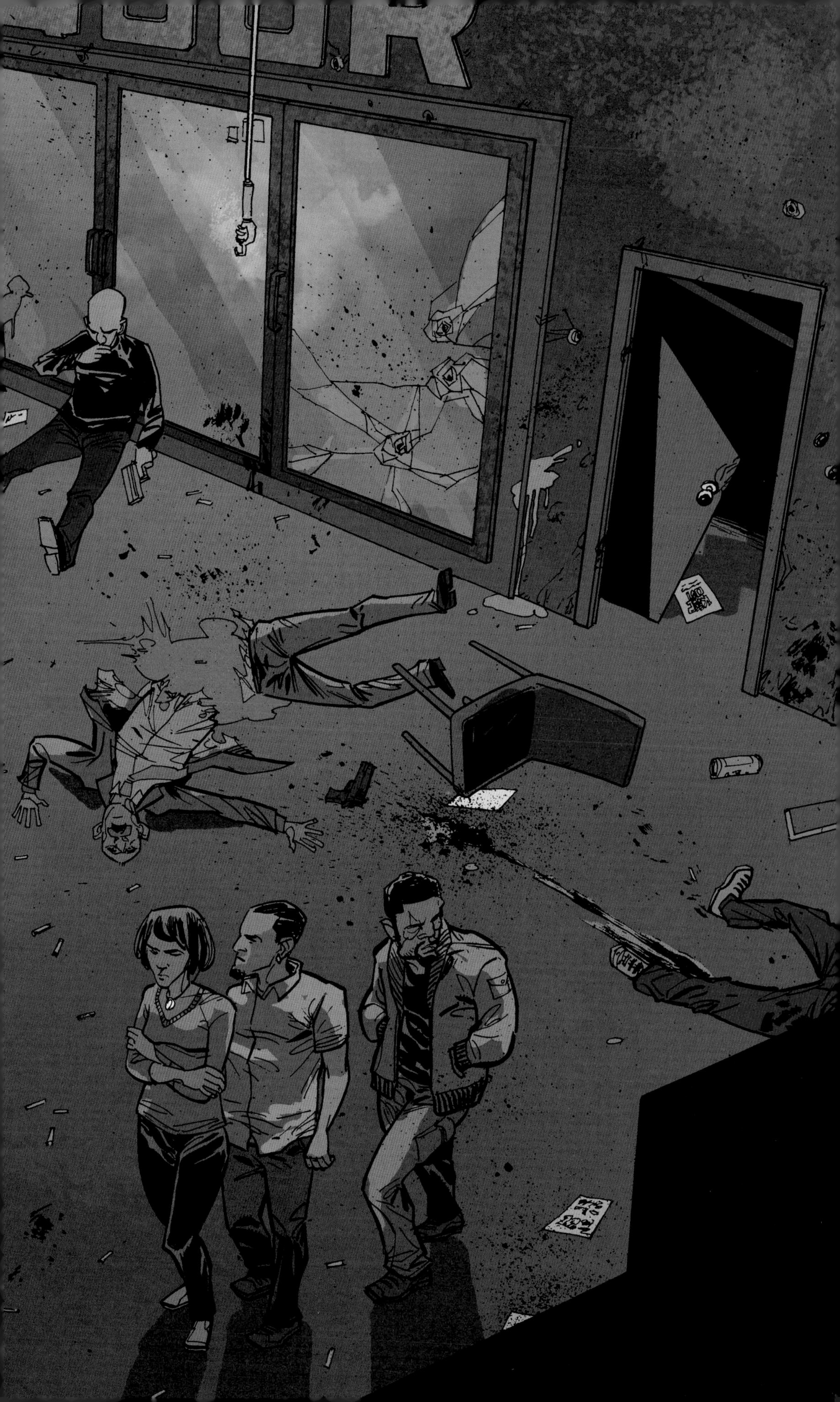

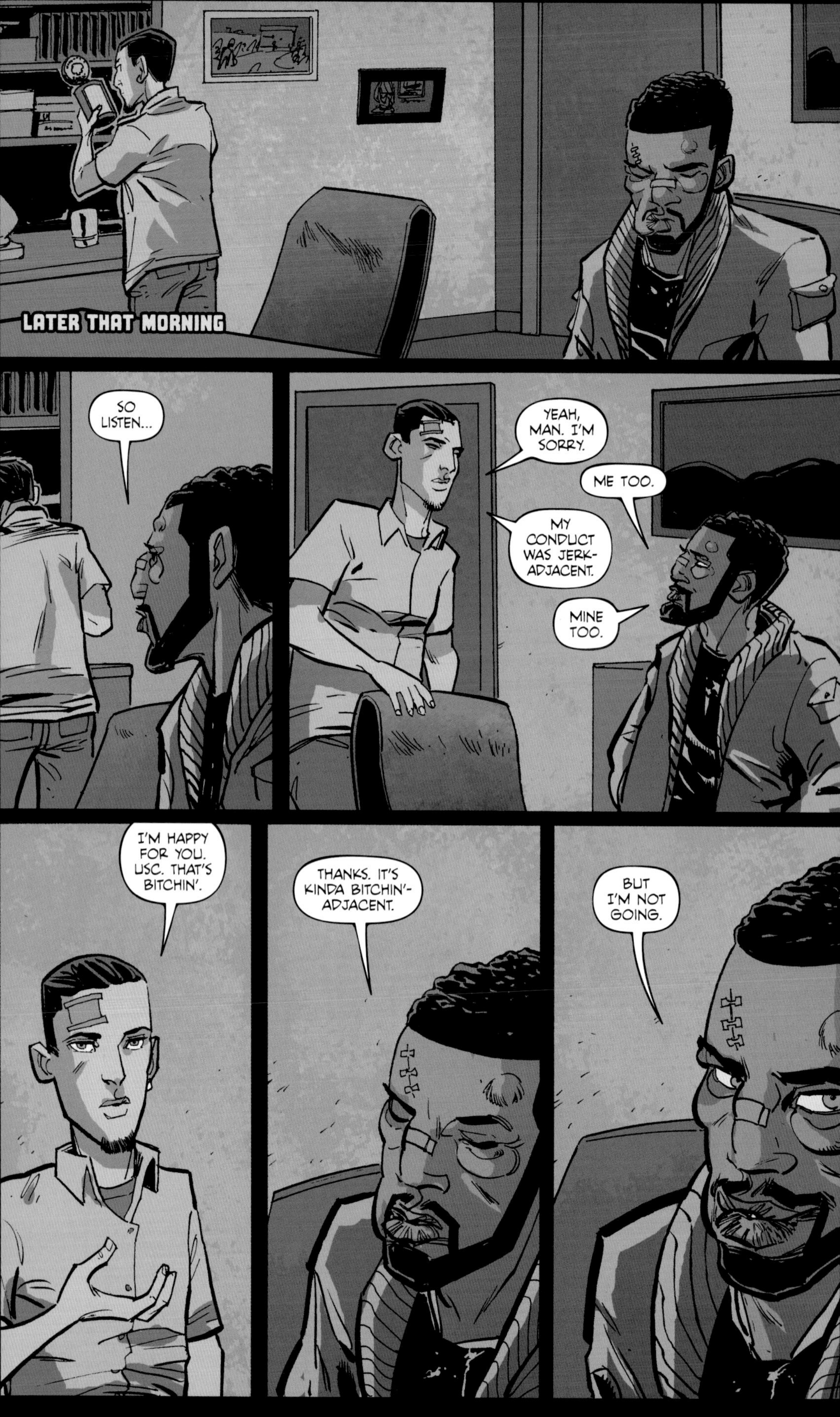
LATER THAT MORNING
SO LISTEN...
YEAH, MAN. I'M SORRY.
MY CONDUCT WAS JERK-ADJACENT.
ME TOO.
MINE TOO.
I'M HAPPY FOR YOU. USC. THAT'S BITCHIN'.
THANKS. IT'S KINDA BITCHIN'-ADJACENT.
BUT I'M NOT GOING.

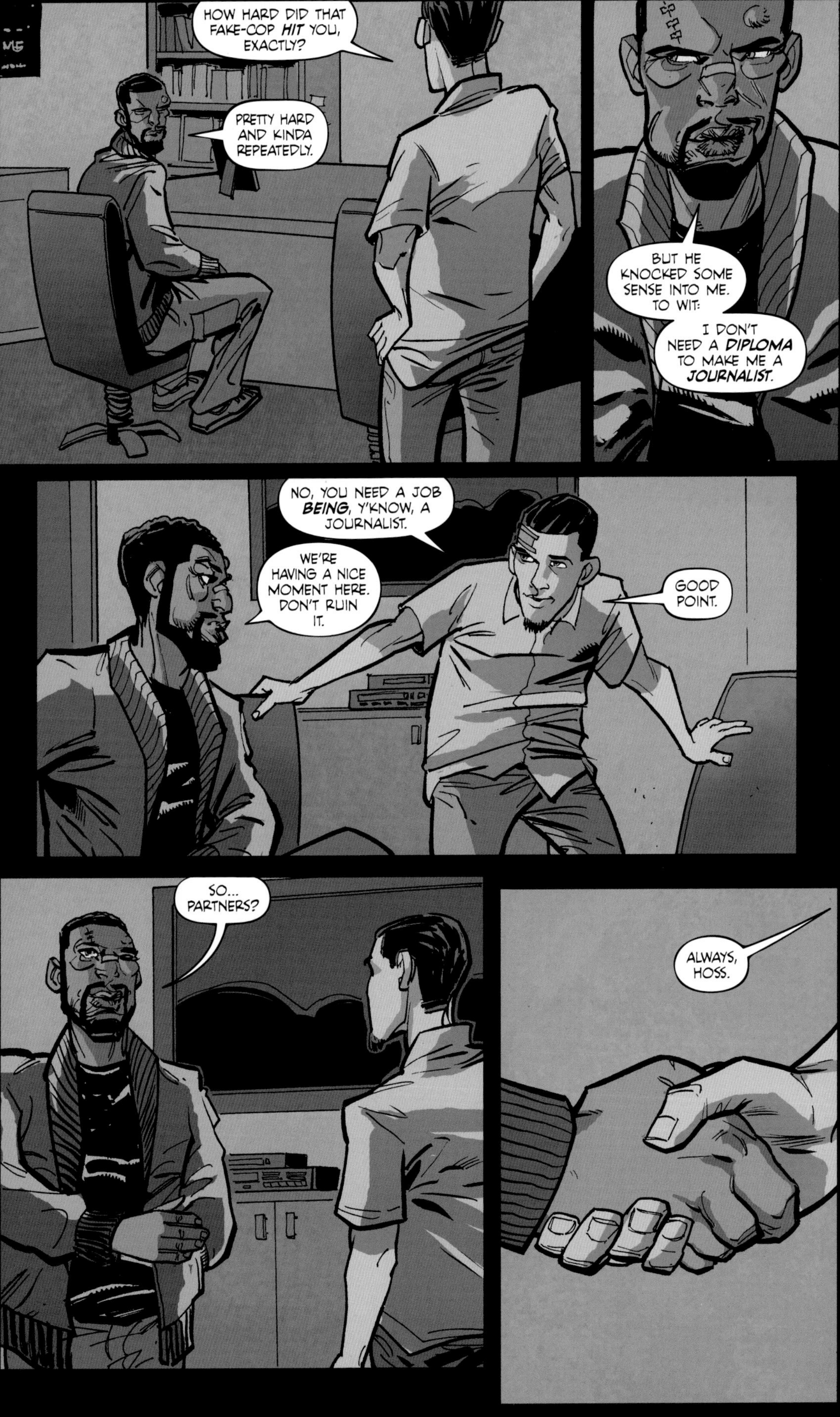
HOW HARD DID THAT FAKE-COP HIT YOU, EXACTLY?
PRETTY HARD AND KINDA REPEATEDLY.
BUT HE KNOCKED SOME SENSE INTO ME. TO WIT:
I DON'T NEED A DIPLOMA TO MAKE ME A JOURNALIST.
NO, YOU NEED A JOB BEING, Y'KNOW, A JOURNALIST.
WE'RE HAVING A NICE MOMENT HERE. DON'T RUIN IT.
GOOD POINT.
SO... PARTNERS?
ALWAYS, HOSS.

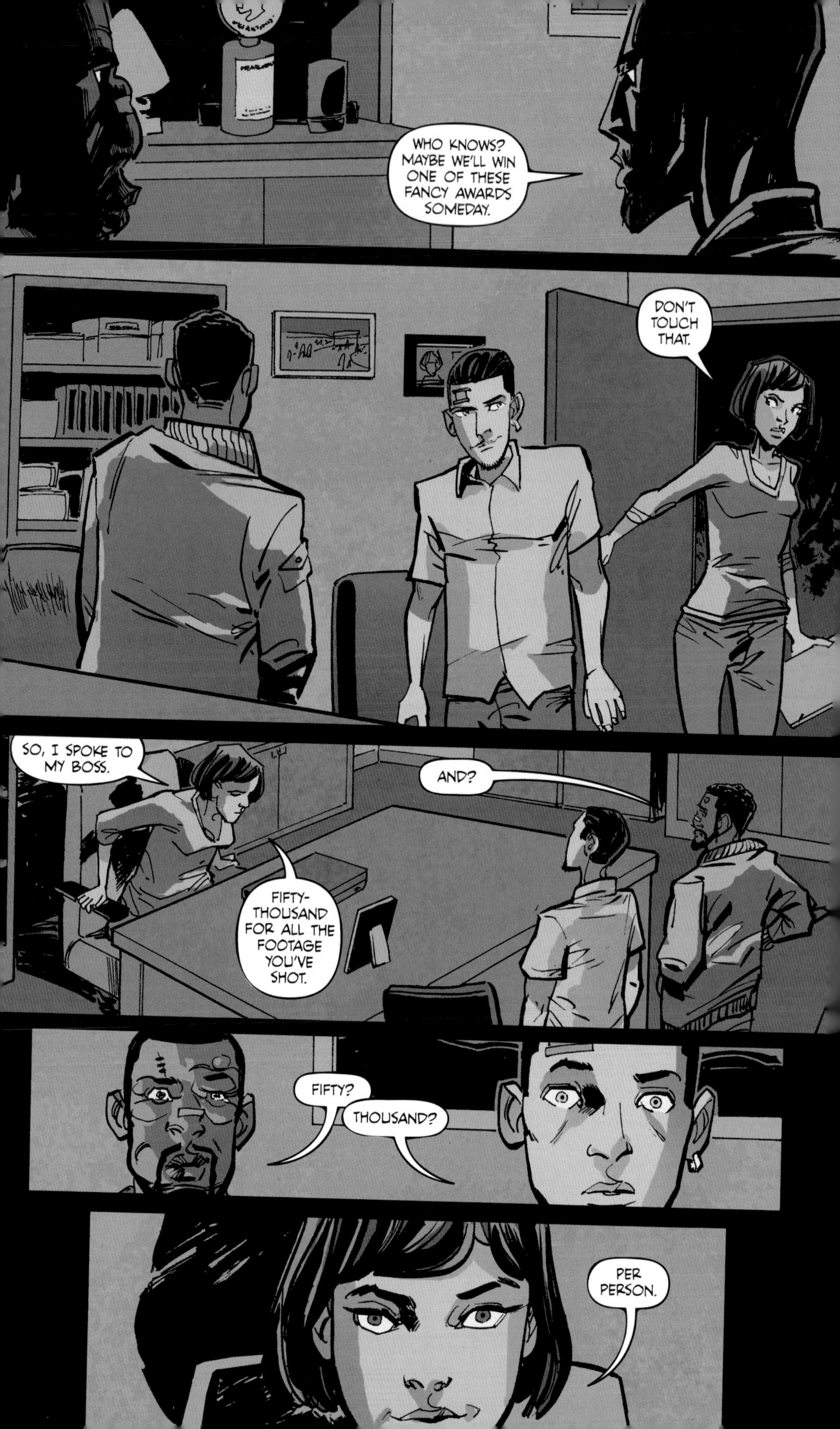
WHO KNOWS? MAYBE WE'LL WIN ONE OF THESE FANCY AWARDS SOMEDAY.
DON'T TOUCH THAT.
SO, I SPOKE TO MY BOSS.
AND?
FIFTY-THOUSAND FOR ALL THE FOOTAGE YOU'VE SHOT.
FIFTY?
THOUSAND?
PER PERSON.

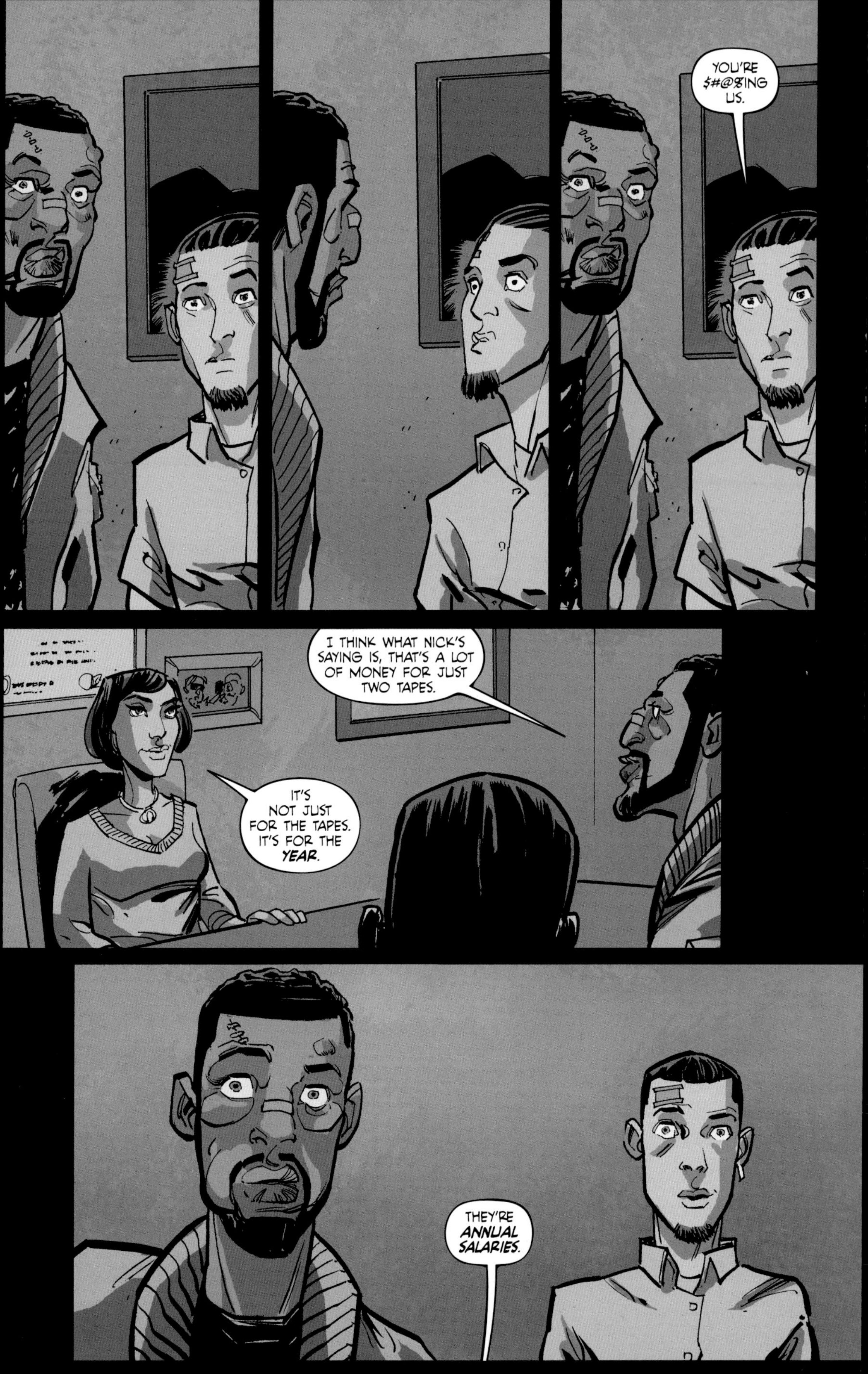
YOU'RE $#@%ING US.
I THINK WHAT NICK'S SAYING IS, THAT'S A LOT OF MONEY FOR JUST TWO TAPES.
IT'S NOT JUST FOR THE TAPES. IT'S FOR THE YEAR.
THEY'RE ANNUAL SALARIES.

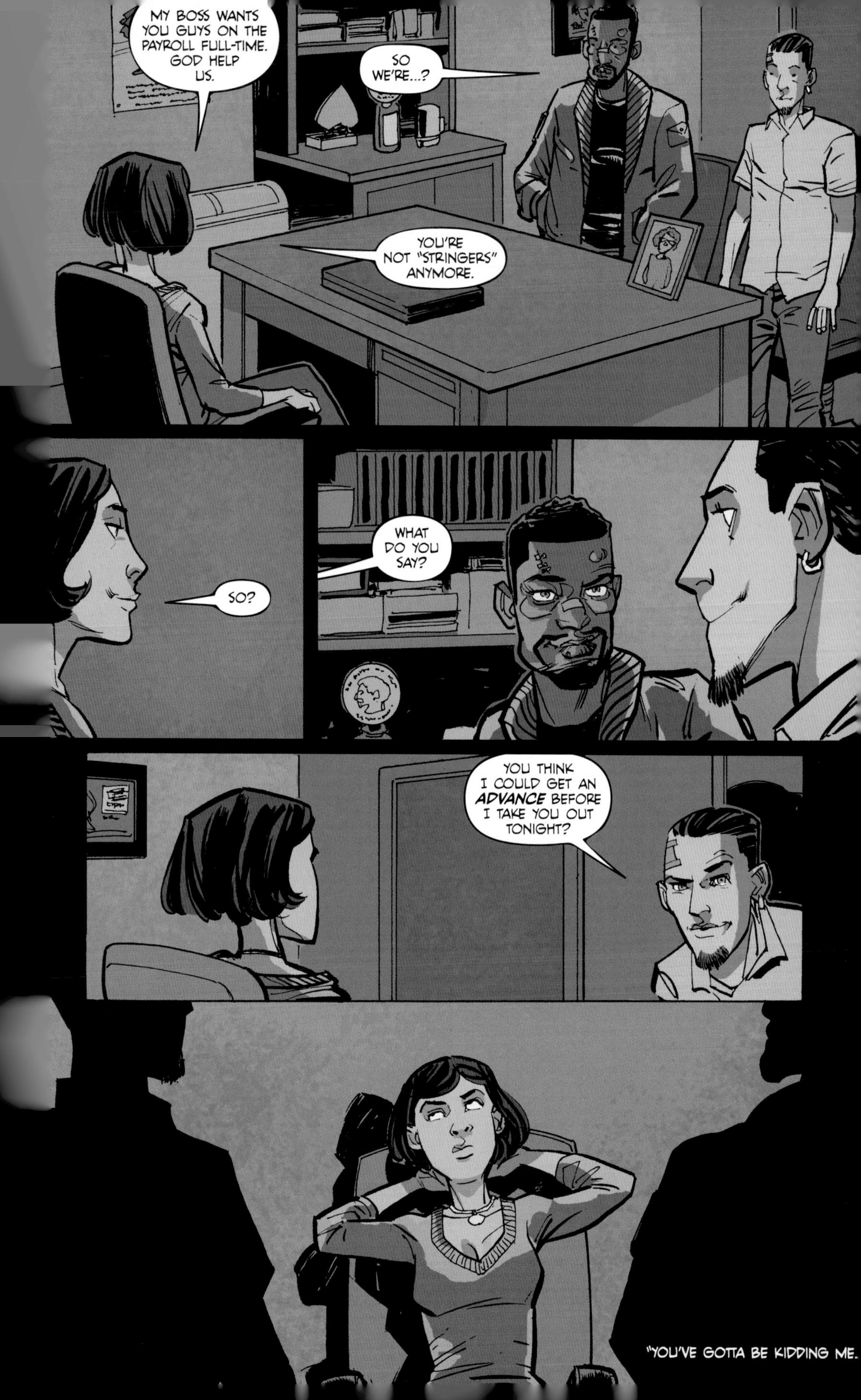

MY BOSS WANTS YOU GUYS ON THE PAYROLL FULL-TIME. GOD HELP US.
SO WE'RE...?
YOU'RE NOT "STRINGERS" ANYMORE.
SO?
WHAT DO YOU SAY?
YOU THINK I COULD GET AN *ADVANCE* BEFORE I TAKE YOU OUT TONIGHT?
"YOU'VE GOTTA BE KIDDING ME.

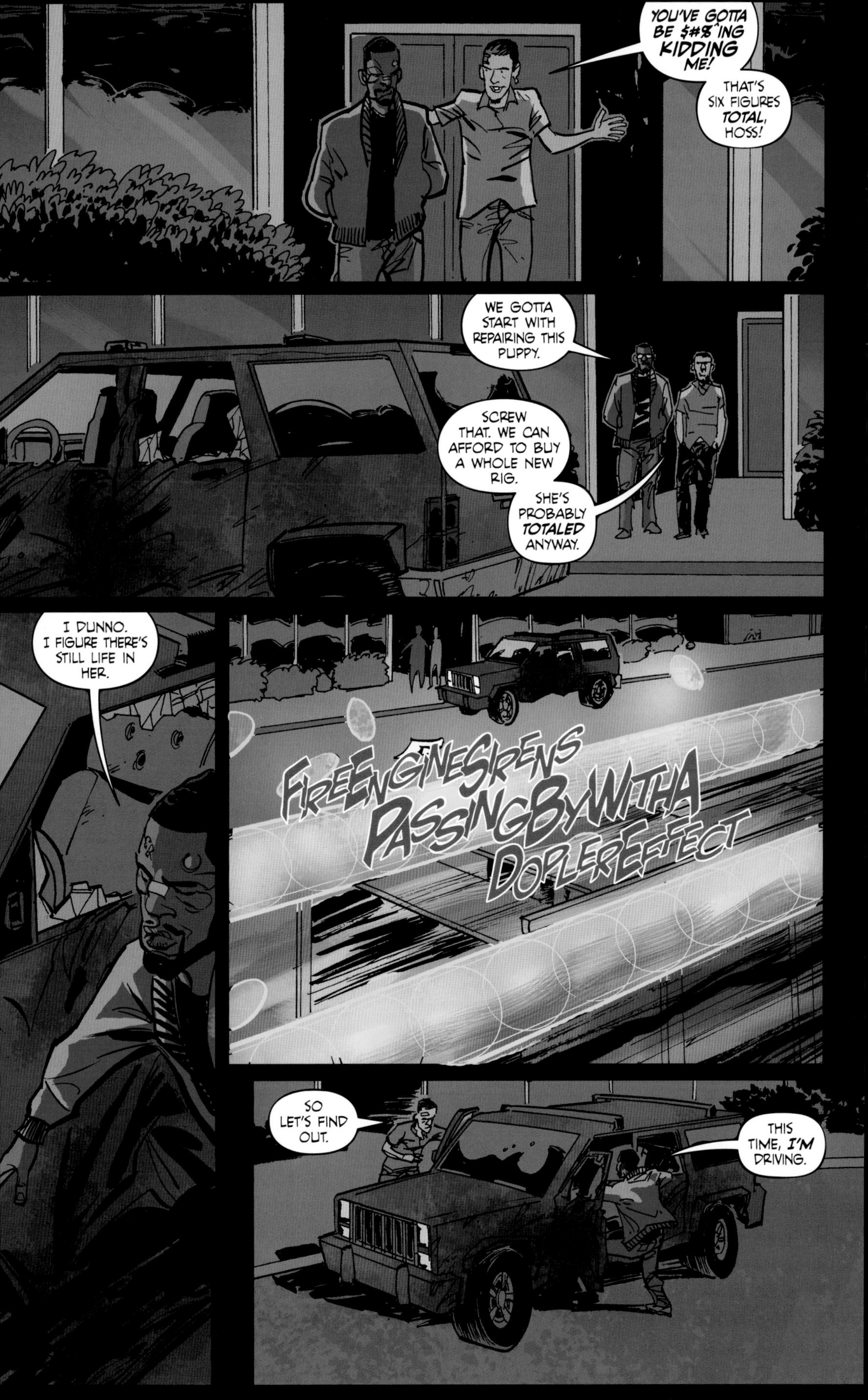
YOU'VE GOTTA BE $#%^ING KIDDING ME!
THAT'S SIX FIGURES TOTAL, HOSS!
WE GOTTA START WITH REPAIRING THIS PUPPY.
SCREW THAT. WE CAN AFFORD TO BUY A WHOLE NEW RIG.
SHE'S PROBABLY TOTALED ANYWAY.
I DUNNO. I FIGURE THERE'S STILL LIFE IN HER.
FireEngineSirens PassingByWithA DoplerEffect
SO LET'S FIND OUT.
THIS TIME, I'M DRIVING.

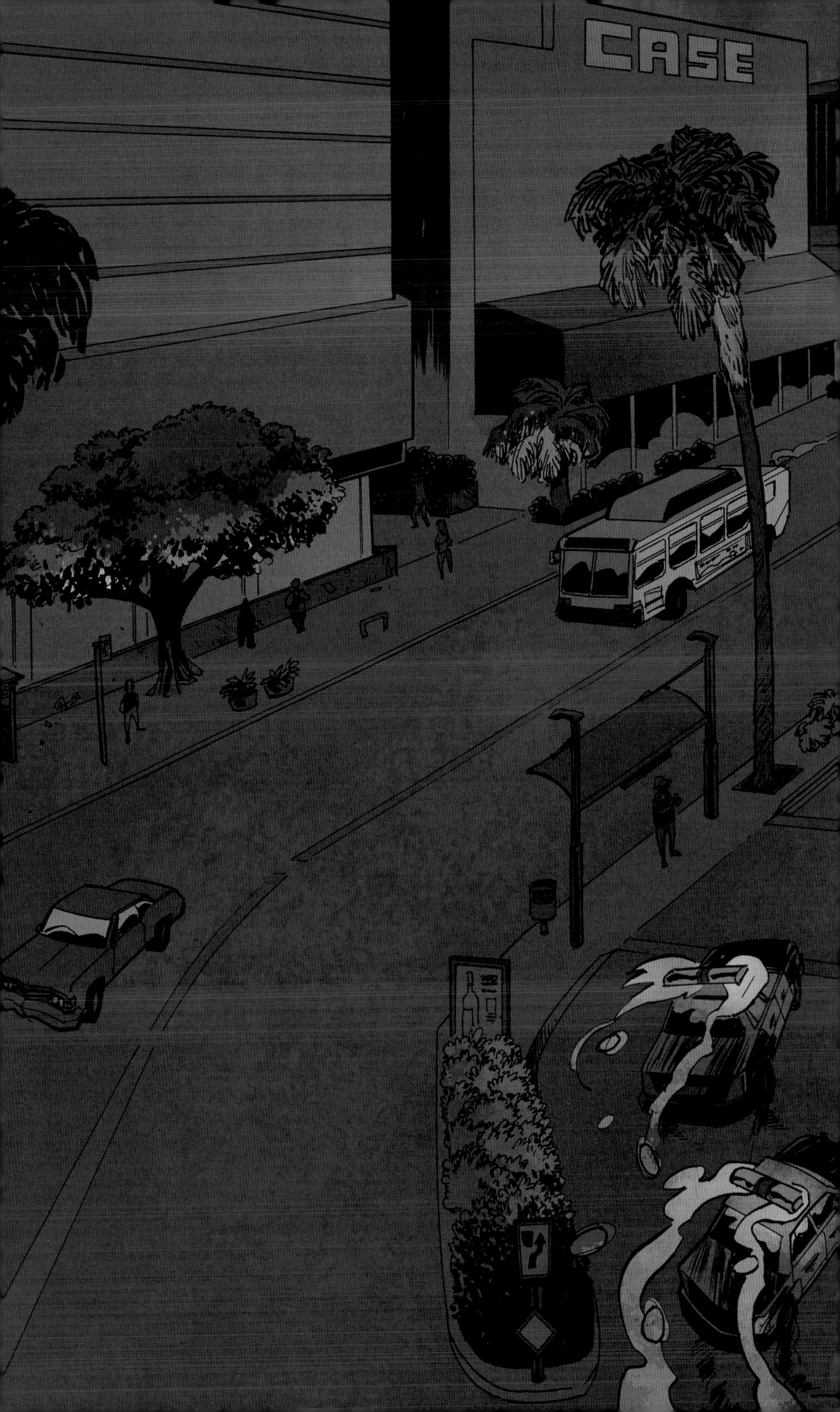
CASE

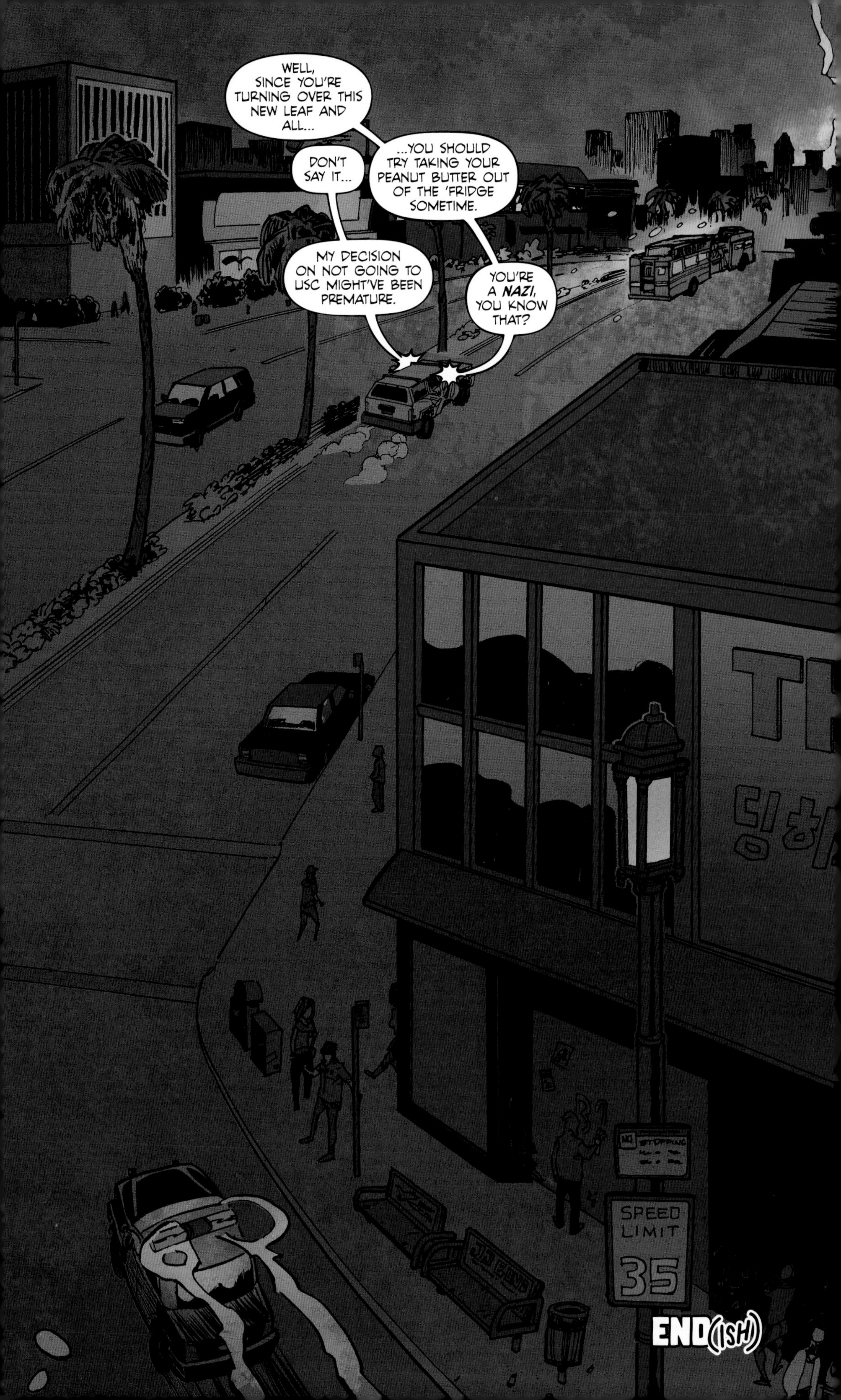

WELL, SINCE YOU'RE TURNING OVER THIS NEW LEAF AND ALL...
DON'T SAY IT...
...YOU SHOULD TRY TAKING YOUR PEANUT BUTTER OUT OF THE 'FRIDGE SOMETIME.
MY DECISION ON NOT GOING TO USC MIGHT'VE BEEN PREMATURE.
YOU'RE A *NAZI*, YOU KNOW THAT?
SPEED LIMIT 35
END(ISH)

COVER GALLERY

STRINGERS #1 RETAIL COVER

ILLUSTRATED BY JUSTIN GREENWOOD AND COLORED BY RYAN HILL

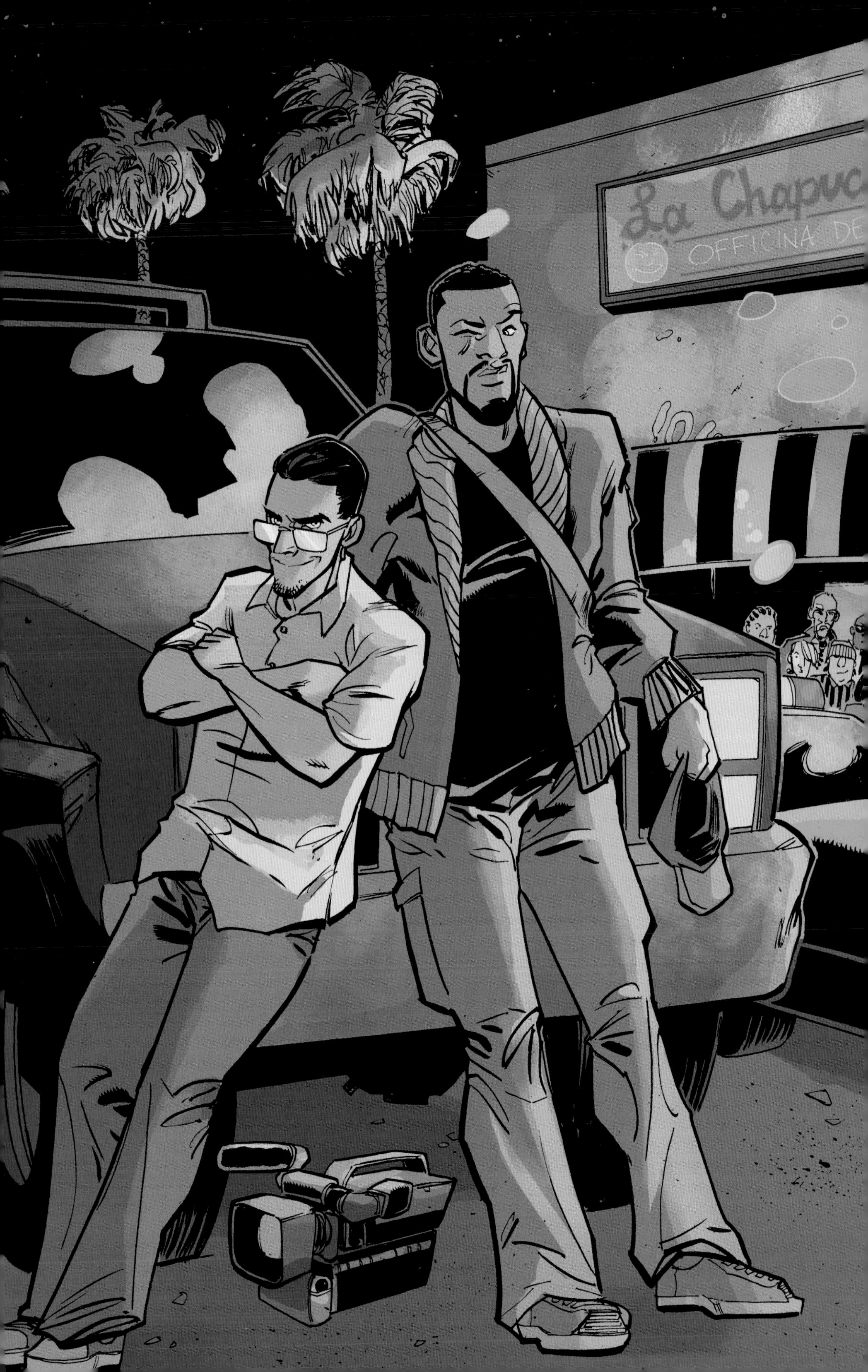

STRINGERS #2 RETAIL COVER

ILLUSTRATED BY JUSTIN GREENWOOD AND COLORED BY RYAN HILL

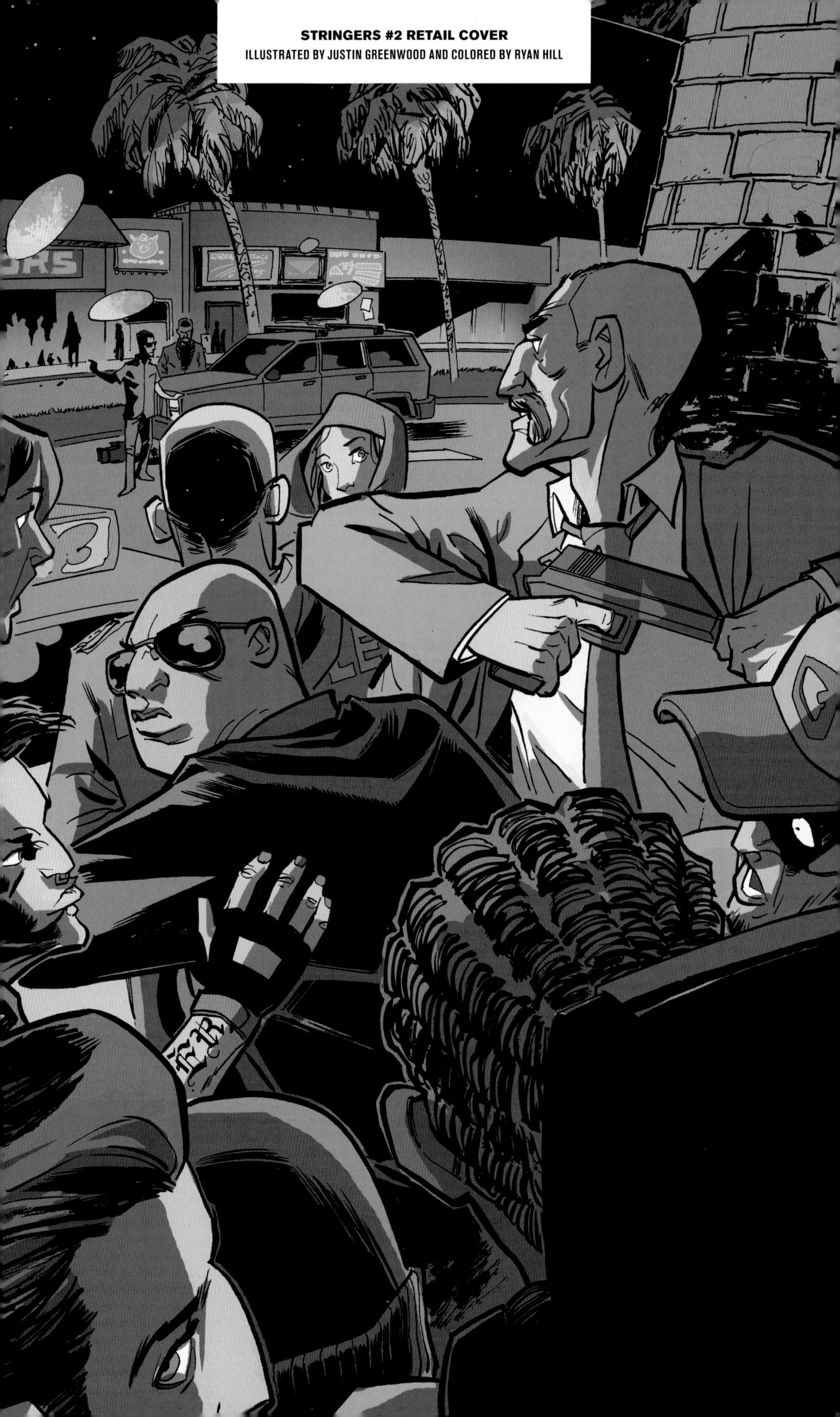

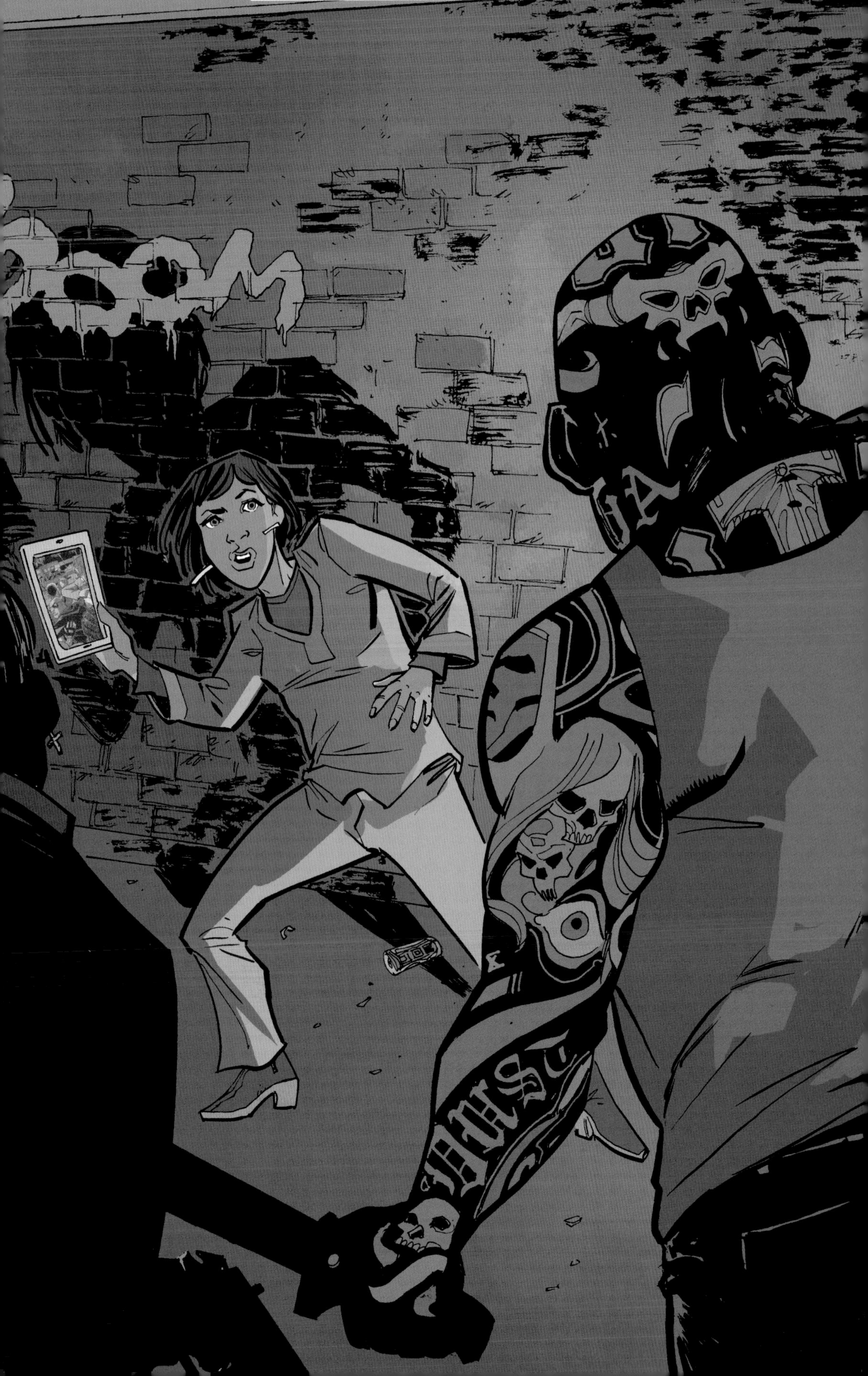

STRINGERS #3 RETAIL COVER

ILLUSTRATED BY JUSTIN GREENWOOD AND COLORED BY RYAN HILL

STRINGERS #4 RETAIL COVER

ILLUSTRATED BY JUSTIN GREENWOOD AND COLORED BY RYAN HILL

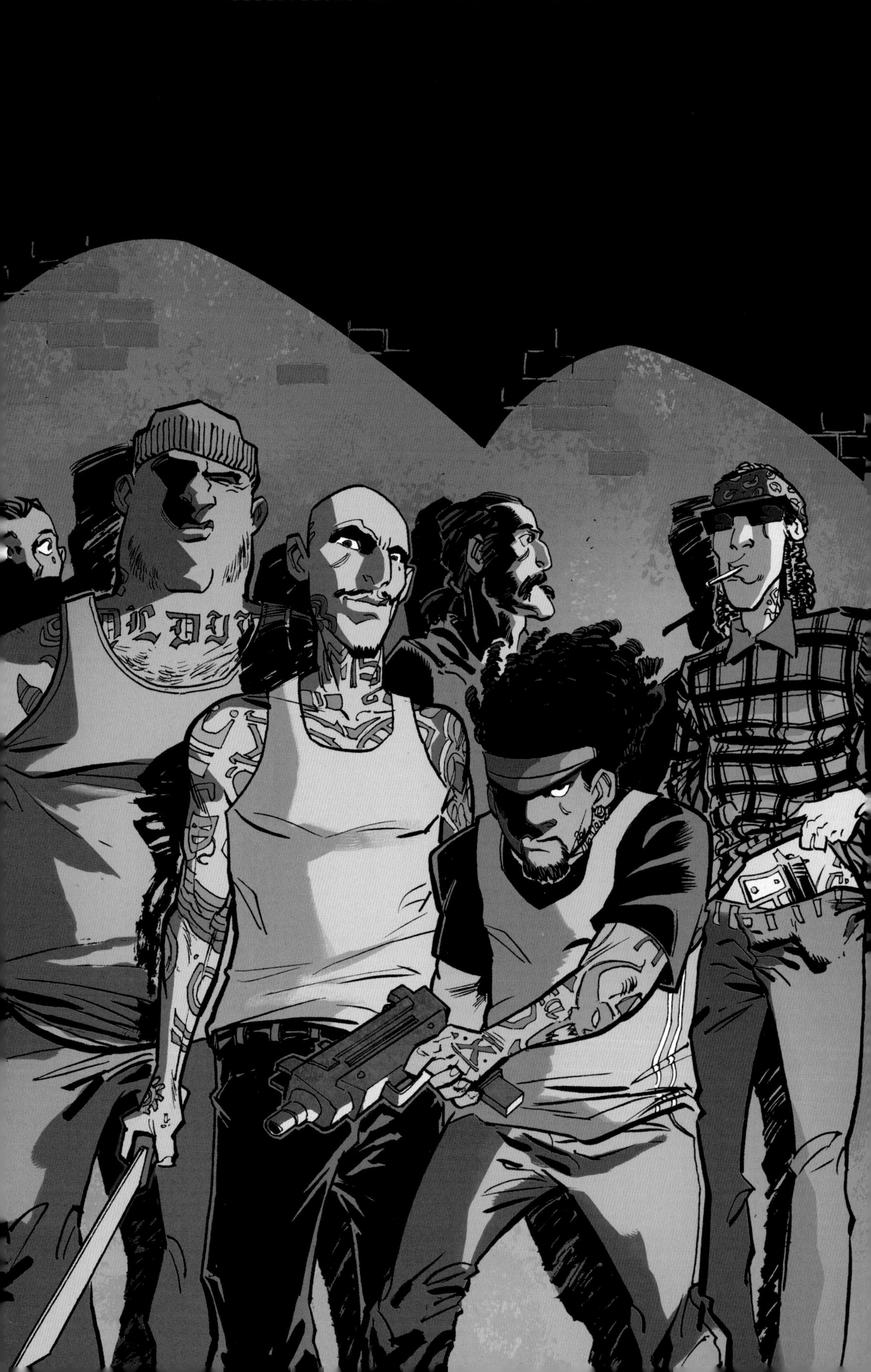

STRINGERS #5 RETAIL COVER
ILLUSTRATED BY JUSTIN GREENWOOD AND COLORED BY RYAN HILL

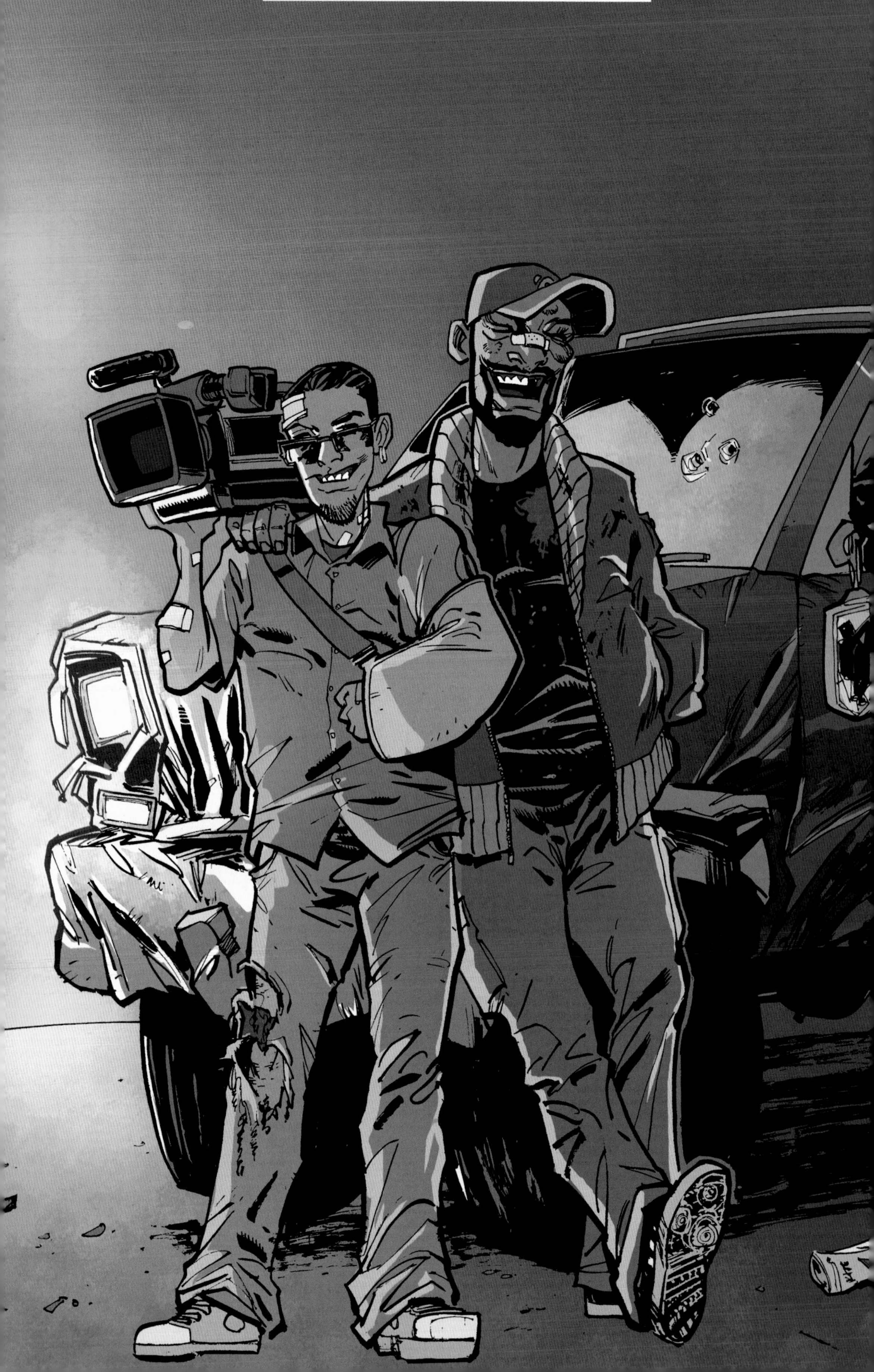

STRINGERS #1 VARIANT COVER
BY ROBBI RODRIGUEZ

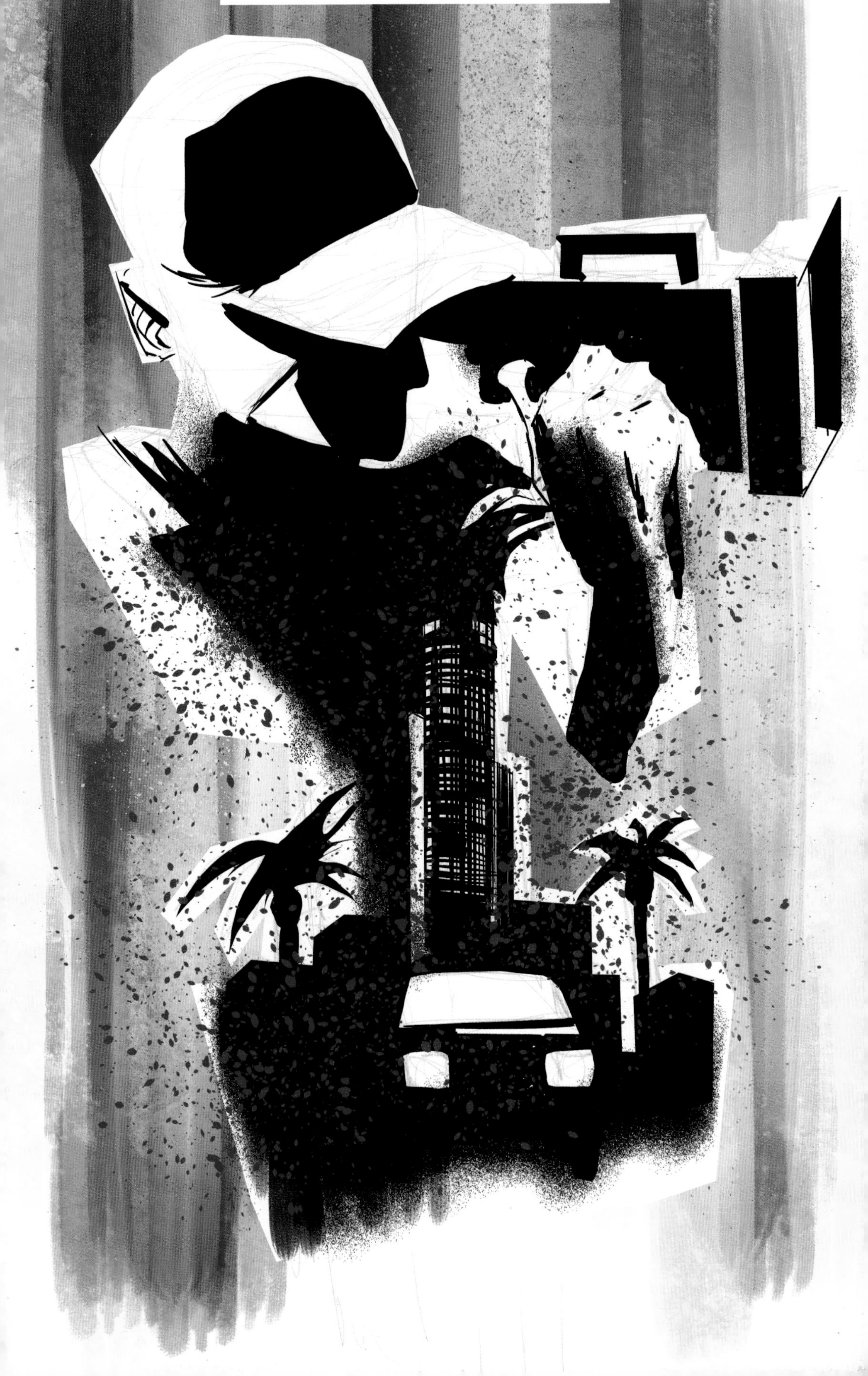

STRINGERS #2 VARIANT COVER
BY BRAHM REVEL

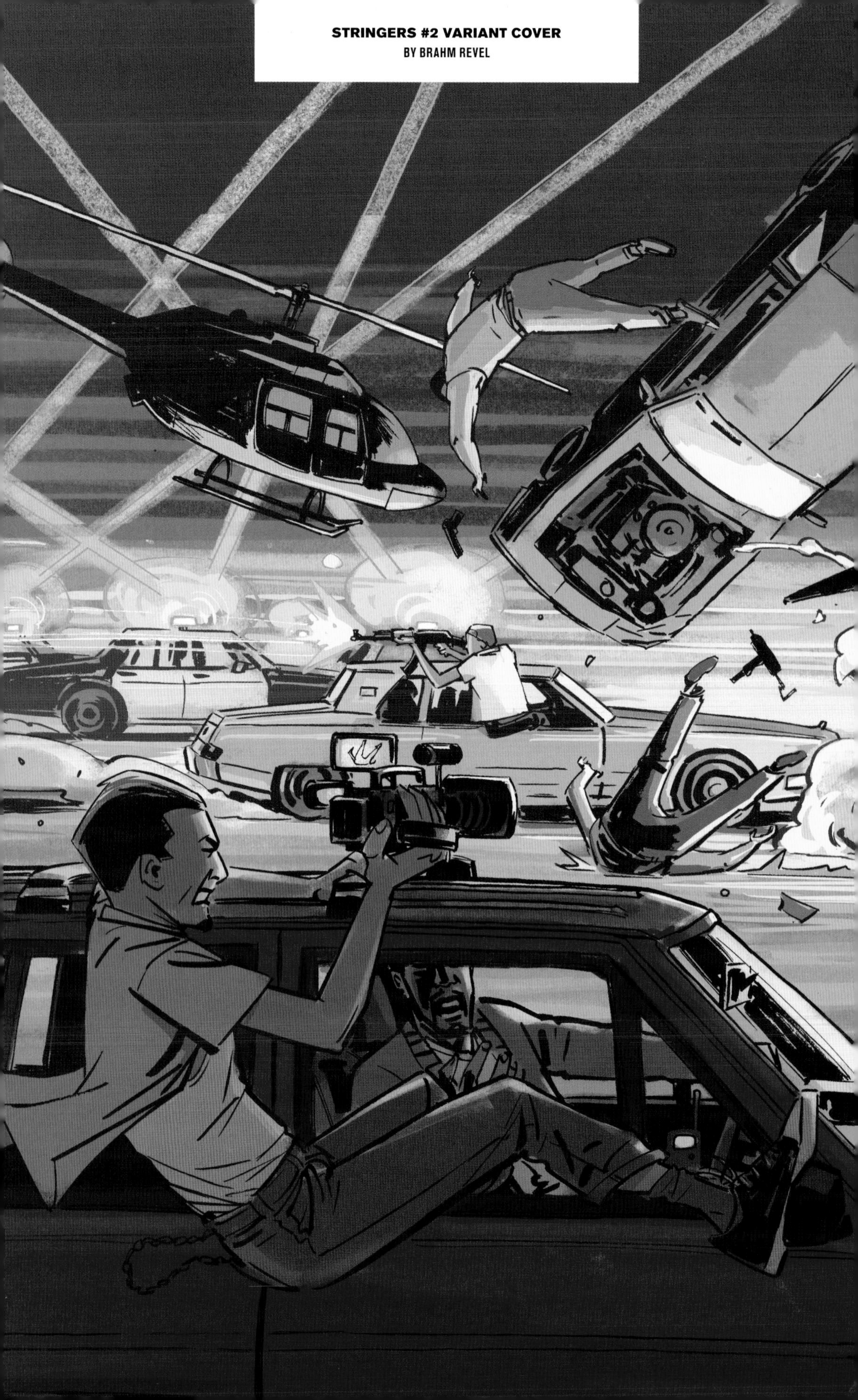

STRINGERS #3 VARIANT COVER

ILLUSTRATED BY JOHNNIE CHRISTMAS AND COLORED BY RYAN HILL

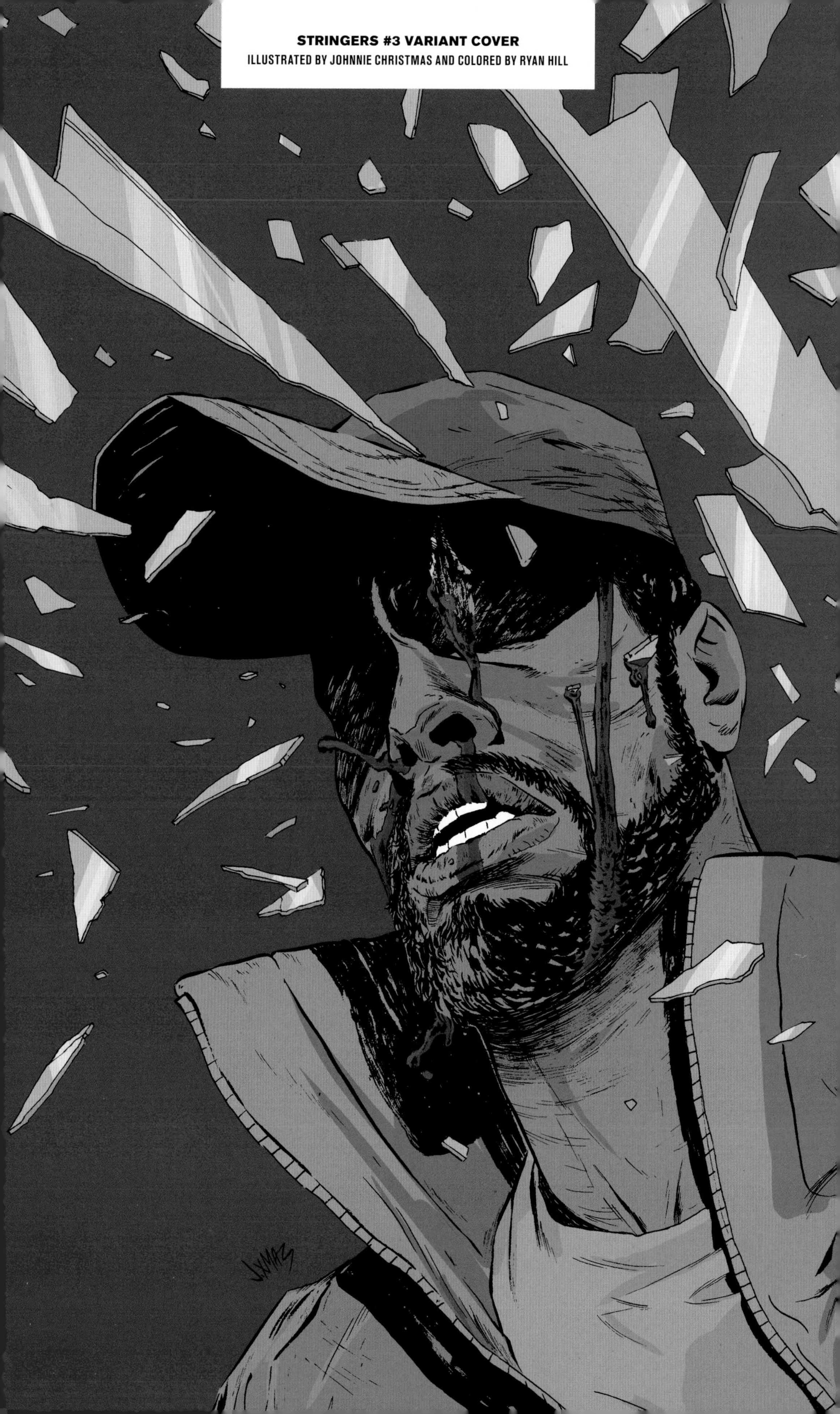

STRINGERS #4 VARIANT COVER
BY TYLER CROOK

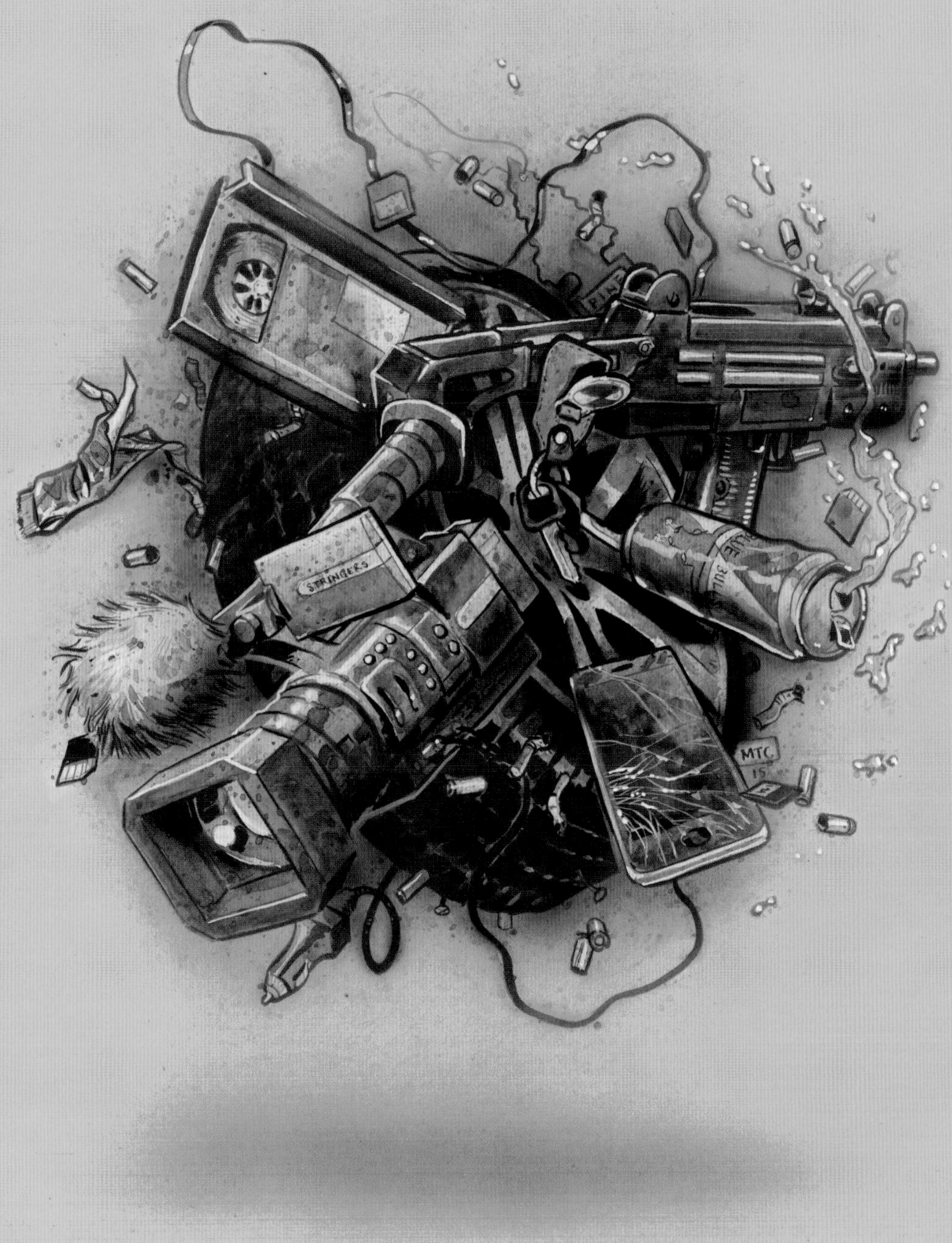
STRINGERS
MTC 15

STRINGERS #5 VARIANT COVER
BY YEHUDI MERCADO

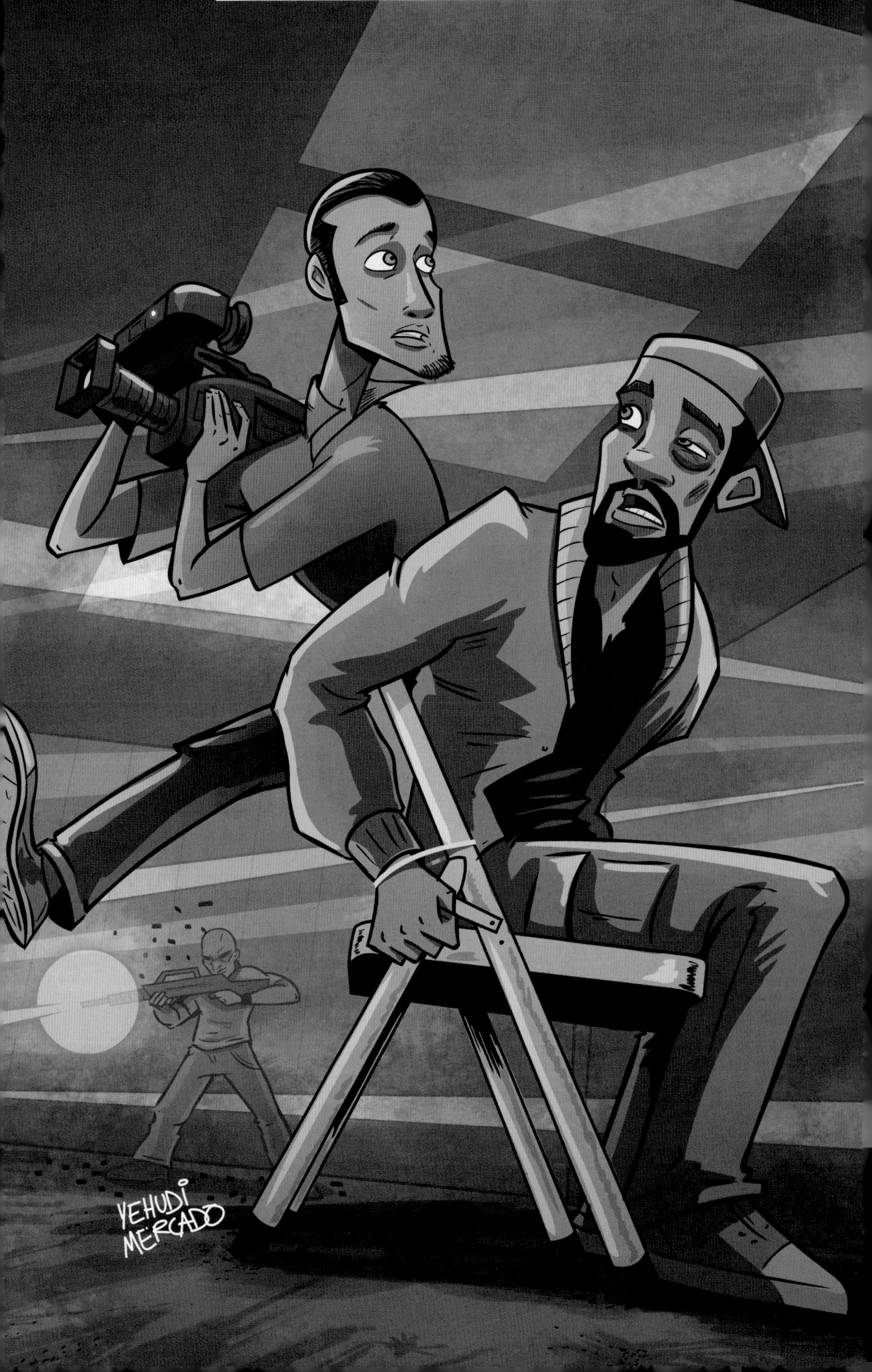
YEHUDI MERCADO

STRINGERS #1 BACK COVER

ILLUSTRATED BY JUSTIN GREENWOOD AND COLORED BY RYAN HILL

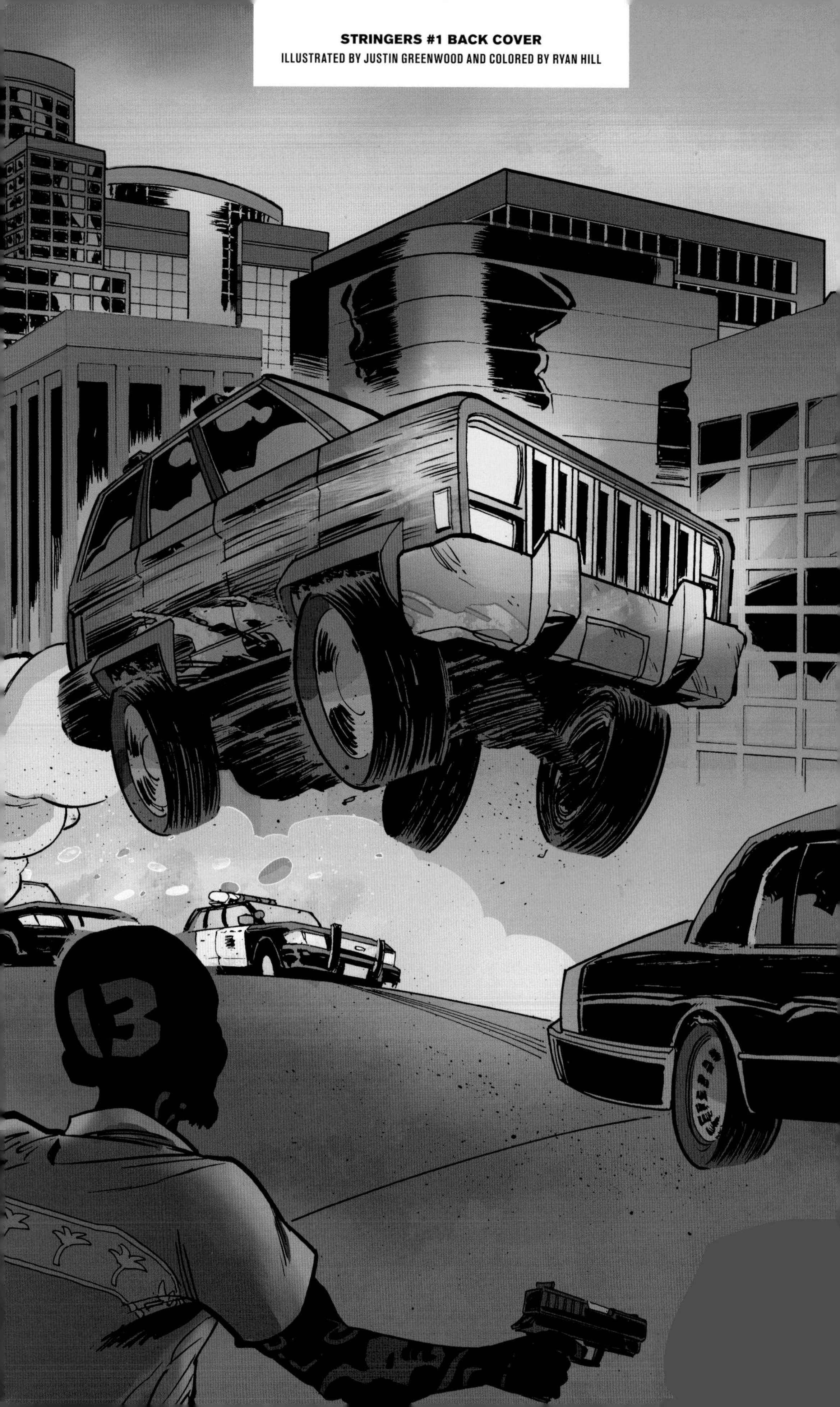

STRINGERS #2 BACK COVER

ILLUSTRATED BY JUSTIN GREENWOOD AND COLORED BY RYAN HILL

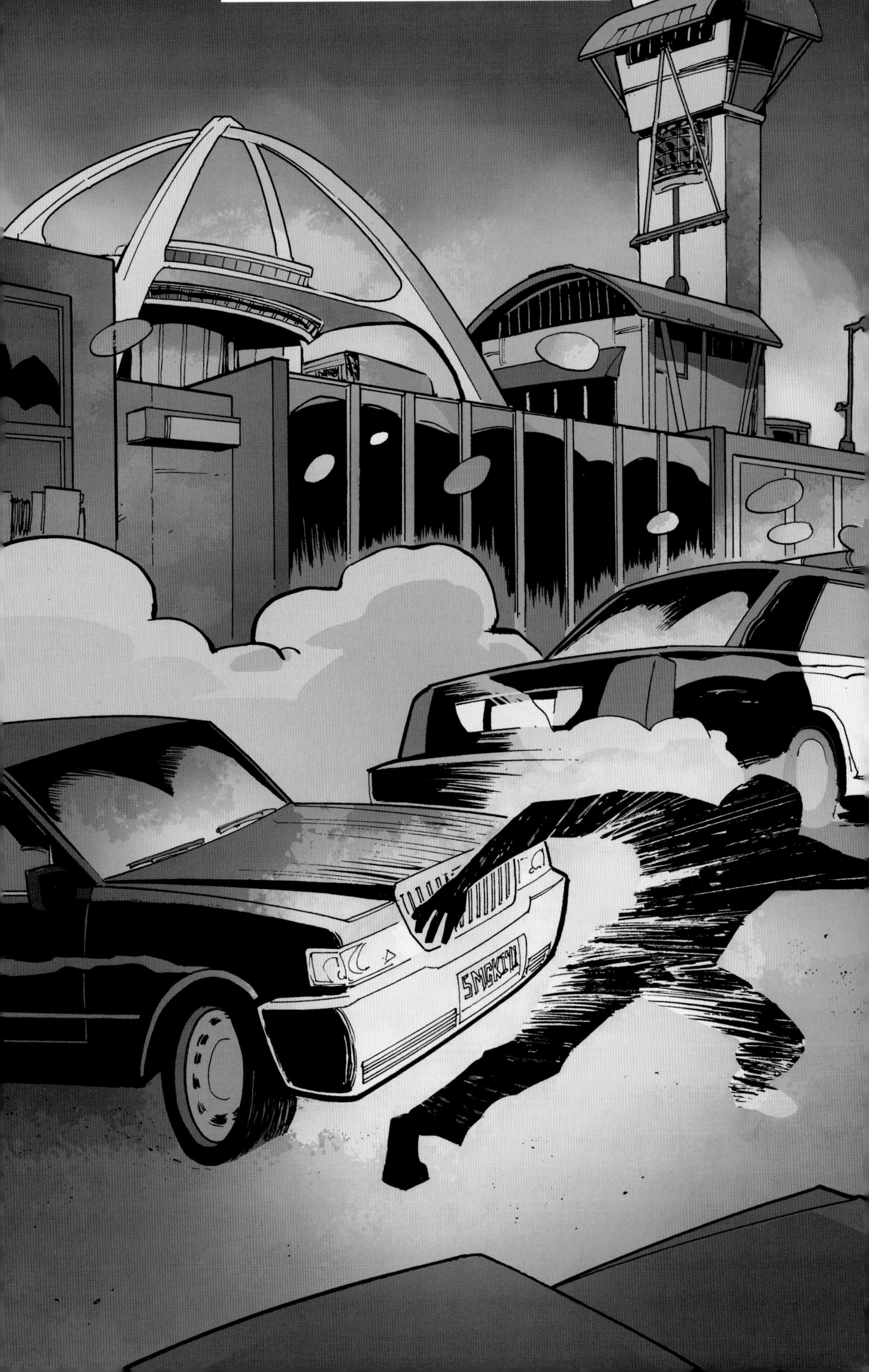

STRINGERS #3 BACK COVER

ILLUSTRATED BY JUSTIN GREENWOOD AND COLORED BY RYAN HILL

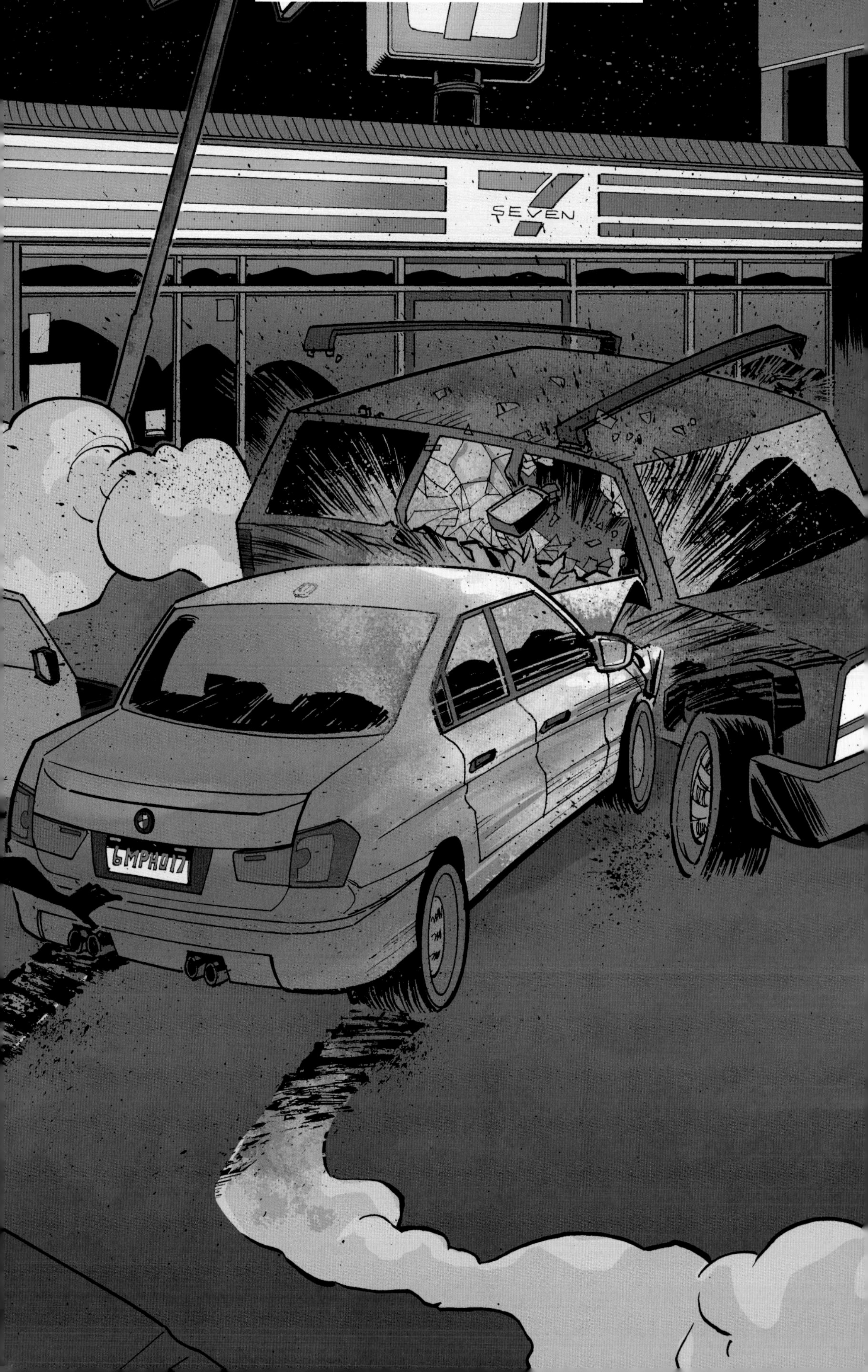
SEVEN
6MPH017

STRINGERS #4 BACK COVER

ILLUSTRATED BY JUSTIN GREENWOOD AND COLORED BY RYAN HILL

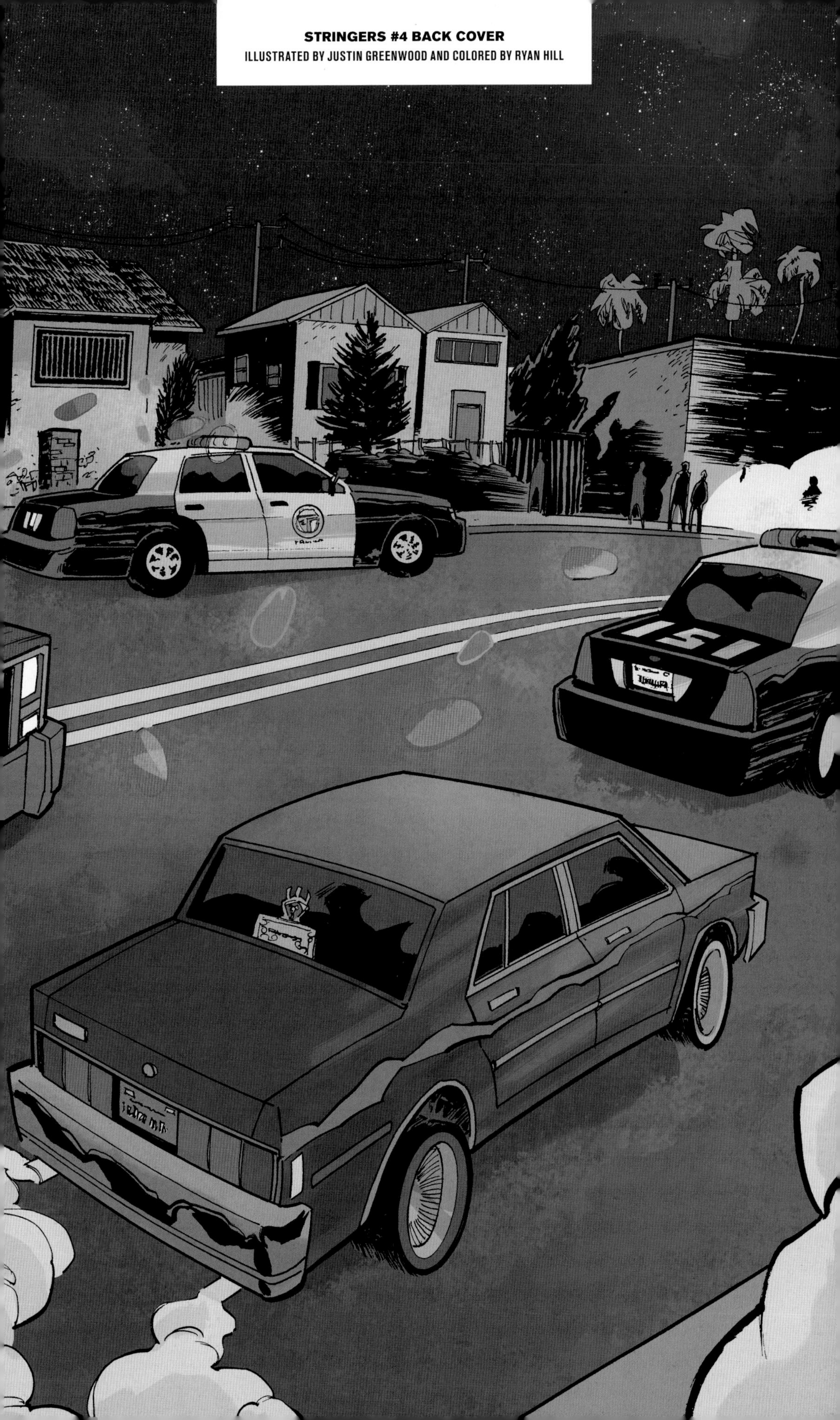

STRINGERS #5 BACK COVER

ILLUSTRATED BY JUSTIN GREENWOOD AND COLORED BY RYAN HILL

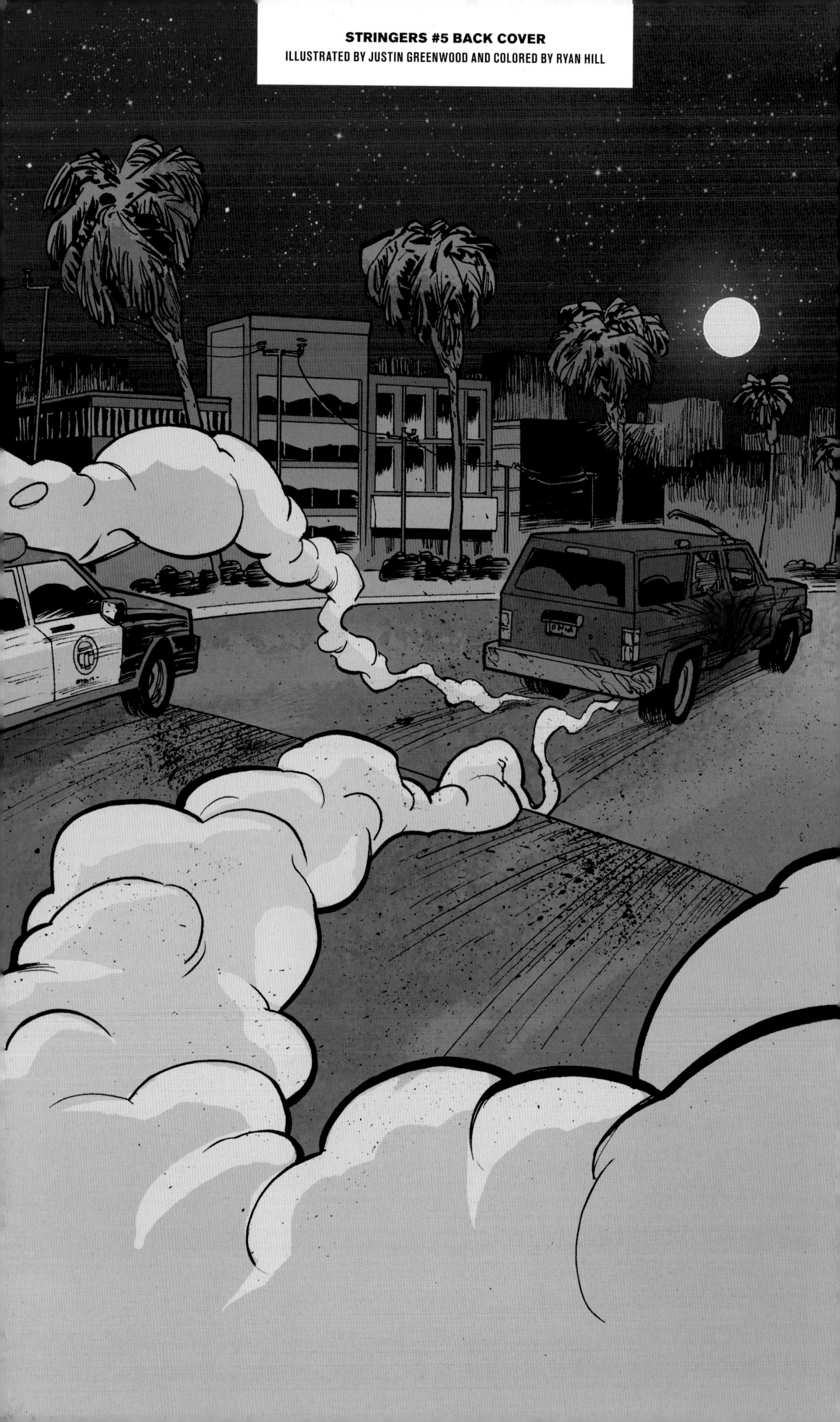

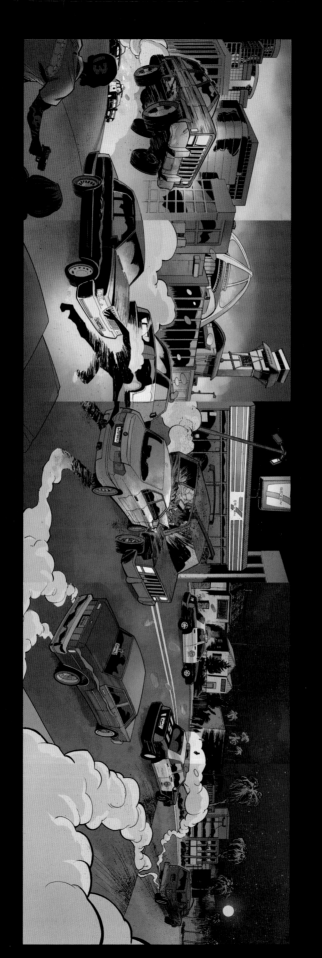

STRINGERS BACK COVER PANORAMA

ILLUSTRATED BY JUSTIN GREENWOOD AND COLORED BY RYAN HILL

@MGUGGENHEIM

MARC GUGGENHEIM co-created and produced the pilot for *Arrow*, which has gone on to become a hit for The CW, and has spun off two shows, *The Flash* and DC's *Legends of Tomorrow*, the latter of which Guggenheim co-created and is currently producing.

A life-long comic book fan, Guggenheim has been writing comics professionally since 2005, writing titles for both Marvel Comics (*Wolverine*, *Blade*, *X-Men*, *Amazing Spider-Man*) and DC Comics (*The Flash*, *Justice Society of America*, *Batman Confidential*). In November 2007, Guggenheim launched his first creator-owned series with Oni Press, entitled *Resurrection*, which he followed up with his own imprint—Collider Entertainment—at Image Comics, where he published *Halcyon* and *The Mission*.

Guggenheim currently lives in Los Angeles with his wife Tara (a fellow TV writer and WGA nominee, who is co-creator of The CW dramedy *Reaper*), their daughters Lily and Sara, and their pets Rocky, Lucky, and a turtle (which may or may not be alive as of this writing).

@JKGREENWOOD_ART

JUSTIN GREENWOOD is a Bay Area comic artist best known for his work on creator-owned series like *Stringers*, *Stumptown*, *The Fuse*, *Wasteland*, and *Resurrection*. When not drawing, he can be found running around the East Bay with his wife Melissa and their dual wildlings, tracking down unusual produce and the occasional card game with equal vigor.